National Identity and Globalization

Is globalization in danger of diluting national identities and "transnationalizing" cultures? How can societies attempt to manage globalization and become developed while maintaining a viable national identity? In a study of three globalizing states and cities in post-Soviet Eurasia – Russia (Astrakhan), Kazakhstan (Almaty), and Azerbaijan (Baku) – Douglas W. Blum provides an empirical examination of national identity formation, exploring how cultures, particularly youth cultures, have been affected by global forces. Blum argues that social discourse regarding youth cultural trends – coupled with official and non-official approaches to youth policy – complement patterns of state–society relations and modes of response to globalization. His findings show that the nations studied have embraced certain aspects of modernity and liberalism, while rejecting others, but have also reasserted the place of national traditions.

DOUGLAS W. BLUM is Professor of Political Science at Providence College and Adjunct Professor of International Studies at the Thomas J. Watson, Jr. Institute of International Studies at Brown University. His research interests center on cultural globalization and the connections between globalization, identity, and security in the former USSR. He has recently edited *Russia and the World: Security and Identity in an Era of Globalization* (forthcoming).

National Identity and Globalization

Youth, State, and Society in Post-Soviet Eurasia

Douglas W. Blum

Providence College

CAMBRIDGE
UNIVERSITY PRESS

CAMBRIDGE UNIVERSITY PRESS
Cambridge, New York, Melbourne, Madrid, Cape Town, Singapore, São Paulo

Cambridge University Press
The Edinburgh Building, Cambridge CB2 8RU, UK

Published in the United States of America by Cambridge University Press, New York

www.cambridge.org
Information on this title: www.cambridge.org/9780521876193

First published 2007

Printed in the United Kingdom at the University Press, Cambridge

A catalogue record for this publication is available from the British Library

ISBN 978-0-521-87619-3 hardback

Contents

Acknowledgments

I arrived at the topic of this book simply by following my curiosity about an intriguing question: how would cultural globalization affect the states of the former USSR, and how would they seek to respond? I had been puzzling over the dynamics of identity formation for some time, and trying – like so many scholars of my generation – to fully comprehend the dizzying changes that had transpired since the fall of the USSR. This topic was useful to me personally, then, inasmuch as it afforded me a way of thinking through the complexities of globalization and post-Soviet nation building more broadly. But far more importantly, I think in retrospect, I was drawn to it simply out of a sense of intellectual fascination, regardless of its theoretical significance or ultimate publishability. After years of struggling to get tenure while working in the evenings as a marketing consultant, what an enormous pleasure it was to simply let my thoughts run! If the result is sometimes undisciplined (both literally and figuratively), I hope the reader will indulge my whims and excesses. I only wish everyone could enjoy their work as much as I have during this project.

I spent a total of almost six years completing the book, and accumulated numerous debts in the process. First and most obviously, I could not have conducted the research presented here without the very generous support of IREX and Providence College. I deeply appreciate it.

Second, I owe tremendous debts to my colleagues. I have been extraordinarily lucky to be able to draw on the collective wisdom of my wonderful fellow members of PONARS (Program for New Approaches to Russian Security), who gamely withstood repeated drafts of my work and provided countless suggestions. In particular, for their helpful comments and reactions to one or more drafts, I wish to thank Jeff Checkel, Matt Evangelista, Henry Hale, Steve Hanson, Ted Hopf, and Jim Richter. And I also want to thank Celeste Wallander, who, after a presentation of my early research, pointed out in her customarily incisive and to-the-point manner: "It's about state–society relations." This was in fact the crucial insight, which had somehow managed to elude me until that moment, and which framed my entire approach from then on. Along the way a number of other people also tried to sharpen my focus, clarify some of my misunderstandings, and steer me in more fruitful directions – hopefully with at least some success. I am very grateful to David Abramson, Laura Adams, Patti Goff, Dietrich Rueschemeyer, Ron Suny, and Nina Tannenwald. Special mention must be given to Rod Hall, who not only offered many superb suggestions but also, without a trace of condescension, first broke the truth to me: "You, my boy, are a sociologist, not a political scientist." I have drawn strength and a measure of consolation from his remarks ever since.

I also benefited greatly from the many insightful comments and questions I received when presenting my work at the Mershon Center at Ohio State University, Harvard University, Brown University, The Center for Strategic and International Studies, the US State Department, the Central Intelligence Agency, and International Studies Association sponsored Workshop on "Identity and International Relations: Beyond the First Wave."

Among the scores of helpful people in Azerbaijan, Russia, and Kazakhstan who assisted me with logistical issues and who donated their time and ideas, I especially want to thank Alexei Vasilev, Rauf Karakazov, Piers Von Berg, Max and Sergei Altantsev, and Elvira Ayapova.

Thanks also to my colleagues in the Political Science Department of Providence College, who – notwithstanding the validity of Rod Hall's observation – gave me their support and useful recommendations. I especially want to single out Sue McCarthy, who read my section on cultural globalization in China and offered only the most tactful suggestions for its improvement. In addition, I was lucky to have fine research assistants: Diane Abramson, Erin Beck, Meridith Hernandez, and Brittany Stalsburg. They not only plowed through vast amounts of primary and secondary material but cheerfully performed all manner of menial tasks, and, most important, helped keep me organized.

I spent many months away from home in the course of my fieldwork. Last, then, I want to thank my pixyish wife Jessie, who magically held everything together during my absences, and my sweet children Joey and Sophie, who always forgave me for missing their birthdays – even when they were young and birthdays still mattered. I suppose I could have written this book without all of you, but it wouldn't have meant very much.

Introduction

Leonid Georgievich Volkov sat in his sparse Astrakhan office and smiled at his guest. Volkov was bemused. As Head of the city government's Department of Youth Affairs, he had never talked to an American about these issues before. How was he to explain the dilemma he faced, in a way that would make sense to this inquiring professor? "Everything has changed," he began. The professor, who said he specialized in the former USSR, presumably already knew this, but still it seemed like an appropriate way to start. "Everything," Volkov repeated, "has completely and utterly changed."

"Now, not only are the economy and society not protected, but neither is the culture." Instead, he explained, the floodgates had opened, and everything – especially the popular culture and the milieu of young people – was suddenly awash in a maelstrom of foreign ideas. "Yes, there has been a huge influence of the West," Volkov commented sadly, shaking his head several times. "An *unfortunate* influence."

And it was easy to understand how this had occurred. "It has taken place through artificial ties, especially films." Hollywood films: violent, sensationalist, tawdry films catering to the lowest common denominator of vulgarity. "This influence affects attitudes and behavior," Volkov went on, "and produces what we can call a 'cult of individualism' instead of any feeling of being part of the collective, of society." It was all so much more complicated, and Volkov wanted the professor to understand this point: there were no simple solutions.

"Individualism is *good* in some ways," he added. This needed to be made clear; after all, Volkov was not some moldy, unreformed Soviet apparatchik. "There *should* be some individualism. Self-sufficiency is a positive thing. Of course, young people need to take care of themselves, and they should contribute to Russia's development." In these ways, he argued, Astrakhan offered wonderful opportunities for young people. "We have oil here," he gestured out the window to the south. "This is the Caspian Sea. We have drilling. We have the market right here."

1

In short, there was nothing wrong with individualism, *per se*. But if everyone was only out for themselves, how would they be able to speak a shared language and come to shared understandings? This was not a black-or-white issue, but rather one of degree. "*Too much* individualism is bad for traditions, it is bad for common understandings, and for the ability to make decisions," Volkov stated solemnly. "And therefore, we must try to choose."

"It is necessary to start in the schools," he proclaimed. "In school, children learn about their culture. They learn their traditions, they learn their own way of life. They already know their own values, and now they learn about them in more depth. Spiritualism. Charity. An Orthodox identity."

"Children are proud, good, self-aware," he continued. Yes, this was the point he had been looking for, and now Volkov warmed to the theme. "Young people know, they *absolutely* know. They *want* Russian culture. They know about the West. Even we knew about the West, the Beatles." Volkov shrugged. So what? "But in the end they naturally want Russian ideas, Russian culture."

But just as naturally, as is always the case with children, it was necessary to provide supervision. And this was Volkov's responsibility. "We have a plan," he informed the professor. "We coordinate with the center; we have our programs here; we meet; the departments work together. And it is not us alone. Everyone, teachers, volunteers, parents are involved. These are all our children. This is our country."

The subject of this book is the connection between state–society relations and national identity formation in post-Soviet Eurasia. "State–society relations" refers here to the entire field of interactions between centralized political institutions and decentralized associations of citizens, to the extent that such interactions arise in regard to shared concerns about collective identity. As such, this book is about the challenges facing people like Volkov, and how they respond to these challenges – independently as well as collaboratively – in the context of globalization.

I begin with the now commonplace observation that identity is a social construction. Indeed, this observation has become so widely accepted as to scarcely occasion notice – especially (but not only) among the legions of constructivist scholars which have sprung up in the past twenty years. And yet this seems to be one of the many situations in which what goes unnoticed also obscures questions which ought to be asked. That is, while abundant scholarship has demonstrated that identity is indeed constructed, remarkably little attention has been paid to the three dimensional *sociality* of identity construction, including the agency involved in conceptualizing, negotiating, and communicating national identity in the context of cultural globalization. How do states and societies respond to foreign cultural flows, and why? Thus, my objective is to understand not simply the *effects* of globalization, but also the *social process* involved in mediating it, and the connections between such processes and specific national identity outcomes. What kinds of actors are involved in constructing national identity; what organizational settings are they located in; what mechanisms do they employ; and within what sorts of interpersonal networks are they embedded? The result is a set of unique, theoretically important insights about the linkage between national identity construction and social-political responses to globalization, which carry far beyond the post-Soviet field.

In problematizing the process of national identity construction, I have chosen to focus on the sub-theme of youth. There are several reasons for making this analytical choice. The first is quite simple: narrowing the scope of inquiry to the youth helps make the sprawling discursive field of national identity formation a bit more manageable. In addition, however, youth identity is a useful proxy for national identity more broadly, inasmuch as it is a particularly sensitive area of collective identity formation. In part this is so because young people are especially attentive to and absorptive of global cultural trends, which helps us understand how the perennial need to re-establish legitimacy is complicated by cultural globalization. As Jean and John Comaroff observe, "youth tend everywhere to occupy the innovative, uncharted borderlands along which the global meets the local."[1] Daunting under any conditions, the inherent difficulties of inter-generational identity transmission become still more problematic amidst the maelstrom of global flows, which call into question established institutions and norms, and thus create sensual temptations among impressionable young people. This raises the other way in which examining youth identity is especially revealing: the contours of youth identity have widely regarded to have enormous implications for national identity as a whole. Perceived changes – or even possible changes – in youth attitudes and behavior therefore generate a tremendous amount of popular anxiety about the prospects for social cohesion, which then becomes the subject of extensive and often contentious public discourse. For these reasons, youth culture is a prominent subject of state policymaking as well as grassroots organization. In short, the official formulation and public enactment of youth identity represents a key modality through which society goes about reproducing itself.

[1] Jean Comaroff and John Comaroff, "Millennial Capitalism: First Thoughts on a Second Coming," *Public Culture*, 12, No. 2 (Spring 2000): 291–343, at p. 308.

This calls for an important qualification: the analytical focus of this book is to explain the *process* of identity construction, not so much its *outcome* – which, as will be discussed in the following chapter, is not particularly unique in any event. The emphasis is thus on the strategic and prescriptive construction of youth identity, as constituting a crucial component of national identity formation under globalization. As we will see below, this has to do with idealized identity constructs and narratives, especially as they are supplied in the course of controlled (or ostensibly controlled) activities deemed healthy and proper for young people. Examples include art exhibits, film forums, reading circles, sporting competitions, and other activities intended for the younger generation at large. The central argument being made here is that attending to such questions yields a set of critical insights into state–society relations, including the way in which state–society relations are worked out through the construction of national identity.

Moreover, to avoid any subsequent misunderstandings, I wish to stress that my proximate analytical goal is *not youth identities in themselves* – i.e., the values, attitudes, outlooks, and characteristic behavior of youth. Not only has this question already been well studied by others,[2] but it fails to engage the particular problem I wish to address, which has to do with the organization of youth socialization and what this reveals about society at large. To be sure, it is impossible to explore these questions fully without considering how the youth themselves respond to the socialization process. Young people are not simply passive recipients, but are actively involved both in engaging – and often contesting – globalization and nation-building. For this reason I consider the views of young people regarding these matters, and I also observe their direct involvement in a number of activities aimed at socializing them. Nevertheless, the actions and attitudes of youth are distinctly secondary themes here. Instead, the main subject under consideration is *the social construction of youth identity, by adults, for the consumption of young people*. I argue that attending to this issue is particularly helpful for coming to grips with a number of key questions related to state–society relations, including the links between state building and nation building under conditions of globalization.

---

[2] Among the important studies to have examined post-Soviet (especially Russian) youth are Hilary Pilkington, ed., *Looking West: Cultural Globalization and Russian Youth Culture* (State College, PA: Penn State University Press, 2002); Fran Markowitz, *Coming of Age in Post-Soviet Russia* (Urbana and Chicago: University of Illinois Press, 2000); Ken Roberts et al., eds., *Surviving Post-communism: Young People in the Former Soviet Union* (Edward Elgar, 2000); James Finckenauer, *Russian Youth: Law, Deviance and the Pursuit of Freedom* (New Brunswick: Transaction Publishers, 1995); and Hilary Pilkington, *Russia's Youth and its Culture: A Nation's Constructors and Constructed* (London and New York: Routledge, 1994).

I have chosen to explore these interconnections by looking at three key post-Soviet states: Russia, Kazakhstan, and Azerbaijan. The former Soviet states are a wonderful laboratory for studying globalization and national identity because since 1992 they have been rapidly inundated by foreign cultural flows, while also having to tackle state building and nation building. With substantially different patterns of political institutionalization and degrees of democratization, they also offer a comparative dimension. However, globalization is largely an urban phenomenon; contestation of and resistance to globalization at the grassroots level takes place mainly in urban centers.[3] For these reasons, I combine my analysis of state-level policymaking regarding national identity with extensive fieldwork in three cities: Astrakhan (Russia); Almaty (Kazakhstan); and Baku (Azerbaijan). Each of these globalizing cities – as regional and/or national centers – provides especially fertile ground for exploring public responses to cultural globalization. Studying them also offers a way of grounding and contextualizing developments which are taking place at the national level in the three countries, and indeed in most countries experiencing globalization. In short, by exploring how globalization and identity formation are mediated by various actors at the national as well as local levels, we are able to grasp what is ultimately at stake for society as a whole with regard to collective identity, social solidarity, and the very nature of the state.

To quickly dispense with definitional issues, for our purposes globalization may be understood in terms of flows: of capital, people, goods, information, and ideas. Moreover, rather than simply referring to the aggregation of such flows, globalization implies an acceleration and intensification of their volume as well as a heightened degree of penetration across nation-state borders. Rather than being merely a structural condition, however, globalization is also a dynamic, intrusive presence, producing constant disruptions in the field of meanings and practices available to actors. One consequence is what has come to be called "deterritorialization," or a loosening of the relationship between culture and place, which in turn complicates the ability of nation-states to conduct their crucial business of nation- and state-building.[4] And yet, collective identity formation is an integral part of the nation and state building business which the post-Soviet states are immersed in, and this highlights the puzzle addressed here: what will be the outcome of this struggle? In short, rather

---

[3] Albert Paolini, *Navigating Modernity: Postcolonialism, Identity, And International Relations* (Boulder: Lynne Rienner, 1999), pp. 9–17.
[4] A critical discussion of this term is John Tomlinson, *Globalization and Culture* (Chicago: University of Chicago Press, 1999), pp. 106–49.

than viewing globalization as an assumed pattern of outcomes, whether homogenization or fragmentation, we are better served by approaching it as an open-ended process. This helps avoid the pitfall of premature closure, or of presuming to understand the ultimate effects of a process which is still very much fluid and fundamentally contested.

As a prelude to examining globalization's effects on identity formation we may begin by considering one of the many insights of Arjun Appadurai, perhaps the most influential writer on cultural globalization today. For Appadurai, the massive flows of ideas across national borders tend to produce supranational attachments, while at the same time diminishing cultural stability.[5] Participation in this process, along with anxiety about its possible effects, sparks a discourse of engagement with globalization which Appadurai calls "imagination as a social practice."[6] Indeed, the focus of this book is the social practice of imagining national identity in the context of globalization. In addition to the content of ideas carried by globalization, the very notion of globalization itself is a part of what gets imagined. As Giddens has argued, this is because globalization is characterized not only by the scope and speed of interconnectedness but also by a "reflexive" self-awareness of being involved in this process.[7] One of the most powerful forms social imagining takes, therefore, has to do with the future of polities which are self-consciously encountering massive international flows, including the questions of whether, or how, they can survive as autonomous entities.

As a result, while neither the particular types of flows nor the social processes associated with national identity formation are fundamentally new, the growing connections between them have, in fact, created something qualitatively new and different with respect to national identity formation. That is, the construction of national identity has been significantly altered by the ever more ubiquitous interference of external forces, and the subsequent need to respond to them systematically through institutional means. This raises the problem of mediation, or how societies attempt to manage the flows of globalization – again, often in quite self-conscious ways.

Perhaps not surprisingly, some of the same deficiencies evident in the literature on globalization are present in the literature on national identity formation. Thus, while the past two decades have seen an outpouring of

---

[5] Arjun Appadurai, *Modernity at Large: Cultural Dimensions of Globalization* (Minneapolis and London: University of Minnesota Press, 1996).

[6] *Ibid.*, p. 31.

[7] Anthony Giddens, *Modernity and Self-Identity: Self and Society in the Late Modern Age* (Stanford: Stanford University Press, 1991), pp. 10–34.

interest in cultural globalization, relatively little work has been devoted to examining how cultural flows produce their effects, including the part played by individual actors in regulating or contesting such flows and their consequences for social identity. To the extent that scholars have considered the problem of mediation at all, they have focused on elites inside and (to a lesser extent) outside of the state.[8] Far less attention has been paid to the role played by non-elite actors in interpreting and adjudicating the influence of foreign ideas. The scholarship to date has also generally emphasized individuals or self-contained groups (i.e., of elites or state officials), rather than examining the relationships between actors embedded in overlapping organizational networks.[9] What tends to be discounted, as a result, is the crucial fact that the "connectivity" engendered by globalization encompasses not only the economic, eco-logical, and technological spheres, but also has a social and institutional dimension.

As should be obvious to the reader by now, I wish to approach the prob-lem of globalization in a quite different way. Empirically, I find an ongoing campaign intended to mediate the effects of cultural globalization, which is joined by state actors at the central and local levels, as well as by activists within various extra-state forms of social organization. Moreover, I find that horizontal and vertical links between all of these actors are common. I argue that by highlighting this social dimension and exploring the link-age between cultural globalization and national identity construction, we gain important insights into the changing nature of state–society relations more broadly. In particular, I would suggest, by focusing on sociality we are able to grasp a fundamental complementarity between state–society relations and modes of collective identity construction, as these become manifest in response to cultural globalization.

State–society relations and national identity formation are mutually intertwined processes; they affect one another in ongoing ways. First, state–society relations influence the process of identity construction by determining the range of actors available to take part in it, the density of interactions across the formal state–society divide, and the prospects for politically consequential cooperation arising from such interactions. Yet the reverse is also true: the very formation of national identity, as a social

---

[8] Examples are Ulf Hannerz, *Cultural Complexity: Studies in the Social Organization of Mean-ing* (New York: Columbia University Press, 1992); Manuel Castells, *The Power of Identity* (Malden, MA: Blackwell, 1997); also David Chaney, *Cultural Change and Everyday Life* (New York: Palgrave, 2002).

[9] An important exception is Aihwa Ong, *Flexible Citizenship: The Cultural Logics of Transna-tionality* (Durham and London: Duke University Press, 1999).

process, not only emerges through state–society relations but also shapes and reshapes these relations. Such processes are always inflected by culture. In the case studies explored here, the dynamic linkage between national identity formation and state–society relations is influenced by two sets of cultural factors: 1) endogenous cultural legacies arising from the Soviet experience, and 2) exogenous cultural flows introduced by globalization, including prevailing ideological interpretations of globalization. This overarching cultural context constrains the processes of identity formation and state–society relations by making certain modalities of organization more likely than others. In these particular cases, therefore, as we will see in detail, the pattern of social response "selected for" by globalization and preexisting cultural legacies is decentralized and flexible, incorporating local grassroots initiatives alongside state policymaking.

Still, the institutional and cultural conditions under which such processes emerge are only part of the story. To understand how identity construction unfolds we also need to come to terms with the actors involved, and the choices they make regarding particular identity constructs and patterns of collaborative action. There is, in other words, no automaticity to the influence of structural factors. Moreover, in engaging the process of identity construction, actors potentially become invested with real agency – as they work out specific constellations of meanings, devise prescriptive patterns for youth socialization, and establish newly appropriate patterns of state–society interaction. While a lesser focus of this study, it should also be noted that youth themselves are obviously implicated in this process through their contestation of the relevant venues and values. In short, by examining identity construction in thick social context, and seeing how actors strategically engaged in it navigate structural conditions as well as how they negotiate particular local outcomes, we gain a nuanced understanding of the agency involved.

In exploring these patterns of social response bound up with the construction of national identity, we encounter a series of ongoing dialogues or social discourses about three main groups of ideas transmitted by globalization. The first group, which carries a distinctly Western pedigree, consists of neoliberal understandings about the desirability of market institutions and of instrumentally rational, efficiency-seeking behavior. The second group, which again emanates largely from the West, comprises various attitudes, values, and lifestyles associated with global pop culture. And yet, as Stuart Hall's conception of "mass popular culture" reminds us, these ideas and attitudes are fostered by the West, but are absorbed and "operate through" local cultural differences, rather than eradicating them.[10] The third group consists of notions of nationalism and state sovereignty, ideas which, over the past two centuries, have become thoroughly global in provenance. These involve assertions of legal and institutional prerogatives as well as imaginings of national solidarity and collective purpose, many of which have their roots in the Soviet period or even earlier, but which are now being rediscovered and/or "reinvented" and pressed into the service of nation-building and state-building schemes.

Of course other ideas circulate within globalization as well. These include various transnational movements, ranging from radical Islamist to anarchist, which express resistance to established institutions and identities. They also include Orthodox, Buddhist, and other spiritual doctrines. Yet the actual influence exerted by these ideas and movements – at least in these countries in general and these cities in particular – remains relatively marginal. While they are of concern to state and society at large, they do not feature prominently in the social discourse of national identity construction and youth socialization. Instead, themes associated with neoliberal individualism, Western pop culture, and nation-state imaginings tend to prevail.

Not surprisingly, these interconnected discourses bound up with marketization, popular culture, and national identity are extensively reflected in state policymaking and diffuse social action. What we discover is that, in each of these cities and countries as a whole, states and social actors have used central ministries as well as decentralized institutions, in order to fight a rearguard cultural battle. This battle is intended not to eradicate Western influence, but rather to limit certain "dangerous excesses" while channeling its perceived beneficial aspects in order to promote certain identity goals and policy purposes. State and non-state elements of society thus respond through a discourse of invented and resurrected traditions, designed to create a historicized image of the ideal citizen as obedient and industrious. This discourse consists of several components. First is an overwhelming preoccupation with Western influences and their identity implications, which are extensively contested. Second, such contestation is repeatedly marked by two fundamental objectives: sanitizing or detoxifying the most virulent strains of globalization in ways consistent with the larger nation-building and state-building project, and coopting its benign or productive features for the same purpose. Third, this

---

[10] Stuart Hall, "The Local and the Global: Globalization and Ethnicity," in Anthony King, ed., *Culture, Globalization, and the World System: Contemporary Conditions for the Representation of Identity* (Minneapolis: University of Minnesota, 1997), pp. 19–39, at p. 28.

preoccupation with the global is mirrored by an obsession with the national, which takes the form of asserting an ostensibly unique, indigenous, and traditional identity, which it is incumbent upon all well-socialized youth to embrace. Along the way, entrepreneurs actively engage in the process of crafting narratives and attempting to mold young people's minds, while also trying to reconcile the contradictions which arise between these "hybrid," or mixed, identity constructs.

This bid is never entirely successful. Instead, in what emerges as a key hallmark of globalization, one finds abundant evidence of contradiction and ambivalence, and slippage between what is sought and attained. This is hardly surprising, since – although the entrepreneurs we encounter would be loath to admit it – the notion of fixity in national identity formation is a deeply illusory one. However, it is still fairly early in the post-Soviet transition, and who knows? Perhaps the outcomes of this effort will be successful, as young people incorporate and reproduce the core of these broadly prescribed national identity constructs. For our purposes, however, the ultimate *outcomes* of youth socialization are far less important than the *process* involved in mediating cultural globalization and national identity formation, as engaged in by state and non-state actors alike.

The remainder of this book is organized as follows. Chapter 1 provides a comparative frame of reference for thinking about the topic of this book, by offering a broad overview of cultural globalization and national identity formation. In addition to sketching out the primary features of "hybridity," I underline the profound similarities in how globalization is responded to in the former USSR and elsewhere in the world. This includes absorption, or a bid to acquire the ideological underpinnings of Western life, such as individual rationality and initiative. At the same time it includes rejection, or the attempt to avoid "excessive" forms of individualism, such as selfishness and sensual indulgence. Finally, it also typically includes assertion, or a plea for retraditionalization, which not only promotes a sense of pride in national aesthetics but also serves as a hedge against harmful foreign influences.

Proceeding from these observations, chapter 2 outlines an interpretive epistemology for explaining identity formation under globalization, by inquiring into the meanings of, and reasons for, specific identity narratives. I offer some tentative reflections on how the typical pattern of national identity response might be explained from various theoretical vantage points, as well as the indeterminacy of such approaches. I argue that it is useful to examine the process empirically, from a discursive and interpretive standpoint, in order to understand the arguments and reasons associated with hybridization in particular settings. I also suggest that tracing how social identity construction takes place offers additional insights into why this process unfolds as it does.

This task is taken up in the following four chapters by turning to the post-Soviet context, in order to explore national identity discourse, policy, cultural entrepreneurship, and everyday interventions into the realm of youth socialization. Chapter 3 turns to a close empirical investigation of the popular discourse concerning national youth identity in the former USSR. As this discourse reveals, the topic – which is fraught with agitation and anxiety – tends to be addressed in the typical global pattern, marked by demands for selective cultural absorption, rejection, and assertion. Chapter 4 considers the official dimension of identity construction by examining, respectively, the form and substance of national youth policy in each of the three countries, including plans for inculcating a uniform identity among the younger generation. Chapter 5 examines the social connections among actors who are involved in implementing official policies at the local level, as well as the degree of cooperation which characterizes their work. Chapter 6 explores the actual interventions undertaken by these actors in everyday contexts, in close interaction with young people.

Having elucidated the process in empirical terms, Chapter 7 returns to the theoretical level. Through a critical review of the literature, and by problematizing assumptions about state–society relations and their relevance for identity formation, I seek to expand the foundation for thinking about national identity construction as a social process. I conclude with some thoughts about the sources of national identity formation, its implications for state–society relations, and the scope of agency within the nation-building process under conditions of globalization.

1   Global responses to globalization

This chapter reviews the literature on cultural globalization. My argument is that globalization produces a strikingly similar pattern, virtually wherever it is encountered. First, the combination of seductive content, disparities in power, and the sheer volume of flows comprising globalization produces a homogenizing tendency, to which post-Soviet elites and mass publics alike are highly sensitive. Rather than being perceived in terms of innocuous "flows," globalization is therefore widely understood as an inundating wave of uniformity that threatens to wash away all cultural difference, undermining the foundation of distinct social and political institutions. Due to the globally dominant discourse of nationalism and the singular legitimacy of the nation-state model, this generates a specific pattern of reaction, marked by desire, anxiety, and the wish to affirm an autonomous (national) self. I illustrate this prevailing response to global cultural flows with examples drawn from a wide variety of countries, and by briefly focusing on the cases of postcolonial India and post-Maoist China. In doing so, I emphasize the deeply ambivalent nature of this process, as well as the abiding ambiguities associated with it.

Comparative hybridization

Much of the controversy over globalization has focused on its ultimate consequences, including the question of whether national identities are likely to be supplanted by local and/or transnational affiliations.[1] A related question is whether, over the *longue durée*, the underlying content of national identities will come to mirror each other through the proliferation

---

[1] For a concise overview of this debate see Manfred Steger, *Globalism: The New Market Ideology* (Lanham, MD: Rowman and Littlefield, 2002), esp. pp. 51–55. See also Tyler Cowen, *Creative Destruction: How Globalization is Changing the World's Cultures* (Princeton and Oxford: Princeton University Press, 2002); Mathew Horsman and Andrew Marshall, *After the Nation-State: Citizens, Tribalism and the New World Disorder* (London: Harper-Collins, 1994); and William Alonso, "Citizenship, Nationality and Other Identities," *Journal of International Affairs*, 48, No. 2 (Winter 1995): 585–99.

of international flows.[2] Those who view current developments in historical perspective are fond of emphasizing the existence of precedents for cultural diffusion. For example, Issawi points out that the high culture of an imperial power was often systematically disseminated throughout the periphery as a means of control, and that under such conditions mass culture tended to follow.[3] Wallerstein has argued that, within the "world system" of capitalist production relations since the sixteenth century, shared and increasingly uniform ideologies have played a key role in stabilizing the system as a whole, lubricating exchange and strengthening commitments despite wrenching social upheavals.[4] Bentley has gone still farther, to propose a general framework for periodizing world history based on cultural interaction as a result of mass migration, imperial campaigns, and long-distance trade.[5] While far from a linear process, according to these and other writers, globalization merely accelerates an historical tendency for the culture of dominant actors to be assimilated in marginal places, thereby facilitating its integration into the prevailing economic and political structure. And it may well be, in very long-term perspective, that the entire trajectory of world history is one of discontinuous yet ultimately massive convergence.[6]

Not surprisingly, this perspective has been countered by a diametrically opposite view. For some scholars, such as Martin Albrow and Andreas Wimmer, globalization leads not to homogeneity or indeed any stable synthesis of ideas, but rather to a radical proliferation of possibilities. Far from producing similarity, this would suggest that the process portends increasingly fragmented, kaleidoscopic identity change, as well as a plethora of overlapping and intermeshing realities.[7] Others have reached a strikingly different conclusion, arguing that cultural globalization almost

[2] For a useful overview of analytical perspectives and projections see David Held, Anthony McGrew, David Goldblatt, and Jonathan Perraton, *Global Transformations: Politics, Economics and Culture* (Stanford: Stanford University Press, 1999), pp. 1–27.

[3] Charles Issawi, *Cross-Cultural Encounters and Conflicts* (New York and Oxford: Oxford University Press, 1998), pp. 23–42.

[4] Immanuel Wallerstein, *The Modern World-System: Capitalist Agriculture and the Origins of the European World-Economy in the Sixteenth Century* (New York: Academic Press, 1974); Wallerstein, *The Modern World-System III: The Second Era of Great Expansion of the Capitalist World-Economy, 1730–1840s.* New York: Academic Press, 1989).

[5] Jerry H. Bentley, "Cross-Cultural Interaction and Periodization in World History," *American Historical Review*, 101, No. 3 (June 1996): 749–70.

[6] G. Eric Hansen, *The Culture of Strangers: Globalization, Localization and the Phenomenon of Exchange* (Lanham, MD: University Press of America, 2002).

[7] Martin Albrow, *The Global Age: State and Society Beyond Modernity* (Stanford: Stanford University Press, 1997), pp. 140–62; also Andreas Wimmer, "Globalizations Avant la Lettre: A Comparative View of Isomorphization and Heteromorphization in an Inter-Connecting World," *Comparative Studies in Society and History*, 43, No. 3 (July 2001): 435–66.

inherently generates a reactionary affirmation of particularism, either because it incites primordial feelings or, more subtly, because in challenging territorial sovereignty it necessitates a compensatory form of social organization.[8]

At least in the near term, there is much to support these ideas. Even where certain imported tastes flagrantly contradict local norms, there is little evidence that their aficionados are inclined to abandon all other traditional attachments. On the contrary, as will be discussed at some length below, clearly in some instances a profound form of rejectionism goes hand in hand with an exclusionary return to tradition. On the whole, however, such extreme responses are the exception. Instead, people situated in globalized settings seem capable of maintaining and moving between multiple, often quite dissimilar identities.[9] As Arnett has argued with respect to youth practices, globalization tends to produce "bicultural identities" which include local as well as global characteristics.[10] The tension between them appears to be most manageable when the enactment of exogenously given identities can be segmented in time and space, or when it involves the consumption of discrete products which represent modernity. While the contrast between these and native customs may be jarring, such differences need not be truly incompatible or unsustainable. For example, as Saldanha observes, Indian youths who participate in psychedelic musical "raves" on the weekend return to their local jobs and traditional social practices during the week.[11]

At least over the medium term, however, with respect to popular culture and national identity, the pattern appears somewhat different. Within this time-frame, the overwhelming trend of globalization – in spite of its many inconsistent and contradictory aspects – is neither homogenization nor backlash; nor is it a dichotomization of sameness and difference. Rather, it is characterized by a form of blending often referred to as hybridization.[12] As a specific mode of cultural mixing, this involves a

[8] Helmuth B. Berking, "Ethnicity is Everywhere: On Globalization and the Transformation of Cultural Identity," *Current Sociology*, 51, No. 3–4 (May 2003): 248–64.

[9] On this point see Peter Kloos, "The Dialectics of Globalization and Localization," in Don Kalb *et al.*, eds., *The Ends of Globalization: Bringing Society Back In* (Rowman and Littlefield, 2000), pp. 281–97; and Jan Aart Scholte, "Globalisation and Social Change (Part II)," *Transnational Associations*, 50, No. 2 (March/April 1998): 62–79.

[10] Jeffrey Jensen Arnett, "The Psychology of Globalization," *American Psychologist*, 57, No. 10 (October 2002): 774–83.

[11] Arun Saldanha, "Fear and Loathing in Goa," *The UNESCO Courier*, 53, No. 7/8 (July/August 2000): 51–3. See also Timothy J. Scrase, "Television, the Middle Classes and the Transformation of Cultural Identities in West Bengal, India," *Gazette: International Journal for Communication Studies*, 64, No. 4 (August 2002): 323–42.

[12] For a critical review of the literature on this concept see Marwan Kraidy, "Hybridity in Cultural Globalization," *Communication Theory*, 12, No. 3 (August 2002): 316–39.

process of "localizing" the products transmitted through globalization. The resulting dynamic, which is nicely described by Hannerz, consists of an active process of "reaching out" to global flows in order to incorporate market and other functional mechanisms, while also adapting them to local institutional contexts and cultural forms.[13] Hybridization therefore not only develops through, but also facilitates, an increased involvement in international flows.[14] It is partly for this reason that critics on the left reject the very term as part of an apologetic and enabling language of neoliberalism.[15]

Setting aside the question of whether globalization is a positive or negative development, however, for the present purposes the point to be underlined is simply that the reflexive awareness of it leads to the strategic pursuit of hybridization – thus constituting yet another standard aspect of globalization. The ensuing discourse, which continually works itself out in local contexts, is marked by three characteristic strands: selective absorption, selective rejection, and the assertion of something quintessentially "national." While in some respects a rather blunt analytical tool, making this tripartite distinction turns out to be quite helpful for grasping the key social and intellectual features of hybridization. The following sections lay out the main contours of this discourse.

Absorption

Globalization is often decried (and sometimes celebrated) for causing the homogenization of almost everything, almost everywhere in the world. This is evident in terms of the standardization of technology, style, attitudes, and economic organization, all within an overarching cultural synthesis rooted in Western urban centers. For some observers, this pattern suggests that not only are disparate places in the world becoming the same, they are in fact being "Westernized" as part of a massive global

---

See also Frederick Buell, *National Culture and the New Global System* (Baltimore: Johns Hopkins University Press, 1994); and Jan Nederveen Pieterse, "Globalization as Hybridization," in Mike Featherstone, Scott Lash, and Roland Robertson, eds., *Global Modernities* (London: Sage, 1995), pp. 45–68.

[13] Ulf Hannerz, "Thinking about Culture in a Global Ecumene," in James Lull, ed., *Culture in the Communication Age* (London and New York: Routledge, 2001), pp. 54–71. Hannerz prefers the term "creolization."

[14] This pattern has led some observers to characterize globalization as leading to a "dialectic" of opposing tendencies, consisting precisely of flow and identity closure. See Birgit Meyer and Peter Geschiere, "Introduction," in Birgit Meyer and Peter Geschiere, eds., *Globalization and Identity: Dialectics of Flow and Closure* (Oxford: Blackwell, 1999), pp. 1–15.

[15] Kraidy, "Hybridity in Cultural Globalization."

movement.[16] Much of this is widely known. Rather than simply providing an endless litany of examples of cultural homogenization, only its most salient aspects will be mentioned here.

At the national and local levels this convergence has been manifested in the striking uniformity of bureaucratic-administrative structures and practices. This includes not only the apparatus of the nation-state, but also the contours of social policy and public administration, as evident for example in the standardization of government retirement plans and old-age social security systems.[17] The same holds for education practices: despite sub-national variation in curricular standards, assessment approaches, and use of information technology, the broad cultural parameters of educational reform are increasingly moving in lockstep all over the world.[18] A central element of this convergence has been the crystallization of a neoliberal policy line, which has functioned as a paradigm for development since the mid to late 1980s, and which by the turn of the century had achieved the nearly unquestioned status of dogma.[19] In all of these functional respects, the cultural artifacts of homogenization may be viewed as manifestations of hegemony, understood as a cultural order associated with power.[20]

Obviously, some of the above forms of homogenization are at least somewhat removed from the areas of youth culture and youth policy which this book will address. Yet although administrative structure and some forms of policy standardization do not directly affect youth, many

[16] Serge Latouche, *Westernization of the World: The Significance, Scope and Limits of the Drive towards Global Uniformity*, translated by Rosemary Morris (Cambridge, MA: Polity Press, 1996).

[17] A wealth of examples can be found in John Boli and George M. Thomas, eds., *Constructing World Culture: International Nongovernmental Organizations since 1875* (Stanford: Stanford University Press, 1999). See also Connie McNeely, *Constructing the Nation-State: International Organization and Prescriptive Action* (Westport, CT: Greenwood Press, 1995); and Alex Inkeles, "Convergence in Societal Systems," in Eliezer Ben-Rafael and Yitzhak Sternberg, eds., *Identity, Culture and Globalization* (Leiden, Boston, and Cologne: Brill, 2001), pp. 161–75.

[18] Martin Carnoy and Diana Rhoten, "What Does Globalization Mean for Educational Change? A Comparative Approach," *Comparative Education Review*, 46, No. 1 (February 2002): 1–9.

[19] Thomas J. Biersteker, "The 'Triumph' of Neoclassical Economics in the Developing World: Policy Convergence and Bases of Governance in the International Economic Order," in James N. Rosenau and Erenst O. Czempiel, eds., *Governance without Government: Order and Change in World Politics* (Cambridge: Cambridge University Press, 1992), pp. 102–31; Rodney Bruce Hall, "The Discursive Demolition of the Asian Development Model," *International Studies Quarterly*, 47, No. 1 (March 2003): 71–99.

[20] As Laitin argues, hegemony understood in this way "yields a set of conflicts that automatically and commonsensically stand at the top of the political agenda." David Laitin, *Hegemony and Culture: Politics and Religious Change among the Yoruba* (Chicago and London: University of Chicago Press, 1986), p. 107.

aspects of neoliberalism and normative change are quite pertinent in this regard, even outside of the educational context. And, as we will see, the underlying emphases on rational efficiency and cosmopolitan awareness are quite central to issues of youth and upbringing.

Even more significant than official-institutional and high culture – especially for youth – is the spread of popular culture from developed to less developed parts of the world. Not only has it become the chief hallmark of globalization, but popular culture also constitutes an important mechanism through which globalization operates on the whole. By far the single most widespread and vivid means of diffusing ideas and identities is the electronic media, within which audiovisual media, including cinema and television (which are still largely dominated by Hollywood) are perhaps especially effective in diffusing Western constructs and commodities.[21] Potent though they are, however, media sources of diffusion are not the only major vehicle for the spread of popular culture, or for absorption more generally. Another important factor is the emergence of transnational networks characterized by high levels of mobility and communication. A growing number of studies suggest that the connections between diasporas and their national homelands are inherently characterized by a kind of cultural arbitrage, whereby novel ideas and practices are negotiated for their prospective fit into local systems of meaning.[22] To some extent such networks promote absorption across a gradient of power, as practices which appear adaptive for making a successful transition to life in the West are appropriated by those hoping either to make such a transition themselves or to recreate the same conditions at home.

It is, of course, important not to assume that global cultural flows are monolithically Western, still less American. As numerous scholars

---

[21] On Hollywood's global dominance see UNESCO, "Survey of National Cinematography," 2000, available online at: http://www.unesco.org/culture/industries; also Cowen, *Creative Destruction*, pp. 73–101. On the related dominance of distribution networks and "movie merchants" see Aida Hozic, "The Political Economy of Global Culture – A Case Study of the Film Industry," in Reneo Lukic and Michael Brint, eds., *Culture, Politics, and Nationalism in the Age of Globalization* (Burlington, VT: Ashgate, 2001), pp. 55–78; also Aviad E. Raz, "Domesticating Disney: Onstage Strategies of Adaptation in Tokyo Disneyland," *Journal of Popular Culture*, 33, No. 4 (Spring 2000): 77–99.

[22] See for example George Lipsitz, *Dangerous Crossroads: Popular Music, Postmodernism, and the Poetics of Place* (London and New York: Verso, 1994); Michael P. Smith and Luis E. Guarnizo, *Transnationalism from Below* (Piscataway, NJ: Transaction Publishers, 1998); Jocelyne Cesari, "Global Multiculturalism: The Challenge of Heterogeneity," *Alternatives: Global, Local, Political*, Supplement, 27, No. 1 (February 2002): 5–19; Peggy Levitt, "Social Remittances: Migration Driven Local-Level Forms of Cultural Diffusion," *The International Migration Review*, 32, No. 4 (Winter 1998): 926–48; Ashley Carruthers, "National Identity, Diasporic Anxiety, and Music Video Culture in Vietnam," in Yao Souchou, ed., *House of Glass: Culture, Modernity, and the State in Southeast Asia* (Singapore: Institute of Southeast Asian Studies, 2001), pp. 119–49.

have pointed out, mass media flows are not unidirectional from core to periphery; on the contrary, cases abound of local culture being brought to the metropole and the West.[23] And certainly Western exports are not the only engine driving globalization. Japanese culture is arguably an important and distinctive challenger to Western hegemony in marketing a global ecumene.[24] Furthermore, as Larkin has observed, the popularity of Indian film among Hausa youth in Nigeria appears to be due to its usefulness in allowing them to test or even transgress cultural constraints "without engaging with the heavy ideological burden of 'becoming western'."[25]

Nevertheless, while serving as a vehicle for disseminating indigenous and traditional styles, the Internet as well as mass media outlets overwhelmingly foster the spread of Western (often American-based) aesthetics. This is perhaps most evident in the tendency for popular cultural artifacts to become rapidly disseminated and imitated. In particular, journalists and academics alike have pointed to the striking tendency for Western tastes, manners, and sensibilities to become dispersed worldwide. Obvious examples include Western fashions, sexualized self-presentation (especially of women), and the everyday trappings of luxurious lifestyles.[26] One result has been the emergence of entire genres of mimesis, even when these are leavened by the incorporation of other native or foreign influences. An example is Arabesk music and popular culture in Turkey, which features extensive and often crass imitation of lowbrow Western lifestyles alongside "Arabian" elements.[27] Even highly successful Japanese products and marketing strategies tend to represent

[23] E.g., Philippe Legrain, "Cultural Globalization is Not Americanization," *Chronicle of Higher Education*, 49, No. 35 (May 9, 2003), B7.

[24] Koichi Iwabuchi, *Recentering Globalization: Popular Culture and Japanese Transnationalism* (Durham: Duke University Press, 2002).

[25] Brian Larkin, "Indian Films and Nigerian Lovers: Media and the Creation of Parallel Modernities," in Jonathan Xavier Inda and Renato Rosaldo, eds., *The Anthropology of Globalization: A Reader* (Malden, MA: Blackwell, 2002), p. 354.

[26] See Hiroshi Narumi, "Fashion Orientalism and the Limits of Counter Culture," *Postcolonial Studies*, 3, No. 3 (November 2000): 293–309; Perry Johansson, "Consuming the Other: the Fetish of the Western Woman in Chinese Advertising and Popular Culture," *Postcolonial Studies*, 2, No. 3 (November 1999): 377–88; Beng-Huat Chua, "World Cities, Globalisation and the Spread of Consumerism: A View of Singapore," *Urban Studies*, 35, Nos. 5/6 (May 1998): 981–1000; G. Pascal Zachary, "The World Gets in Touch with its Inner American," *Mother Jones*, 24, No. 1 (January 1999): 50–6; Helena Norberg-Hodge, "The March of the Monoculture," *Ecologist*, 29, No. 3 (May/June 1999): 194–7.

[27] Meral Ozbeck, "Arabesk Culture: A Case of Modernization and Popular Identity," in Sibel Bozdogan and Resat Kasaba, eds., *Rethinking Modernity and National Identity in Turkey* (Seattle: University of Washington Press, 1997), pp. 211–32.

cultural translations, intended either to compete with Western products in Western markets or to adapt Western products to Asian tastes.[28]

Such absorptive tendencies are notoriously pronounced among the youth, who are both highly attuned to popular cultural trends and massively exposed to foreign-based media. Most important are cinema, popular music, and youth magazines, all of which are nearly universal in scope and message.[29] Consequently, the more a given region is exposed to globalization the more intense the absorption of Western culture (especially popular culture) tends to be among the younger generation. In a place like Bangalore, India, the typical result is that young elites who can afford to do so reproduce Western advertising, fashion, film, dance, the macho car culture of "driving around," and the social scene of "going out" to private parties. In these and other symbolic ways they thereby repudiate the backwards, traditional-oriental India, and instead embrace the West and, along the way, reconstruct India as modern and even – ideally – as part of the West.[30] Interestingly, this response of young people appears to run somewhat contrary to that of adults, who are arguably less susceptible to the iconic allure of Western goods or the challenges posed to engrained culture and institutions (including gender) by global narratives.[31]

[28] Harumi Befu, "Globalization Theory from the Bottom Up: Japan's Contribution," *Japanese Studies*, 23, No. 1 (May 2003): 3–22.

[29] Pam Nilan, "Young People and Globalizing Trends in Vietnam," *Journal of Youth Studies*, 2, No. 3 (October 1999): 353–70; Jack Banks, "MTV and the Globalization of Popular Culture," *Gazette*, 59, No. 1 (1997): 43–60; Hilary Brown, "American Media Impact on Jamaican Youth: A Cultural Dependency Thesis," in Hopeton S. Dunn, ed., *Globalization, Communications and Caribbean Identity* (New York: St. Martin's Press, 1995), pp. 56–82; and Lynette Lashley, "Television and the Americanization of the Trinbagonian Youth: A Study of Six Secondary Schools," in *ibid.*, pp. 83–97; Mark Liechty, "Media, Markets and Modernization: Youth Identities and the Experience of Modernity in Kathmandu, Nepal," in Vered Amit-Talai and Helena Wulff, eds., *Youth Cultures: A Cross-Cultural Perspective* (London and New York: Routledge, 1995), pp. 166–201.

[30] Arun Saldanha, "Music, Space, Identity: Geographies of Youth Culture in Bangalore," *Cultural Studies*, 16, No. 3 (May 2002): 337–50. See also Suman Verma and T. S. Saraswathi, "Adolescence in India: Street Urchins or Silicon Valley Millionaires?" in B. Bradford Brown, Reed W. Larson, and T. S. Saraswathi, eds., *The World's Youth: Adolescence in Eight Regions of the Globe* (New York: Cambridge University Press, 2002), pp. 105–40.

[31] Srinivas argues that because India is a relatively developed country with substantial prior exposure to the West, commodities need not be consumed simply in order to demonstrate an affinity with things Western and modern. In making this claim Srinivas appears to overlook the contrary experience of young people. Tulasi Srinivas, "A Tryst with Destiny: The Indian Case of Cultural Globalization," in Peter Berger and Samuel Huntington, eds., *Many Globalizations: Cultural Diversity in the Contemporary World* (New York: Oxford University Press, 2002), pp. 89–116. See also Steve Derné, "The (Limited) Effect of Cultural Globalization in India: Implications for Culture Theory," *Poetics*, 33, No. 1 (February 2005): 33–47.

In addition to media flows, popular culture is not only marked but to a significant extent actually caused and constituted by the flow of consumer goods, along with their "commodified narratives" of values and understandings about social and economic organization.[32] These obviously influence young and old alike. Again, while such flows (in the form of trade) have an ancient pedigree as a source of cultural mixing, they have been intensified in recent decades by the instantaneous availability of goods advertised in the global media. A facilitating factor is the proliferation of urban shopping malls, in which indigenous as well as cosmopolitan lifestyles and commodities commingle with a stylized blend of traditional and modern architecture, further increasing the possibilities for cultural borrowing and transformation.[33] In the mall and elsewhere, the mimicry of modern architecture is significant in its own right as a symbol of intercultural literacy, thereby contributing to the emergence of hybrid lifestyles. And like the mall, the creation of trendy waterfront districts (often fronted by post-industrial lofts) provides a vivid experience of modern, urbane sophistication, all of which works not only to reproduce class distinctions but also to propagate materialist-acquisitive values and to link them to commercialized symbols.[34]

Rejection

Despite the profound allure of the West, this modernizing and homogenizing trend is only one part of the overall pattern of hybridization. A counter-trend of rejection arises in direct response to foreign practices which conflict with established local practices and values, and which, if left unchecked, threaten to homogenize national culture.[35] Only to a minor extent can this be understood as a fundamentalist reaction, such as that expressed by militant Islamists or other groups philosophically opposed to globalization *per se*.[36] Rejection does not, in other words, generally arise as an abstract commentary on foreign culture, but is

---

[32] Frederic Jameson, "Globalization as a Philosophical Issue," in Frederic Jameson and Masao Miyoshi, eds., *The Cultures of Globalization* (Durham and London: Duke University Press, 1998), pp. 54–77.

[33] Mona Abaza, "Shopping Malls, Consumer Culture and the Reshaping of Public Space in Egypt," *Theory, Culture and Society*, 18, No. 5 (October 2001): 97–122.

[34] Caglar Keyder, "The Housing Market from Informal to Global," in Caglar Keyder, *Istanbul: Between the Global and the Local* (Lanham, MD: Rowman and Littlefield, 1999), pp. 143–71; Emanuela Guano, "Spectacles of Modernity: Transnational Imagination and Local Hegemonies in Neoliberal Buenos Aires," *Cultural Anthropology*, 17, No. 2 (May 2002): 181–210.

[35] Gregory Jusdanis, *The Necessary Nation* (Princeton: Princeton University Press, 2001), pp. 188–92.

[36] The prospect of an Islamic backlash was popularized by Samuel Huntington's thesis of a "clash of civilizations" as well as by Benjamin Barber's sketch of the opposing tendencies,

instead a direct response to the immediate practice of absorption. As such it is also intertwined with assertion. Within the hybridization narrative, then, rejection serves three complementary purposes: 1) to facilitate assertion; 2) to limit absorption; and 3) paradoxically, to allow further absorption.

Some of these functions of rejection are intrinsic to nationalism more broadly. After all, the bid to proclaim and defend national uniqueness, almost by definition, requires limiting change in those practices most constitutive of national identity. It is very much this concern which underlies the popular Argentine humorist Alejandro Dolina's routines about "modernization." For Dolina modernization poses a threat to traditional culture, ranging from the tango to native festivals and foods, and ultimately to national identity itself.[37] The fact that his depictions of cultural change have so much popular resonance in Argentina suggests that the comedian's anxieties are widely shared. Furthermore, resistance to the loss of identity often transcends narrow instrumental issues. Similar concerns are triggered by mimicking the West almost regardless of the quality of the practices involved. Thus, Brazilian critics have also voiced strenuous resistance to the excessive imitation of Hollywood film techniques, quite aside from the question of whether such techniques might enhance viewer satisfaction.[38]

The crux of the matter, though, is almost always shared values. At times, as in much of modernizing Asia, the focus of rejection is on the laziness and decadence of Western culture, which is contrasted with the Asian "work ethic."[39] But everywhere, rejection is expressed in the form of anxiety about the potentially corrupting effects of global mass media, with its perceived emphasis on violence, sexuality, consumerism, and other forms of moral lassitude. Typical responses – i.e., of haranguing young people and trying to counter Western influences by substituting

---

"Jihad" and "McWorld." It has since been the subject of countless scholarly and journalistic analyses. Samuel P. Huntington, *The Clash of Civilizations and the Remaking of World Order* (New York: Simon and Schuster, 1996); Benjamin Barber, *Jihad vs. McWorld: How Globalism and Tribalism are Reshaping the World* (New York: Ballantine Books, 1995). See also Stephen Vertigans and Philip W. Sutton, "Globalisation Theory and Islamic Praxis," *Global Society*, 16, No. 1 (January 2002): 31–46. On the anti-globalization movement in general see Frederick Buttel, "Some Observations on the Anti-Globalization Movement," *Australian Journal of Social Issues*, 38, No. 1 (February 2003): 95–116.

[37] Rita De Grandis, "The Voice of Alejandro 'Negro' Dolina: Towards a Repositioning of Populist Discourse," *Studies in Latin American Popular Culture*, 16 (1997): 127–45.

[38] Maria Helena Braga e Vaz da Costa, "Representation and National Identity in Rio de Janeiro: Walter Salles, Jr.'s, *A Grande Arte*," *Studies in Latin American Popular Culture*, 20 (2001): 165–85.

[39] Alastair Bonnett, *The Idea of the West: Culture, Politics and History* (New York: Palgrave, 2004), pp. 107–22.

indigenous programming – can be found all over the world.[40] Because these social pathologies are so widely manifest in youth culture, and because of the stake all societies have in their youth, there tends to be particular sensitivity to the effects of globalization in this area.

In response to such perceived or anticipated influence, authorities have launched massive programs to counter permissive attitudes toward drug use, sex before marriage, and violent or other anti-social behavior.[41] Curtailing such influence often involves extensive policing in an effort to prevent offensive or cultural corrosive content from appearing in the media. Even short of drastic rejectionist measures such as those taken in Iran, examples of such state intervention abound, particularly throughout Asia. Examples include censorship in Singapore, official denunciations in India and Indonesia, and Malaysia's ban on unlicensed satellite dishes (lifted in 1996). As then Information Minister Mohamed Rahmat stated, "We can ill-afford the influx of foreign elements which could be detrimental to our efforts in nation-building."[42] At times such policies have been highly specific in seeking to filter out certain especially nefarious elements. For example, in Vietnam in 1995–6 the state responded to a perceived invasion of negative Western influences by carrying out "cultural purity" and "cultural cleansing" drives, including the confiscation and destruction of hundreds of thousands of cassettes and CDs.[43] In 1997 the South Korean broadcasting service launched a short-lived attempt to ban performers with dyed hair, dreadlocks, tattoos, exposed midriffs, male earrings, and sexually provocative dress, while in Malaysia the state has attempted to prohibit hip hop and heavy metal music.[44]

[40] For example, see Kavitha Cardoza, "Parental Control Over Children's Television Viewing in India," *Contemporary South Asia*, 11, No. 2 (July 2002): 135–61.

[41] Kuldip Rampal, "Cultural Bane or Sociological Boon? Impact of Satellite Television on Urban Youth in India," in Yahya Kamalipour and Kuldip Rampal, eds., *Media, Sex, Violence, and Drugs in the Global Village* (New York: Rowman and Littlefield, 2001), pp. 115–30.

[42] Monroe Price, *Media and Sovereignty: The Global Information Revolution and its Challenge to State Power* (Cambridge, MA: The MIT Press, 2002), p. 12. While restrictions have been relaxed since 1996 in Malaysia, many remain in place and have been subject to far less social challenge than in neighboring Indonesia. See Philip Kitley, "Subject to What?: A Comparative Analysis of Recent Approaches to Regulating Television and Broadcasting in Indonesia and Malaysia," *Inter-Asia Cultural Studies*, 2, No. 3 (December 2001): 503–14.

[43] Carruthers, "National Identity, Diasporic Anxiety, and Music Video Culture in Vietnam," pp. 132–4.

[44] Keith Howard, "Exploding Ballads: The Transformation of Korean Pop Music," in Richard King and Timothy Craig, eds., *Global Goes Local: Popular Culture in Asia* (Vancouver: University of British Columbia Press, 2002), pp. 80–95; Rüdiger Korff, "Globalisation and Communal Identities in the Plural Society of Malaysia," *Singapore Journal of Tropical Geography*, 22, No. 3 (November 2001): 270–83.

Without resorting to outright censorship state policing may take the form of behind-the-scenes pressure, as with the South Korean government encouraging network executives to produce more family-friendly shows.[45] Similarly, several Asian states have moved to restrict Internet access, ranging from extreme ban in North Korea and Myanmar to more moderate screening, pressure, and surveillance in China, Vietnam, and Singapore.[46] Nor have such interventions been limited to states espousing what was referred to in the 1990s as the "Asian Values" model of national identity. In Latin America, concern over dependence on US imports in the television and movie industries has led Argentina and Brazil to impose market restrictions, and the Organization of American States has explored the possibility of a regional cultural policy in order to manage globalization.[47] Throughout the former USSR, one can detect steps in the direction of state control over media content. Thus in Uzbekistan, the closure of a television station in 1999 was justified in part by the station's practice of showing "films that contradict national ideology, propagandizing violence and moral indecency (Hollywood films)."[48] Likewise, while official steps to restrict morally questionable content in media have not been taken in Ukraine, nationalists there tend to hold similar views on the desirability of such censorship.[49]

Here again, however, the impulse to protect national culture and to safeguard the younger generation is hardly a new one. On the contrary, such efforts have always been linked to the project of nationalism. Already by the early nineteenth century the goal of producing well-socialized, nationally identified citizens led to an increasing focus on children, and this was accompanied by recurrent popular panics over the supposedly ruinous effects of popular culture on youth. The importance of a proper moral upbringing began to be stressed in the context of nationalism. As

[45] Jong Kang, "Lethal Combination: Sex and Violence in the World of Korean Television," in Kamalipour and Rampal, eds., *Media, Sex, Violence, and Drugs in the Global Village*, (New York: Rowman and Littlefield, 2001), pp. 153–65.

[46] Nina Hachigian, "The Internet and Power in One-Party East Asian States," *Washington Quarterly*, 25, No. 3 (Summer 2002): 41–58.

[47] OAS, "Cultural Industries in the Latin American Economy: Current Status And Outlook In The Context Of Globalization," available online at: http://www. oas.org/culture/pub.html.

[48] Cited in Ivan Sigal and Joshua Machleder, "Independent Media and Alternative Narratives in Central Asia," unpublished paper presented at the Central Eurasian Studies Society annual conference, October 2003.

[49] Stephen Shulman, "Cultures in Competition: Ukrainian Foreign Policy and the 'Cultural Threat' from Abroad," *Europe-Asia Studies*, 50, No. 2 (March 1998), p. 293. As discussed below, similar ideas have circulated in the other post-Soviet states considered in this study.

Mosse notes, to some extent this was attributable to jockeying among classes. The bourgeoisie sought to distinguish itself from the profligate aristocracy and vulgar masses, and to underpin its claim to status, by emphasizing a new set of "proper" sexual mores. Yet this movement was also inextricable from the project of nationalism, since self-control was considered necessary for social cohesion and order, which in turn were explicitly related to the requirements of nationhood.[50] These developments led to a new representation of the state as paternalistic guardian of social morality, which culminated in the institutionalization of an entire apparatus charged with overseeing the raising of children.[51] The main difference today is that much of the popular cultural threat to youth and societal values comes from the outside world, and threatens to elude the state's regulatory ability. In response, states have mobilized propaganda campaigns to counter the impact of Western messages on impressionable minds.

Even this, in fact, is not entirely new. In Indonesia under Suharto, for example, proponents of forging a new national identity were highly sensitive to cultural flows that might undermine desirable patterns of socialization. By the early 1970s elites were warning of the "estrangement" of youth from national culture due to increasingly deviant, and highly Westernized, expressions of social and sexual attitudes.[52] In the Soviet Union already by the mid-1950s, official ideologues railed against the tendency for young people to "blindly imitate foreign fashion and bow before the 'American way of life.'"[53] Under full-blown globalization, however, both the challenges to national identity and the organized responses they evoke are considerably magnified. Consequently, inasmuch as globalization is nearly a ubiquitous process, resistance to absorption (as a strand of cultural hybridization) has become pervasive as well. Therefore while it is easy to imagine radical Islam or the policies pursued by Turkmenistan as being quintessentially rejectionist, in fact such responses are merely extreme. Selective rejection is practiced in most, if not all, contemporary societies experiencing globalization.

[50] George Mosse, *Nationalism and Sexuality: Respectability and Abnormal Sexuality in Modern Europe* (New York: Howard Fertig, 1985). Thanks to Jim Richter for drawing my attention to this point.

[51] John Springhall, *Youth, Popular Culture, and Moral Panics: Penny Gaffs to Gangsta-Rap, 1830–1996* (New York: St. Martin's Press, 1998); Sylvia Schafer, *Children in Moral Danger and the Problem of Government in Third Republic France* (Princeton: Princeton University Press, 1997).

[52] Benedict Anderson, *Language and Power: Exploring Political Cultures in Indonesia* (Ithaca: Cornell University Press, 1990), pp. 183–90.

[53] Alan M. Ball, *Imagining America: Influence and Images in Twentieth-Century Russia* (New York: Rowman and Littlefield, 2003), p. 183.

Apropos of this point it is striking that some scholars of Japan tend to attribute unusually resistant qualities to Japanese culture. For example, Mayumi Itoh has suggested that Japanese culture contains intrinsically reactive qualities which help national uniqueness persevere in the face of homogenizing trends. Accordingly, past some point, a tendency for openness (*kokusaika*) triggers an offsetting and especially powerful tendency for insularity (*sakoku*).[54] Pursuing a related theme, Gerard Delanty argues that the imposition of Americanization without colonization meant that key aspects of Japanese culture remained essentially intact, as a result of which "Americanization . . . affirmed existing identities rather than leading to the creation of new ones." Moreover, as a reflection of this cultural resilience, "Instead of mass consumption of Americanized products, characterized by convenience, newness and a desire for material comforts, a new generation of Japanese are emerging who are more discriminating. . . ."[55] In a similar vein, it is possible to interpret recent legislation to restore the prewar flag and anthem as a typically bristling Japanese reaction to global encroachments.[56]

Such arguments appear to be highly selective in focusing on rejectionism while overlooking or discounting the significance of absorptive tendencies. Some recent scholarship has begun to highlight the latter. Thus, despite strenuous efforts by the elite to preserve Japan's "core cultural values," the encroachments of globalization appear to be steadily eroding both the sense and actuality of national distinctiveness.[57] It is even possible to argue that the self-conscious emergence of Japanese traditional symbolism since the 1990s represents not only resistance in its superficial content, but more subtly in its commodified forms and institutional contours actually reflects the triumphant march of globalization.[58] The notion of Japanese exceptionalism is therefore probably best

---

[54] Mayumi Itoh, *The Globalization of Japan* (New York: St. Martin's Press, 2000).

[55] Gerard Delanty, "Consumption, Modernity and Japanese Cultural Identity: The Limits of Americanization?" in Ulrich Beck, Nathan Sznaider, and Rainer Winter, eds., *Global America? The Cultural Consequences of Globalization* (Liverpool: Liverpool University Press, 2003), pages 117 and 124, respectively.

[56] See Gavan McCormack, "New Tunes for an Old Song: Nationalism and Identity in Post-Cold War Japan," in Roy Starrs, ed., *Nations Under Siege: Globalization and Nationalism in Asia* (New York: Palgrave, 2002), pp. 137–67.

[57] Neil Renwick, "Japan.com," *National Identities*, 3, No. 2 (July 2001): 169–85. An important example of this is the Japanese Ministry of Education's embrace of standard curricular models. See Lynn Parmenter, "Internationalization in Japanese Education: Current Issues and Future Prospects," in Nelly Stromquist and Karen Monkman, eds., *Globalization and Education: Integration and Contestation Across Cultures* (Blue Ridge Summit, PA: Rowman and Littlefield, 2000), pp. 237–54.

[58] Tomiko Yoda, "A Roadmap to Millennial Japan," *The South Atlantic Quarterly*, 99, No. 4 (Fall 2000): 629–68; and see Kenichi Ohmae, *The End of the Nation State: The Rise of Regional Economies* (New York: The Free Press, 1995), pp. 35–9.

understood as part of a subjective reading of Japanese society which reflects the resilience of national mythology more than the actual resilience of indigenous culture. What to make of the embrace of rap music, where performers have not only adopted dreadlocks but have even altered language patterns and idioms to accommodate rap rhythms? And yet, as will be discussed further below, to some extent the question is hard to answer objectively; much depends on which aspects the observer attends to. Thus it can also be argued that Japanese rap reveals the persistence of traditional themes, as the lyrics tend to reflect national and parochial issues.[59]

Perhaps it is simply too early to say; it may indeed be the case that Japan displays extraordinary resistance to outside enculturation. It may also prove to be the case that Japan has found a way to transcend the homogenizing aspects of globalization by refashioning foreign influences into an inimitable (and highly marketable) manifestation of "national cool."[60] For the time being, however, the vigor and even the apparent successes of its assertion and rejectionism should not be taken to imply that Japan is unique in contesting cultural globalization. Even a cursory, comparative survey of national responses suggests that the self-conscious rejection of foreign culture has become a normal, everyday part of delineating identity boundaries all over the world.

Assertion

The final feature of hybridization consists of articulating a coherent national identity based on traditional elements intermingled with modern-global norms and institutions, as a way of integrating society while simultaneously facilitating international integration.[61] This typically involves the elaborate uncovering and revival of indigenous values and practices. Here we typically encounter the state attempting to present itself as the guardian of national tradition, even when doing so requires

---

[59] Ian Condry, "The Social Production of Difference: Imitation and Authenticity in Japanese Rap Music," in Heide Fehrenbach and Uta G. Poiger, eds., *Transactions, Transgressions, and Transformations: American Culture in Western Europe and Japan* (New York: Berghahn Books, 2000), pp. 166–84; Dave Laing, "The Music Industry and the 'Cultural Imperialism' Thesis," *Media, Culture and Society*, 8 (1986): 331–41.

[60] Douglas McGray, "Japan's Gross National Cool," *Foreign Policy*, No. 130 (May/Jun 2002): 44–54.

[61] Shampa Biswas, "W(h)ither the Nation-State? National and State Identity in the Face of Fragmentation and Globalisation," *Global Society: Journal of Interdisciplinary International Relations*, 16, No. 2 (April 2002): 175–98; Robert J. Foster, "Making National Cultures in the Global Ecumene," *Annual Review of Anthropology*, 20 (1991): 235–60; Jerome Vogel, "Culture, Politics, and National Identity in Côte d'Ivoire," *Social Research*, 58, No. 2 (Summer 1991): 439–56.

extensively "reinventing" and popularizing that same tradition.[62] A hallmark of this effort is what Alger terms the "creation of culture," in which reworked traditional themes provide the basis for innovative and adaptive responses to outside influences.[63]

The above statements about the assertive strand of hybridization require some qualification. First, not all assertions of traditional culture take place as part of a strategic response to globalization. The expression of collective identity is always central to social reproduction, independent of the degree of international integration or the trajectory of modernization; that is, it is part of the powerful allure of nationalism.[64] Within this time-honored and now nearly ubiquitous process of identity formation, the mobilization of tradition fosters in-group cohesion by expressing collective identity in relative terms, as consisting of some essential quality lacking in Others.[65] For instance, in numerous South Pacific islands the notion of *kastom*, or indigenous custom, is used to signify age-old practices that separate local inhabitants from outsiders.[66] The problem of cohesion arises especially urgently in areas populated by diverse ethnic groups, where exposure to heightened flows of capital, trade, and information might exacerbate social cleavages and possibly provide fuel for separatist leanings. One way of countering such tendencies is by promoting a synthetic identity capable of integrating disparate cultures.[67] Conversely, it is also possible to find assertions of native culture for reasons of separatism, as in the case of the Basque or Kurds, where state and national projects are pitted against local and sub-state forces.[68]

---

[62] See Eric Hobsbawm and Terence Ranger, eds., *The Invention of Tradition* (Cambridge and New York: Cambridge University Press, 1983); also Anderson, *Imagined Communities*, pp. 178–84. Anderson makes this argument with particular reference to the museum.

[63] Chadwick Alger, "Local Response to Global Intrusions," in Zdravko Mlinar, ed., *Globalization and Territorial Identities* (Brookfield, VT: Ashgate, 1992), pp. 77–104.

[64] In recent centuries, the nationalist idea has become so powerful and ubiquitous because it works on several levels at once: it not only fulfills a deep social psychological need for solidarity, but it also offers potential empowerment through identification with national tradition and glory. Rodney Bruce Hall, *National Collective Identity: Social Constructs and International Systems* (New York: Columbia University Press, 1999), pp. 34–44; and see also Castells, *The Power of Identity*.

[65] As Benedict Anderson observes regarding post-colonial Indonesia, "defining what is national can only be a complex project of juxtapositions and separations between the 'foreign' and the 'indigenous'." Anderson, *Language and Power*, p. 166.

[66] Roger Keesing, "Creating the Past: Custom and Identity in the Contemporary Pacific," *The Contemporary Pacific*, 1, No. 1 (1989): 19–42.

[67] On nationalism as providing such a synthetic national culture as well as fostering the "collective amnesia" needed for ethnic reconciliation, see Ernest Gellner, *Culture, Identity, and Politics* (Cambridge: Cambridge University Press, 1987), pp. 6–28.

[68] In such cases, as Appadurai argues, "[N]ations . . . seek to capture or co-opt states and state power, [while] states simultaneously seek to capture and monopolize ideas about

Obviously too, in areas where globalization has exerted relatively less pressure, traditional culture may be used for various state-building or domestic political purposes without rejection or absorption being involved. This essentially domestic political function may be seen in the formation of a "Club for the Development of Culture" by young men living in Guinea-Bissau, in a community experiencing decline due to economic collapse and migration. The danger in this context is a form of anomie, as established values are delegitimized by their association with failing economic policies, yet without any alternative basis for holding the group together. Accordingly, the Club challenges the prevailing practices associated with the community's elders, and at the same time promotes replacement values – based on ostensibly traditional practices – as a basis for reconsolidating society. On the other hand, given the level of underdevelopment in the region there is no immediate concern with absorbing or rejecting ideas coming from outside.[69] Another instance would appear to be the drafting of a *National Charter* in Eritrea in 1994, with its broad goals of national unity, democracy, development, social justice, and cultural revival. In this case the promotion of national unity and cultural revival were overwhelmingly linked with domestic goals of state building, as local elected assemblies were replaced by a hierarchical system of presidential appointments, and land reform was undertaken to uproot the previous, patrilinear system of local rotation of small holdings. In short, mediating globalization was far less important than other, more insular matters.[70] In both the Guinea-Bissau and Eritrean cases tradition is "reinvented" as part of an adaptation of legitimating ritual to underlying social change.[71]

nationhood." Appadurai, *Modernity at Large*, p. 39. See also Joseph Camilleri, "State, Civil Society, and Economy," in Joseph Camilleri, Anthony Jarvis, and Albert Paolini, eds., *The State in Transition: Reimagining Political Space* (Boulder, CO: Lynne Rienner, 1995), pp. 209–28.

[69] Eric Gable, "The Culture Development Club: Youth, Neo-Tradition, and the Construction of Society in Guinea-Bissau," *Anthropological Quarterly*, 73, No. 4 (October 2000): 195–203. Reference to similar initiatives can be found in Mamadou Diouf, "Engaging Postcolonial Cultures: African Youth and Public Space," *African Studies Review*, 46, No. 2 (September 2003), pp. 7–9.

[70] Kjetil Tronvoll, "The Process of Nation-Building in Post-War Eritrea: Created from Below or Directed from Above?" *Journal of Modern African Studies*, 36, No. 3 (September 1998): 461–82.

[71] As Hobsbawm argues, this practice is most likely to occur "when a rapid transformation of society weakens or destroys the social patterns for which 'old' traditions had been designed, producing new ones to which they were not applicable, or when such old traditions and their institutional carriers and promulgators no longer prove sufficiently adaptable and flexible, or are otherwise eliminated . . ." Eric Hobsbawm, "Introduction: Inventing Traditions," in Hobsbawm and Ranger, eds., *The Invention of Tradition*, pp. 4–5.

Nevertheless, in parts of the world buffeted hard by globalization, the ordinary processes of national identity formation have been immensely complicated by the need to manage the massive flows of ideas – selectively adopting positive elements and deflecting negative ones – while also reconciling these actions with a parallel narrative of traditionalism. Along the way national identity assertion plays several distinct roles as part of the strategic response to globalization. Indeed, following Robertson, it is possible to argue that the "universalization of the particular" is itself an essential feature of globalization.[72]

For one thing, assertion works to consolidate customary practice in the face of new, dislocating practices, and thereby assists in the balancing act of becoming modern without sacrificing the sources of social cohesion. In Fiji the widespread, daily practice of *sevusevu* has evolved to offer just such a means of reasserting community values versus the new, acquisitive-individualist ethos. As Karen Brison has argued, this represents a change in the symbolic meanings associated with the custom, which involves the ritual drinking of a kava root preparation, accompanied by elaborate speeches with mythological references. In contrast to the past, when *sevusevu* was primarily a means of reinforcing social hierarchy, today it serves to consolidate collective traditional identity in the face of international homogenizing pressures.[73] Such ideas are thus intentionally reproduced alongside – and indeed largely because of – the official pursuit of neoliberal, integrationist development policies.[74] Much the same motivation is evident in Mexico, where, with the increasing intrusion of American capital following the NAFTA accord, the notion of historical purity has been loudly invoked. Within this "neo-indigenismo" discourse, traditional culture helps inoculate against social disintegrative trends brought on by the loss of rural jobs and mass displacement to the cities and the north.[75] In this sense national-traditional assertion represents a cultural "counterattack."

As part of hybridization understood as the strategic adaptation to globalization, however, assertion may be employed simply to limit, or

---

[72] Roland Robertson, *Globalization: Social Theory and Global Culture* (London: Sage, 1992), pp. 174–80.
[73] Karen J. Brison, "Constructing Identity through Ceremonial Language in Rural Fiji," *Ethnology*, 40, No. 4 (Fall 2001): 309–27.
[74] Ernest A. Duff, "Attack and Counterattack: Dynamics of Transculturation in the Caribbean," *Studies in Latin American Popular Culture*, 12 (1993): 195–202.
[75] *Ibid.*; see also Stephen D. Morris, "Between Neo-liberalism and Neo-indigenismo: Reconstructing National Identity in Mexico," *National Identities*, 3, No. 3 (November 2001): 239–55. See also Lois Hecht Oppenheim, "Latin America and the Cultural Consequences and Contradictions of Globalization," *Perspectives on Global Development and Technology*, 2, No. 1 (2003): 54–76.

otherwise manage, the identity effects of foreign influences introduced by absorption. An example is the wide-ranging public discussion in Thailand regarding the possibility of embracing Western culture without losing touch with traditional Thai ways, which was institutionalized by the state's designation of 1994 as the "Year to Campaign for Thai Culture." Thus, as strategic defenders of Thai national identity claimed, it is possible to remain "Thai" in one's cultural or spiritual essence regardless of how many foreign-made goods one consumes.[76] Similarly, Delanty notes that in Japan, "traditional festivities" such as viewing cherry blossoms "exist alongside modern consumer cultures, providing in part an enchantment destroyed by modernity."[77] In this way, depending on the particular issue and cultural practice at hand, the goal may be to compensate for the intrusion of foreign influences. This in turn makes it (theoretically) possible to participate in international economic arrangements without abandoning crucial social attachments and thereby forfeiting stability and perhaps even political autonomy.

Comparison with Japan underscores the point that the defensive aspects of cultural assertiveness are not limited to the post colonial and developing world. Essentially similar efforts are underway even in the world's most developed states, often marked by similar responses to globalization. In Canada and France, for example, although cultural traditions need not be invented anew or differentiated from a Western oppressor, they must still be persuasively reproduced, distanced from various competing identities, and successfully imparted to the younger generation. Doing so requires drawing what Patti Goff calls "invisible borders," or self-conscious cultural repertoires with which states can attempt to regulate the production of citizenship.[78]

Besides safeguarding natural citizenship (i.e., preventing the loss of ostensibly primordial identity markers), another common reason for mobilizing tradition is to defend against inimical values. Singapore offers a case in point, in the form of the "Shared Values" campaign, through which the state has attempted to fashion a melange culture from Indian, Chinese, and Malay elements. Beginning in the 1980s, the Singapore government distilled supposedly key traditional characteristics of each

---

[76] Kasian Tejapira, "The Post-Modernization of Thainess," in Yao Souchou, ed., *House of Glass: Culture, Modernity and the State in Southeast Asia* (Singapore: Institute of Southeast Asian studies, 2001), pp. 150–70.

[77] Delanty, "Consumption, Modernity and Japanese Cultural Identity," p. 121. Again, despite Delanty's claims to the contrary, the assertion of traditional practices appears a nearly ubiquitous form of national identity reproduction, rather than something remarkable about Japan.

[78] Patricia M. Goff, "Invisible Borders: Economic Liberalization and National Identity," *International Studies Quarterly*, 44, No. 4 (December 2000): 533–62.

culture and then distilled them in the form of "shared values" common to each: community, family, consensus-seeking, and inter-ethnic harmony. Clearly one of the chief goals here was to foster stable ethnic relations, but the specific choice of values reveals that more was involved. That is, in addition to promoting general social cohesion the emphasis placed on "family" and "community" was part of an effort to set limits on the permissible bounds of individualism.[79]

Similar projects were common throughout Southeast Asia during the 1990s, as states sought to frame national identity in such a way as to promote values and competencies tailored to global economic requirements. As part of the "Asian Values" campaign, this typically took the form of promoting a "developmental state" model alongside communitarian institutions such as the "mutual aid society." Whereas the developmental state model emphasized modernity, efficiency, and productivity, the mutual aid society – derived from Confucianism and laced with traditional symbols – emphasized stability and affective ties.[80] In places like Malaysia where Confucian associations had limited resonance, appropriate adjustments were made. The state introduced a modulated policy of Islamicization calculated to achieve the same goals, i.e., to foster disciplined and morally stable citizens. Accordingly, the thrust of educational policy (as reflected in the Malaysian national curriculum) was to promote computer literacy and English language as well as values of compassion, self-reliance, and cooperation.[81] Despite such local variations, the typical approach was to blend ostensibly traditional norms of family cohesion, self-discipline, thrift, and hard work, which were presented as key to finding a separate path of development.

One response to the problem of identity formation under current global conditions is to establish official vehicles for enculturation, such as national media services. Thus although American media products have become extraordinarily pervasive, many countries have moved to expand domestic content in television broadcasting. For example, Islamic fundamentalist reaction to the sensual excesses of MTV spurred the Egyptian government to create Nilesat, which provides a wide range of programming, including national as well as international broadcasts and religious

---

[79] See Beng-Huat Chua, "Between Economy and Race: The Asianization of Singapore," in Ayse Oncu and Petra Weyland, eds., *Space, Culture and Power: New Identities in Globalising Cities* (London: Zed Books, 1997), pp. 23–41.

[80] Robert W. Compton, Jr., *East Asian Democratization: Impact of Globalization, Culture, and Economy* (Westport and London: Praeger, 2000), pp. 56–63; Beng-Huat Chua, "'Asian-Values' Discourse and the Resurrection of the Social," *positions*, 7, No. 2 (Fall 1999): 573–92; Ong, *Flexible Citizenship*, pp. 193–213.

[81] Molly Lee, "The Impacts of Globalization on Education in Malaysia," in Stromquist and Monkman, eds., *Globalization and Education*, pp. 315–32.

as well as secular content. At the same time, Nilesat allows the Egyptian government to purvey a national image of being both African and cosmopolitan.[82] In addition to creating media outlets or facilitating public and local broadcasting, states also endeavor to mediate globalization by promoting cultural standards over the airwaves. Thus, throughout China and Southeast Asia national governments have created their own broadcasting services and have periodically attempted to license satellite dishes. A case in point is the establishment of an official advertising code by the Malaysian Ministry of Information, according to which ads should promote national morality by championing the importance of good citizenship, educational achievement, and traditional family values.[83]

Despite these conservative and defensive aspects of national identity assertion, then, the mobilization of tradition is flexible enough to allow, and even encourage, the adoption of certain new practices. In this way it may function as a complement to absorption, as "traditional" culture is extensively recast to facilitate market-based development and international integration. The thrust of this approach, which is often referred to as "glocalization," is to interpret indigenous values as being essentially convivial to neoliberal ideas. As part of this strategy, in Aihwa Ong's words, elites "appropriate 'Western' knowledges and re-present them as truth claims about their own countries."[84] This kind of strategic elasticity has been evident in the Solomon Islands, where a widely circulated narrative of national identity (based on allegedly ancient values) emphasizes self-sufficiency and industriousness. In the 1990s, as the Asian Development Bank and other IGOs pushed the new development philosophy, the same narrative was reinterpreted as being essentially conducive to marketization.[85] Of course, insisting that traditional and modern elements are actually syncretic does not make it true, as the Solomon Islands case also attests. The persistence of established (and decidedly illiberal)

---

[82] Hussein Amin and Hanzada Fikry, "Media, Sex, Violence, and Drugs: Egypt's Experience," in Kamalipour and Rampal, eds., *Media, Sex, Violence, and Drugs in the Global Village*, pp. 219–33; Robert A. Metzger, "King of the Nilesat," *Wired*, 6, No. 10 (October 1998), available online at: http://www.wired.com/wired/.

[83] Todd J. M. Holden and Azrina Husin, "Moral Advertising in Malaysian TV Commercials," in Richard King and Timothy Craig, eds., *Global Goes Local: Popular Culture in Asia* (Vancouver: University of British Columbia Press, 2002), pp. 138–59; Ien Ang, "Desperately Guarding Borders: Media Globalization, Cultural Imperialism; and the Rise of 'Asia'," in Yao Souchou, ed., *House of Glass: Culture, Modernity, and the State in Southeast Asia* (Singapore: Institute of Southeast Asian studies, 2001), pp. 27–45.

[84] Ong, *Flexible Citizenship*, p. 35, emphasis in the original. A related stratagem, which Robertson refers to as the "particularization of universalism," consists of paving the way for absorption by translating Western cultural flows into a form suitable for local consumption. Roland Robertson, "Mapping the Global Condition: Globalization as the Central Concept," *Theory, Culture and Society*, 7, Nos. 2/3 (1990): 15–30.

[85] Edward LiPuma, "History, Identity and Encompassment: Nation-Making in the Solomon Islands," *Identities* 4, No. 2 (December 1997): 213–44.

practices coupled with unrest caused by the spread of the Asian financial crisis eventually forced the government to abandon or at least postpone its original plans.[86] Still, the crucial issue here is the extent to which traditional elements may be intentionally manipulated in order to foster absorption.

Another example (this time from Singapore) pertains to the pop music of Dick Lee, which mixes traditional motifs and American rock in a didactic call for hybrid modernization. In Lee's hortatory lyrics, "traditional" Asian values of family, self-control, frugality, and collective identity are presented as crucial for national progress.[87] In this way the perceived need to adjust to the market not only translates into the acquisition of Western cultural and symbolic content, but also, paradoxically, into its opposite. Roughly equivalent objectives may also be pursued in strictly symbolic ways. An example is the 1998 "Miss Vietnam" beauty pageant, in which all contestants appeared in traditional *ao dai* outfits adorned with modern, chic accoutrements. Because it was a state-sponsored event, this fashion mélange constituted a vivid official endorsement for combining national and cosmopolitan sensibilities.[88] Of course, the appropriated symbolism need not be Western. In New Zealand, pressures for regional economic integration led the state to espouse the idea that the country was really "Asian-Pacific" in character rather than European.[89] Details aside, however, the general point is the same: cultural traditions are selectively and systematically mobilized to create a pseudo-historical image of the citizen as industrious, obedient, grounded in place, and yet also (sometimes jarringly) modern.[90]

---

[86] For background see Jane Turnbull, "Solomon Islands: Blending Traditional Power and Modern Structures in the State," *Public Administration and Development*, 22, No. 2 (May 2002): 191–201.

[87] C. J. W.-L. Wee, "Representing the Singapore Modern: Dick Lee, Pop Music, and the New Asia," in Yao Souchou, ed., *House of Glass: Culture, Modernity, and the State in Southeast Asia* (Singapore: Institute of Southeast Asian Studies), pp. 243–69.

[88] Nilan, "Young People and Globalizing Trends in Vietnam."

[89] This also took the form of rewriting history to show that the country had been settled by numerous, multicultural waves of immigrants rather than mainly by modern Europeans. Mark Laffey, "Adding an Asian Strand: Neoliberalism and the Politics of Culture in New Zealand," in Jutta Weldes et al., eds., *Cultures of Insecurity: States, Communities, and the Production of Danger* (Minneapolis and London: University of Minnesota Press, 1999), pp. 233–60.

[90] Not only economic modernization but also political modernization may be legitimated, or rather used in the service of identity formation, through imaginative flights of national self-assertion. A striking instance of this is the Crimean Tatar national movement's claim that "traditional" democratic practices on the part of the khanate between the fifteenth to eighteenth centuries served historically as a model for *Western* countries to emulate. See Greta Uehling, "Social Memory as Collective Action: The Crimean Tatar National Movement," in John Guidry, Michael Kennedy, and Mayer Zald, eds., *Globalization and Social Movements: Culture, Power, and the Transnational Public Sphere* (Ann Arbor: University of Michigan Press, 2000), pp. 260–87.

What is at stake in assertion can be demonstrated by a counter-example of not marshaling legitimacy in national terms. In Turkey under the Kemalists, beginning in the 1930s, elites linked to the state attempted to impose modernization-as-Westernization fairly indiscriminately and without systematically incorporating local culture into the bargain. This state-led program failed to resonate with the popular perception of modernization and Westernization as socially, economically, and culturally dislocating. This gap between elite discourse and practice, on the one hand, and popular attitudes on the other, generated mass resistance to the modernizing process.[91] As this case illustrates, efforts to achieve development by relentlessly pursuing absorption alone, or in the relative absence of assertive retraditionalization, run a serious risk of failure.

Strategic hybridization I: postcolonial India

The example of Kemalist Turkey raises the point that the cultural dynamic of modern nationalism is in many ways similar to strategic hybridization in the context of globalization. This is apparent in the rise of Indian nationalism, which was articulated as resentment over discriminatory policies and, perhaps even more, as a critique of the cultural self-abnegation widely practiced by well-socialized Indians. This in turn led to an eruption of hostility toward the English and the infusion of English culture into everyday life, as a direct reaction to the previous, precisely opposite tendency to disparage the indigenous while glorifying everything Western.[92] As the nationalist tide gathered strength it also spawned several smaller movements which attempted to spark interest in Indian history and to reanimate traditional culture as well as Hindu religion. Beyond providing a firm basis for cohesive social identity, such nationalist musings also worked to justify the rejection of imposed political rule and their accompanying "artificial" identities, as being incompatible with the supposedly pure, primordial Indian self.[93] Thus, one feature of the decolonization

---

[91] Caglar Keyder, "Whither the Project of Modernity? Turkey in the 1990s," in Bozdogan and Kasaba, eds., *Rethinking Modernity and National Identity in Turkey*, pp. 37–51. Bahrampour, while emphasizing the role of economic problems, also notes that the Kemalists "failed to sell" their radical Westernizing program to the masses, which likely reflected the very absence of offsetting assertive and rejectionist moves. Firouz Bahrampour, *Turkey: Social and Political Transformation* (Brooklyn: Theo. Gaus' Sons, 1967), p. 17 and pp. 14–36, passim.

[92] A candid, nearly contemporaneous acknowledgment is Chitra Fernando, "Asian Xenophobia against the West," *Annals of the American Academy of Political and Social Science*, 318 (July 1958): 83–88.

[93] On the development of such ideas prior to independence, including the bitter rift between Extremist and Moderate factions in the Indian National Congress, see

movement was a widespread commitment to uncovering the nation's deep cultural and spiritual foundations.[94]

In addition to rejection and assertion, however, absorption must not be under-emphasized in assessing the Indian national movement. One of the paramount aims of the National Congress program was economic independence, which necessarily meant pursuing industrialization. This was widely considered essential for overcoming the backwardness which many attributed to British colonial rule.[95] Furthermore, especially in the years leading up to and immediately following independence – i.e., at exactly the same moment that rejectionism was most potent – imitation was also carefully practiced as a way of conveying sophistication and maturity. Elites strove to assimilate British forms not only in technical and bureaucratic proficiency, but also modes of education, dress, and expression, and even in formal ceremonial displays during the early period of the national movement.[96] Even when such practices were extensively indigenized, as Appadurai argues was the case with cricket, they still represented modes of civilized and civilizing behavior suitable for integrating the country, and for presenting it to the world in a manner consistent with the demands of modernity and sovereignty.[97] In fact, the Hinduist wave emerged later largely in opposition to the imitative essence of the early nationalist movement.[98]

Constructions as well as various manipulations of traditionalism played a critical role in this process. Of course, within the cacophony of voices vying for influence in the Indian independence movement there were relative modernists and traditionalists, the latter of whom certainly included Gandhi. Still, even Gandhi and his supporters were not fundamentally hostile to modernity and industrial technology; they simply sought to limit or tame its practical as well as spiritual implications for Indian

R. Suntharalingam, *Indian Nationalism: An Historical Analysis* (New Delhi: Vikas Publishing, 1983), pp. 134–68.

[94] Sagarika Dutt, "Identities and the Indian State," *Third World Quarterly*, 19 No. 3 (September 1998): 411–35.

[95] Paul R. Brass, *The Politics of India Since Independence*, second edn. (Cambridge and New York: Cambridge University Press, 1994), pp. 10–12.

[96] Bernard S. Cohn, "Representing Authority in Victorian India," in Hobsbawm and Ranger, eds., *The Invention of Tradition*, pp. 165–210; Brass, *Politics of India Since Independence*, pp. 1–28. Brass also notes the presence of Soviet central planning and redistributive principles.

[97] Appadurai, *Modernity at Large*, pp. 89–113. On cricket's integrative function see Ramachandra Guha, "Cricket and Politics in Colonial India," *Past and Present*, No. 161 (November 1998): 155–190.

[98] Bipin Chandra Pal, "Hinduism and Indian Nationalism," in Elie Kedourie, ed., *Nationalism in Asia and Africa* (New York and Cleveland: The World Publishing, 1970), pp. 338–52.

society. Toward this end, Gandhi explicitly marshaled tradition, in his famous 1908 work *Hind Swaraj*, understood as the embodiment of human dignity, respect for nature and for others, and humility. With the aid of such understandings, he suggested, it might be possible to become at least reasonably developed, but without sacrificing the quintessentially Indian framework of values.[99] For many others within the Indian elite, however, such ideas of traditionalism could be easily molded into an instrument for achieving rapid technological change. For them, the rhetoric and symbolic practice of tradition were important not only in their own right, but also for demonstrating the nationalist credentials of all associated policies, and thus for legitimating the establishment of foreign practices. Nor was it necessary to be cynical in order to advance such views; it was enough to be deeply nationalistic. Indian national activists presented Sanskrit literature as a cultural anchor and as a fount of practical knowledge, including remarkably advanced insights in the fields of agriculture, commerce, the sciences, and jurisprudence.[100] The point – as with the examples from other states discussed earlier – was that ancient (but lamentably forgotten) indigenous values were actually entirely consistent with modernization.

Of course, following independence the tenor of such narratives shifted somewhat; Nehru's focus was clearly on modernization (though with a distinctly socialist and Soviet-inflected approach). Yet while he was critical of "pure traditionalism" in the Gandhian sense, even Nehru sought to combine certain traditional aspects of national identity within his development project, albeit for the purpose of consolidating unity rather than as a distinct philosophy of modernization.[101] Nevertheless, despite these changes, national identity narratives of the early postcolonial period were characterized by a key element of continuity. The consensually recognized need for "cultural autonomy" thus included, often very self-consciously, a novel synthesis of modern and indigenous constructs.[102] Nationalist expressions of this kind were often marked by what Von Laue has called "anti-Western Westernization." As practiced by Nehru (and his Bandung

---

[99] Suresh Sharma, "*Hind Swaraj* as a Statement of Tradition in the Modern World," in Vasudha Dalmia and Heinrich Von Stietencron, eds., *Representing Hinduism: The Construction of Religious Traditions and National Identity* (Thousand Oaks, CA: Sage Publications, 1995), pp. 283–305.

[100] Radha Mookerji, *Nationalism in Hindu Culture* (Delhi: S. Chand and Co., 1957), pp. 76–88.

[101] Balkrishna Govind Gokhale, "Nehru and History," *History and Theory*, 17, No. 3 (October 1978): 311–22; Balraj Madhok, *Indianization* (New Delhi: S. Chand and Co., 1970).

[102] Makarand Paranjape, "Reworlding Homes: Colonialism, National Culture, and Post-National India," in Geeti Sen, ed., *India: A National Culture?* (Thousand Oaks, CA: Sage Publications, 2003), pp. 114–26.

generation of postcolonial leaders), this meant not only industrializing and adopting Western organizational forms, but also insisting on socialist and other cultural practices whereby the nation could be starkly distinguished – and thereby protected – from its previous masters.[103]

Chatterjee brilliantly examines how this process was worked out in drama, literature, education, and family life in India during and after British rule. The key, as he argues, was an understanding that "[t]he greater one's success in imitating Western skills in the material domain . . . the greater the need to preserve the distinctiveness of one's spiritual culture." Consequently, under postcolonialism, "nationalism launche[d] its most powerful, creative, and historically significant project: to fashion a 'modern' national culture that is nevertheless not Western."[104] In short, this was a "two step process" in which the material attainments of the West were embraced along with their immediate cultural manifestations, while folklore, ritual practices, and other "spiritual" constructs were also cultivated for their ability to unify and, paradoxically, as a way of legitimating such change. Accomplishing the latter feat involved the resuscitation of traditional popular culture (as well as its sanitization and classicization) and its representation as a timeless "repository of national truth."[105] Such efforts epitomize strategic hybridization, understood as the systematic propagation of hybrid, or blended, national identity constructs, containing the key features of absorption, rejection, and assertion.

Strategic hybridization II: post-Maoist China

One further example which illustrates how the three trends of hybridization are intertwined, this time outside the postcolonial context, is offered by China today. Here again the prevailing policy is one of encouraging technological modernization and foreign investment while trying to manage the attendant cultural influences. And once again this is being attempted by representing Chinese national identity as something intrinsic, coherent, and hopefully enduring.[106]

---

[103] Theodore H. Von Laue, *The World Revolution of Westernization: The Twentieth Century in Global Perspective* (New York: Oxford University Press, 1987), pp. 239–71.

[104] Partha Chatterjee, *The Nation and its Fragments: Colonial and Postcolonial Histories* (Princeton: Princeton University Press, 1993), p. 6.

[105] Chatterjee, *Nation and its Fragments*, pp. 72–75. I abstract from Chatterjee's analysis of the gendered nature of this identity discourse.

[106] Yunxiang Yan, "Managed Globalization: State Power and Cultural Transition in China," in Berger and Huntington, eds., *Many Globalizations*, pp. 19–47; Arif Dirlik, "Markets, Culture, Power: The Making of a 'Second Cultural Revolution' in China," *Asian Studies Review*, 25, No. 1 (March 2001): 1–33.

In pursuit of this goal the ruling Communist Party tries to check critical intellectual tendencies, and maintains a state media sector in television, cinema, and publishing. The Party also seeks to limit the worrisome and increasingly prevalent signs of "social dislocation, money worship, hedonism, individualism, corruption" and other problems. Beginning in the early 1990s this took the form of a campaign for "socialist spiritual civilization," which included an increase in formal censorship as well as the extension of an informal system of ideological watchdogs throughout society in an effort to root out "rotten capitalist values."[107] At the same time, in a bow to reality, the government allowed Western media to circulate while trying to mix it with traditionally Chinese as well as socialist revolutionary themes.[108] Increasingly, as market-oriented reform accelerated after 1992, the state sought to accommodate a degree of modernization, including cultural Westernization, while at the same time curbing its excesses and counterbalancing its identity effects.

To a significant extent this policy proceeds by way of internalized restraint. Thus although a substantial amount of policing does occur, including on the Internet, much of it appears to be self-imposed or anticipatory.[109] This is important in light of the state's lack of capacity to impose its preferences on consumers. The establishment of a "socialist market economy" and the attendant pursuit of profits, combined with the tremendous expansion of communication infrastructure, makes it effectively impossible to control the decentralized transmission of uncensored material.[110] As a result the icons of American popular culture have become trendy among young people, just as everywhere else in the world. In special export processing zones, even openly hedonistic forms of self-expression are tolerated as providing a social safety valve, so long as they pose no threat to the Party's leading position.[111] The upshot is a seemingly contradictory pattern of openness and control, which has culminated in an official countertrend of anti-Westernization (especially

---

[107] Feng Chen, "Rebuilding the Party's Normative Authority," *Problems of Post-Communism*, 45, No. 6 (November/December 1998): 33–41.

[108] Mercedes Dujunco, "Hybridity and Disjuncture in Mainland Chinese Popular Music," in King and Craig, *Global Goes Local*, pp. 25–39.

[109] On active surveillance, see Howard W. French, "Despite an Act of Leniency, China Has its Eye on the Web," *New York Times*, June 27, 2004, Section 1, p. 6; on self-monitoring see Shanthi Kalathil and Taylor C. Boas, *Open Networks, Closed Regimes: The Impact of the Internet on Authoritarian Rule* (Washington, DC: Carnegie Endowment for International Peace, 2003), pp. 13–42.

[110] Daniel C. Lynch, *After the Propaganda State: Media, Politics, and "Thought Work" in Reformed China* (Stanford, CA: Stanford University Press, 1999).

[111] Ong, *Flexible Citizenship*, pp. 55–83.

anti-Americanization). As Yu argues, this is not simply an opposing extreme of Westernization but is actually bound up with it as part of an overall strategy.[112]

Accordingly, rejectionist, absorptive, and assertive tendencies are systematically combined in the project of national identity formation, in a way geared to promoting market conditions without relinquishing social stability or Party control. An important mechanism through which this is occurring is the mobilization of traditional culture, despite lingering Marxist/Maoist suspicions. The result is a series of state-led programs designed to cultivate – yet also manage – supposedly authentic expressions of the popular soul. Accordingly, since the 1990s the Party has attempted to identify historical roots of an indigenous Chinese nationalism, or "national sentiments," notwithstanding the fact that such elements are considered potentially retrograde and threatening to the state (for which reason the latter must supervise the entire process).[113] An intellectual movement to revive Confucianism gathered strength, precisely in order to promote non-Western modernization. By 1995 this movement garnered state support, as leading officials began to praise Confucianism as a force capable of consolidating the nation.[114] There is also renewed enthusiasm for minority ethnic traditions. For example, as Ralph Litzinger shows, local Yao traditions are being rediscovered with state encouragement, and are cast as a repository of social morality which might be combined with the Party's bid for rational order. Prominent themes include respect for one's place in the social hierarchy, generosity and cooperation with neighbors, and strict social sanctioning and discipline. The result has been the "civilized village" campaign under which the state seeks to delegate social supervision to heads of the village along with party functionaries, who engage in detailed behavioral accounting and policing justified as a return to traditional standards. In this way Yao

---

[112] Keping Yu, "Americanization, Westernization, Sinification: Modernization or Globalization in China?" in Beck, Sznaider, and Winter, eds., *Global America?*, pp. 134–49.

[113] To a significant extent this was a reaction to the Tiananmen uprising. Samuel S. Kim and Lowell Dittmer, "Whither China's Quest for National Identity?" in Lowell Dittmer and Samuel S. Kim, eds., *China's Quest for National Identity* (Ithaca: Cornell University Press, 1993), pp. 237–90. See also Anbin Shi, "Toward a Chinese National-Popular: Cultural Hegemony and Counterhegemony in Maoist and Post-Maoist China," *Social Semiotics*, 10, No. 2 (August 2000): 201–10.

[114] Seong Hwan Cha, "Modern Chinese Confucianism: The Contemporary Neo-Confucian Movement and its Cultural Significance," *Social Compass*, 50, No. 4 (December 2003): 481–91. On state support of the neo-Confucian movement see Chen, "Rebuilding the Party's Normative Authority," p. 39. Thanks to Sue McCarthy for alerting me to this point.

culture functions as a site for the construction of state power and state-led society.[115]

In addition, much as we have seen in post-colonial India and elsewhere, cultural indigenization (or "sinification") has often been used as a vehicle for smuggling in, and assimilating, foreign and Western ideas geared to promoting development.[116] Thus, McCarthy's analysis of state policy toward the Bai and Dai nationalities in Yunnan province reveals how authorities are closely engaged in supporting the revival of local traditions, folk festivals, and handicrafts, while also harnessing this movement to the goals of modernization. This means not only fostering tourism and foreign investment, including suppressing "backward" superstitions, and attempting to influence the expression of tradition in terms suitable for efficient development work.[117] These same themes are also evident in the recent, intense debate over Zeng Guofan, a prominent nineteenth-century writer, general, and Qing Dynasty official. While Zeng's legacy is invoked for a variety of reasons, central among them appears to be his utility in representing traditional (Confucian) Chinese culture in a way conducive to modernity, morality, and pan-ethnic unity.[118] Similar too is the official discourse of "leisure culture," according to which the state's goals of promoting consumption, computer and technological literacy, and social cohesion are achieved by making leisure into a normatively acceptable and circumscribed set of public activities (going to the museum, sports, shopping, learning computers and English). As Wang argues, this also helps to prevent social dislocation as well as public immorality associated with self-indulgent forms of private pleasure and increasing disparities of wealth.[119]

The point to be stressed here is that China is not fundamentally different from Thailand or most other states in its posture toward mediating globalization. To be sure, China's level of control over certain flows of ideas exceeds that imposed in most countries. This has to do not with claims about national essence but rather with the state's authoritarian political structure, quite apart from any broader cultural orientation.

---

[115] Ralph Litzinger, "Reimagining the State in Post-Mao China," in Weldes *et al.*, eds., *Cultures of Insecurity*, 293–318. See also Yu, "Americanization."

[116] Jing Wang, *High Culture Fever: Politics, Aesthetics, and Ideology in Deng's China* (Berkeley: University of California Press, 1996), pp. 236–42.

[117] Susan McCarthy, "Gods of Wealth, Temples of Prosperity: Party-State Participation in the Minority Cultural Revival," *China: An International Journal*, 2, No. 1 (March 2004): 28–52.

[118] Yingjie Guo and Baogang He, "Reimagining the Chinese Nation," *Modern China*, 25, No. 2 (April 1999): 142–70.

[119] Jing Wang, "The State Question in Chinese Popular Cultural Studies," *Inter-Asia Cultural Studies*, 2, No. 1 (April 2001): 35–52.

Such an interpretation is at odds with the argument made by Lynch, to the effect that China represents a "guardian" state, which, as such, is characterized by a historically established commitment to maintaining the centrality (in global terms) of its imagined collective identity. In contrast, Lynch presents Thailand as a paradigmatic "gatekeeper" state, which has therefore "accepted a non-central position in the new world order" and is "otherwise wide-open to outside influences and even to fundamental reconstitution at the level of identity."[120] Even setting aside definitional problems, however, this is an unsustainable claim. The fact is that China pursues hybridization: it absorbs much of Western culture – popular, economic, and administrative – with enormous alacrity; vigorously rejects certain unacceptable aspects of that same Western culture; and asserts the importance of Confucian as well as minority ethnic traditions. And all of this is done in the name of reconciling diversity within an overarching narrative of development and "harmony."[121] In all of these ways China is essentially like most states in the world, including Thailand. The real exceptions, such as Myanmar, Turkmenistan, and North Korea, are those where truly dictatorial regimes have acted to drastically limit all global flows. In these very few cases we find no strategic hybridization.

The ambivalence of hybridization

Clearly, tradition and modernity cannot be regarded as polar opposites, incapable of coexisting stably and forever threatening to supplant one another.[122] And yet this should not be taken to mean that the fusion of these elements is unproblematic. On the contrary, beyond understanding its political costs and benefits (as well as grasping the discursive legitimation of its component parts), hybridization cannot be entirely understood without appreciating the ambivalence at its core, which is in fact its most quintessential characteristic. From this perspective the dynamic interrelatedness of hybridization does not arise from the sequential collision of each of its strands with the others, but is instead very much an immanent and inescapable tension at the very heart of being modern.[123] This

---

[120] Daniel C. Lynch, "International 'Decentering' and Democratization: The Case of Thailand," *International Studies Quarterly*, 48, No. 2 (June 2004): 346–47 and passim.
[121] On these (as well as other) uses of "harmony" see William A. Callahan, "Remembering the Future: Utopia, Empire, and Harmony in 21st-Century International Theory," *European Journal of International Relations*, 10, No. 4 (December 2004): 579–80.
[122] Joseph R. Gusfield, "Tradition and Modernity: Misplaced Polarities in the Study of Social Change," *The American Journal of Sociology*, 72, No. 4 (January 1974): 351–62.
[123] Bauman makes a somewhat similar argument. See Zygmunt Bauman, "Modernity and Ambivalence," in Mike Featherstone, ed., *Global Culture: Nationalism, Globalization and Modernity* (London: Sage Publications, 1990), pp. 143–69.

element of ambivalence, it may be suggested, helps explain why seemingly contradictory patterns of absorption and rejection (and assertion) are so continuously followed. On one level, then, the acquisition of modern "civilized" modes of behavior is obviously a source of considerable pride. And yet inevitably the decision to adopt more efficient or otherwise superior foreign ideas produces a deep sense of abasement and cultural inferiority. Manthia Diawara's insights on globalization in Africa are relevant here:

> The concept of Western technology involves a masked essentialism and immanence that cement the relationship between the European and modern technology and posits that any participation in the technological revolution must necessarily import European culture . . . The states in Africa have surrendered to the notion of the superiority of European rationality and internalized the stereotype of African experiences . . . as discontinuous with the interest of the new man.[124]

This sense of cultural inferiority also immediately becomes a political problem by undermining the state's ability to mobilize nationalist sentiments on its own behalf, in its role as preeminent defender of the nation's unique identity. This threatens to gravely compromise the prospects of successful state building.[125] In sum, the absorption of Western practices and values inherently generates opposition on both collective psychological and political grounds. Understanding how this unfolds, and why the social-psychological and political dimensions are interrelated, offers a way of grasping Edward Said's insight: that cultural identities are "contrapuntal ensembles" which follow a particular logic.[126]

As we have already seen, rejection of particularly offensive or otherwise uncomfortably alien practices is a central feature of hybridization. This does not arise simply as part of an official plan or through the efforts of nationalistic elites, but is also expressed in the form of widespread revulsion over perceived aping of foreign (especially Western) styles, especially when unaccompanied by an adequate dose of native cultural leavening. Ayse Oncu's analysis of cartoon images in Istanbul is relevant in this context, particularly with regard to the popular characterization of Others. In numerous popular publications these cartoons take several forms, each depicting a category of social perversion: the greedy, libertine slob [*maganda*]; the gaudy, self-conscious imitation of Western (and

---

[124] Manthia Diawara, "Toward a Regional Imaginary in Africa," in Jameson and Miyoshi, eds., *The Cultures of Globalization*, p. 119.

[125] As Mazrui and Tidy observe, one of the chief problems faced by those seeking to retraditionalize African culture in service of the state has been precisely the "compulsive urge to imitate and emulate the West." Ali Mazrui and Michael Tidy, *Nationalism and New States in Africa from about 1935 to the Present* (London: Heineman, 1984), p. 298.

[126] Edward Said, *Culture and Imperialism* (New York: Vintage Books, 1994), p. 52.

other) debased styles [*arabesk*]; and the ostentatious posturing of the nouveau riche [*haciaga*]. Each is exposed as not only morally bankrupt, but also derivative, and therefore degrading insofar as it reveals a lack of personal and national pride.[127] And yet, as Oncu has also shown, such rejection takes place within a larger context of embracing Western, consumer-based standards of social status, such as the well-equipped home and the high-tech TV set as necessities for a fully modern and therefore desirable lifestyle.[128] The fundamental ambivalence of this collective fantasy is revealed by the fact that cultural imitation is provisionally accepted, but only so long as it is not expressed in "immoderate" terms.

To some extent national identity assertion is bound up with this aspect of rejection. In other words, in addition to the "translation" of Western rock patterns, we also see ambivalence in the decision by Malaysian pop singers to employ traditional images in their music, as part of a larger effort to detoxify and domesticate Western ideas.[129] From this standpoint, too, the tendency to naturalize Western institutions (or to depict them as essentially indigenous) represents an effort to legitimate what would otherwise be an embarrassing degree of assimilation, since it would signify something dangerously close to a renunciation of national identity. In contrast, if cultural innovations geared to facilitating modernization can plausibly be claimed as national, questions about the authenticity of "national" identity need not arise. Past some point, then, acts of absorption understood as subordination tend to result in (collective) ego-affirming and socially stabilizing reactions, expressed as claims of national integrity and even historical grandeur.[130]

Here it is worth considering again the insights of Edward Said, unquestionably one of the most brilliant observers of national identity formation as it is bound up with the mediation of foreign culture and international

---

[127] Ayse Oncu, "Istanbulites and Others: The Cultural Cosmology of Being Middle Class in the Era of Globalism," in Caglar Keyder, ed., *Istanbul: Between the Global and the Local* (Lanham, MD: Rowman and Littlefield, 1999), pp. 95–119.

[128] Ayse Oncu, "The Myth of the 'Ideal Home' Travels Across Cultural Borders to Istanbul," in Oncu and Weyland, eds., *Space, Culture and Power*, pp. 56–72.

[129] Eric Thompson, "Rocking East and West: The USA in Malaysian Music (An American Remix)," in King and Craig, *Global Goes Local*, pp. 58–79. Thompson also notes that the traditional-modern mix is part of a broad-based marketing strategy designed to appeal to both urban and rural people.

[130] See Ashis Nandy, *The Intimate Enemy: Loss and Recovery of Self under Colonialism* (Delhi: Oxford University Press, 1983). Nandy perceptively (yet also, as an interested participant of the Indian national recovery experience, revealingly) emphasizes cultural traits which in his view enable post-colonial societies to potentially avoid the homogenizing effects of globalization: the ability to locate self-in-society, spirituality, and general depth of culture.

belonging. As Said remarked with regard to postcolonialism, nationalism is fundamentally the quest for a true, independent identity, but one that can only be attained by coming to terms with what has been borrowed. "To achieve [self] recognition," he argues, "is to rechart and then occupy the place in imperial cultural forms reserved for subordination, to occupy it self-consciously, fighting for it on the very same territory once ruled by a consciousness that assumed the subordination of a designated inferior Other."[131] For this reason, in their struggle for autonomy nationalist writers tend to express a common theme:

The post-imperial writers of the Third World therefore bear their past within them – as scars of humiliating wounds, as instigation for different practices, as potentially revised visions of the past tending toward a post-colonial future, as urgently reinterpretable and redeployable experiences, in which the formerly silent native speaks and acts on territory reclaimed as part of a general movement of resistance, from the colonist.[132]

And as we will see vividly in the cities of the former Soviet Union, such reactions are readily evident – not only in the identity politics of earlier postcolonial states, but also within the ongoing dialectic of globalization and national identity response.

In sum, as a speculative generalization we might suggest that ambivalence is a crucial, driving engine of cultural hybridization, as absorption ultimately demands a compensatory response in the form of rejection and national identity assertion. At the same time, ironically, the absorption of technological, institutional and symbolic-cultural forms of modernity is actually useful for efforts to salvage the past, because it allows the reanimation of tradition to be cast as part of a progressive project rather than as something merely reactionary and atavistic. The same is true in reverse: rejection of what the nation is *not* creates a foundation for claims about what the nation actually *is*, and both provide an implicit sanction for adopting Western practices which are not proscribed as antithetical to the core essence of the nation. Somewhat counterintuitively, then, the twin practices of rejection and assertion help to consolidate national identity in ways that often contribute to international integration and modernization.

The persistent ambiguity of hybridization

Before moving on to address explanations for this pattern of ambivalent hybridization, it is worth briefly considering the possibility that much

---

[131] Said, *Culture and Imperialism*, p. 210.   [132] *Ibid.*, p. 212.

of the literature on globalization is nothing more than a normatively informed debate on development policy, in which scholars marshal interpretation as a tool for advancing their policy preferences. From this perspective, accounts of local responses to globalization may reveal more about the authors themselves than about the actual meanings of ideas and practices within local contexts.

For example, there is a running argument about whether what looks like homogenization is really homogenization at all. A number of scholars have suggested that the need to translate foreign cultural imports in order to make them intelligible within local systems of meaning actually involves transforming their content far more than is often appreciated. This observation applies, for example, to Western rock music: while ravenously consumed by young audiences all over the world, it is typically interpreted in light of native cultural values and meanings, or blended with indigenous elements to produce a vehicle for expressing common emotions or attitudes toward establishment culture. "Rai" music in Algeria furnishes one such instance of cultural mixing, in which young singers use Western instruments, combine local popular rhythms with American songs, and reflect traditional Islamic values as well as a fascination for Western youth culture.[133] In such ways, while partaking of a global "rock aesthetic" derived from a canon of formative work dating to the 1960s and 1970s, "rockization" also allows creative, even self-consciously original and national cultural expression.[134]

A result is the creation of cultural blends, such as fashions that incorporate local and Western styles, or fusion music that combines indigenous traditional themes with pop or American rock. In this way what may be an originally Western genre becomes consumed locally through its combination with native or traditional styles, leading to distinctly local forms such as Korean reggae or Chicano rap.[135] Similarly, although the rise of "black ethnicity" in El Salvador reveals a recourse to traditional culture, even this act of assertion and apparent resistance is leavened by the incorporation of global-modern elements, such as funk and hip-hop

---

[133] Marc Schade-Poulsen, "The Power of Love: Rai Music and Youth in Algeria," in Amit-Talai and Wulff, eds., *Youth Cultures*, pp. 81–113.
[134] Motti Regev, "'Rockization': Diversity within Similarity in World Popular Music," in Beck, Sznaider and Winter, eds., *Global America?*, pp. 219–21.
[135] Howard, "Exploding Ballads"; Fernando P. Delgado, "Chicano Ideology Revisited: Rap Music and the (Re)articulation of Chicanismo," *Western Journal of Communication*, 62, No. 2 (Spring 1998): 95–113. See also Mark Fenster, "Understanding and Incorporating Rap: The Articulation of Alternative Popular Musical Practices within Cultural Practices and Institutions," *Howard Journal of Communications*, 5, No. 3 (Spring 1995): 223–44.

styles as well as consumer-oriented technological symbols.[136] In fact, even the consumption of completely unaltered and unadorned Western commodities may carry quite specific, culturally conditioned meanings. For example, as Winter points out, the seemingly passive reception of American television shows in Trinidad is often a "communal activity," involving extensive arbitrage and accommodation which alters the original meaning of broadcasts.[137] Therefore what appears at first glance to be sameness is often far more complex and variegated in terms of its social and subjective experience. In short, what gets counted as absorption may actually be a subtle form of assertion through which local audiences (including young people) "display agency."[138]

And yet the insistence on cultural autonomy may also be highly misleading. James Ferguson makes this point in reviewing the case of two Guinean boys who were found dead in the landing gear of an airplane, having tried to smuggle themselves into Belgium. Along with the boys' bodies was a letter in which they beseeched Europeans for help to "become like you." Ferguson incisively juxtaposes this naked expression of mimicry with the common tendency among scholars to deny the reality of such a humiliating practice. "The dominant anthropological solution to the embarrassment of African mimicry," Ferguson suggests, "has been to interpret colonial- and postcolonial-era imitations of Europeans as some combination of parody and appropriation and to insist that such 'mimesis' is therefore in fact a gesture of resistance to colonialism."[139]

Underneath such gestures of respect often lies a commitment to countering the demeaning view of non-Western peoples as being helplessly subject to the domination of imperialist powers, and therefore incapable of contesting global culture on their own terms.[140] For analysts who

---

[136] Vivian Schelling, "Globalisation, Ethnic Identity and Popular Culture in Latin America," in Ray Kiely and Phil Marfleet, eds., *Globalisation and the Third World* (London: Routledge, 1998), pp. 141–62.

[137] Rainer Winter, "Global Media, Cultural Change and the Transformation of the Local: The Contribution of Cultural Studies to a Sociology of Hybrid Formations," in Beck, Sznaider, and Winter, eds., *Global America?*, pp. 206–21. See also David Howes, ed., *Cross-Cultural Consumption: Global Markets, Local Realities* (London: Routledge, 1996).

[138] Mary Bucholtz, "Youth and Cultural Practice," *Annual Review of Anthropology*, 31 (2002): 525–52; Henry Jenkins, "Pop Cosmopolitanism: Mapping Cultural Flows in an Age of Media Convergence," in Marcelo Suarez-Orozco and Desirée Qin-Hilliard, eds., *Globalization: Culture and Education in the New Millennium* (Berkeley: University of California Press, 2004), pp. 114–40; Peter Jackson, "Local Consumption Cultures in a Globalizing World," *Transactions of the Institute of British Geographers*, 29, No. 2 (June 2004): 165–78.

[139] James G. Ferguson, "Of Mimicry and Membership: Africans and the New World Society," *Cultural Anthropology*, 17, No. 4 (November 2002): 551–71.

[140] See John Tomlinson, *Cultural Imperialism: A Critical Introduction* (London: Pinter, 1991). A similar insight provides the premise for Abu-Lughod's discussion of

approach globalization from this perspective, the very act of interpreting cultural exchange as Western-led homogenization itself reproduces the notion of developing countries and peoples as subordinate, and therefore unwittingly facilitates hegemonic behavior.[141] Despite the apparent ideological allure of this position, however, a dispassionate look at absorption suggests that much of it is indeed assimilative. This is not to suggest that assimilation need extend all the way to the erasure of national identity; on the contrary national narratives remain very much alive, as this book's examination of three former Soviet cities attests. It is also quite possible, as Boulanger argues with respect to Borneo, to utilize national culture actively as a way of managing the process of modernization, thus potentially curtailing its erosive effects on collective identity.[142] Yet this ought not to obscure the point that globalization does generate an enormous amount of confluence in institutions and the attitudes associated with them.

The same cautionary note applies to inferring the underlying values expressed in hybridization. Bollywood provides a good case in point. As already noted, middle-class, urban Indian youth appear to be powerfully attracted to Western lifestyles and symbols. Nonetheless, many commentators have pointed out the surprising resilience of Indian indigenous media, including the ability of Bollywood to hold its own against Hollywood since the lifting of import restrictions in 1992. Thus, for Tyrrell, the popularity of Bollywood films expresses cultural resistance; their characteristic song and dance numbers can be read as "opposition to Western cultural imperialism."[143] A deeper look at the content of such films tells a somewhat different story, however. Underneath its thematic musical choreography and family values, Bollywood increasingly reveals incursions of consumerism and a capitalist–individualist ethos, which allow it to be consumed as an enactment of national identity while at the same time masking the accommodation of hegemonic values. While this may be

resistance as revealing of power – and perhaps of submission to particular manifestations of power. Lila Abu-Lughod, "The Romance of Resistance: Tracing Transformations of Power through Bedouin Women," *American Ethnologist*, 17, No. 1 (February 1990): 41–55.

[141] Tomlinson, *Globalization and Culture*, pp. 81–8. On this point see also Buell, *National Culture and the New Global System*, esp. pp. 1–13; and García Néstor Canclini, *Hybrid Cultures: Strategies for Entering and Leaving Modernity* (Minneapolis: University of Minnesota Press, 1995).

[142] Clare L. Boulanger, "Inventing Tradition, Inventing Modernity: Dayak Identity in Urban Sarawak," *Asian Ethnicity*, 3, No. 2 (September 2002): 221–31.

[143] Heather Tyrrell, "Bollywood versus Hollywood: Battle of the Dream Factories," in Tracey Skelton and Tim Allen, eds., *Culture and Global Change* (London: Routledge, 1999), p. 262.

especially true of the diaspora, for whom Bollywood represents a classic "culture industry," it would appear applicable in India as well.[144]

It thus seems necessary to regard claims of local resistance to absorption with a certain degree of skepticism. Although the reproduction of Western culture frequently takes on local nuances and meanings, the thrust of popular culture everywhere increasingly reflects conspicuous materialism, sensual indulgence, and individualism, all of which are quintessentially modern and Western values. As Shlegel suggests, it may well be the case that "ideology [is] implicit in the artifacts" of cultural globalization.[145] This appears also to be true of the global consumption of Hollywood cinema, which often appears to convey American perceptions and assumptions even when indigenized by non-American audiences.[146] At a still deeper level, Martin-Barbero observes that regardless of how much "glocalization" occurs, seemingly parochial content is actually subservient to neoliberal practice. Thus, while it is possible to find indigenous, creative expressions of Latino perspectives and social tensions in the popular Latin American *telenovos*, by employing native cultural nuance such shows work to naturalize global themes of international market integration, upward and downward mobility, and individualism (expressed through divorce as well as the emancipation of women).[147] In such cases the apparent increase in "cultural diversity" takes place only on a superficial level, and masks the general absorption of Western values and practices. While this in no way contradicts the importance of rejectionist and (especially) assertive strands of hybridization, it does suggest that efforts to discount the profundity of absorption may be politically motivated. On the other hand, the same may be said of arguments that local culture is being relentlessly eroded by international capital.

---

[144] Anthony C. Alessandrini, "'My Heart's Indian for All That': Bollywood Film between Home and Diaspora," *Diaspora: A Journal of Transnational Studies*, 10, No. 3 (Winter 2001): 315–40; Ashish Rajadhyaksha, "The 'Bollywoodization' of the Indian Cinema: Cultural Nationalism in a Global Arena," *Inter-Asia Cultural Studies*, 4, No. 1 (April 2003): 25–39.

[145] Alice Shlegel, "The Global Spread of Adolescent Culture," in Lisa J. Crockett and Rainer K. Silbereisen, eds., *Negotiating Adolescence in Times of Social Change* (New York: Cambridge University Press, 2000), p. 80. See also Mel van Elteren, "Conceptualizing the Impact of US Popular Culture Globally," *Journal of Popular Culture*, 30, No. 1 (Summer 1996): 47–89; Mel van Elteren, "US Cultural Imperialism: Today Only a Chimera," *SAIS Review*, 25, No. 3 (Summer/Fall 2003): 169–88; Marat Cheshkov, "Globalizatsiia: sushchnost, nyneshniaia faza, perspektivy," *Pro et Contra*, 4, No. 4 (Fall 1999), available online at http://pubs.carnegie.ru/.

[146] Ulf Hedetoft, *The Global Turn: National Encounters with the World* (Aalborg, Denmark: Aalborg University Press, 2003), pp. 89–107.

[147] Jesus Martin-Barbero, "Transformations in the Map: Identities and Culture Industries," *Latin American Perspectives*, 27, No. 4 (July 2000): 27–48.

And yet, what ultimately matters is the perception of those participants actually involved in mediating cultural flows. Thus (to cite the opposite of cultural borrowing by recipients in the developing world), in at least certain cases, foreign media productions which incorporate local cultural themes may be experienced as largely affirming, rather than undermining, unique identity constructs. An example is the *kung fu* movies and soap operas which are made in Hollywood and are enormously popular among native as well as diasporan Asian audiences. Instead of eroding traditional identities, according to Ong, a close reading of the popular experience of such films suggest that they operate to normalize cultural specificity, albeit within an overarching context of transnational capitalism and market-based values.[148] While not denying the importance of power in the global transmission of ideas, this perspective suggests the possibility of a stable, hybrid synthesis that balances modernization with autonomous political and identity outcomes. More importantly, however, it serves as a warning against making assumptions about the outcome of globalization or the meaning of various responses to it. On the contrary, the negotiation of national identity under globalization is an empirical matter, one which remains largely unexplored at the level of process and meanings. These issues are taken up in the following chapters.

[148] Ong, *Flexible Citizenship*, pp. 161–69.

2   Theoretical assumptions and methods

Theories of hybridization

In one sense, "explaining" hybridization is far beyond the scope of this book. After all, even accounting for absorption, rejection, or assertion alone, in an empirically grounded fashion, requires a truly intimidating amount of cross-cultural and comparative research. One might, of course, reduce each strand to a small sub-set of concrete referents in order to simplify the analytical problem, but only at the expense of eliding the interconnectedness among ideas and practices which is so essential to globalization and the social response it engenders. Moreover, as the above discussion suggests and as the remainder of this book will argue in greater detail, the distinct strands of hybridization are best understood as *interrelated*, meaning that any effort to comprehend each separately is doomed to failure. This, I would suggest, is because there is something truly foundational about the dialectic described by the patterned responses to globalization – which explains why the pattern recurs so widely all over the world. That is, the combination of absorption, rejection, and assertion represents a basic imperative of national identity formation, which consists of becoming an integral part of global society while at the same time remaining unique. And yet, this process operates at such a high level of abstraction that falsification becomes virtually impossible: alternative explanations are not only equally plausible, but are equally supportable in general terms. Attempting to explain the entire pattern of hybridization thus seems bound to lead to rather bland theoretical insights. Nevertheless, briefly thinking through some of the issues involved in conducting such an inquiry is helpful in suggesting a different avenue of approach.

To start with absorption – of public institutions as well as high and low Western culture – explaining even this one strand of hybridization as it works itself out in local contexts is essentially equivalent to accounting for the global trend of convergence. This question alone has attracted a massive amount of scholarly attention and spawned a number of distinct theoretical approaches. One set of explanations revolves around functionalism, in the sense of pragmatic adaptations designed to address concrete organizational goals. From this standpoint homogenization occurs as a result of the global replication of what "works," ranging from technological modernization to management practices to international economic integration and standardization, all driven by the pursuit of efficiency and economies of scale.[1] This quest for efficiency, in turn, has been variously explained. For example, neorealist theory highlights competitive pressures arising from international anarchy. According to this interpretation, "hard" or material power constitutes a large part of the success which evokes functional mimesis among developing states, even when the institutions being borrowed are not directly related to military potential.[2] Alternatively, the functionalist impulse may be attributed to the state's domestic institutional interests, including the requirements of governance and tending to the general welfare.[3] Finally, from a discursive perspective, the very construction of institutional convergence as something "inevitable" is itself part of the explanation for why it occurs.[4]

Still other theories contend that states absorb Western ideas and practices for reasons of legitimacy. Once again, however, there are very different ways of thinking about what is involved here. From one perspective, legitimacy constitutes a key *political commodity* which nation-states seek to acquire by wielding the symbols of modernity – ranging from the formal

---

[1] Held *et al.*, *Global Transformations*, esp. pp. 327–75; for an historical perspective see Craig N. Murphy, *International Organization and Industrial Change: Global Governance Since 1850* (New York: Oxford University Press, 1994).

[2] Without attempting to cite an enormous literature, a useful overview as well as discussion of this point is Randy Schweller and David Priess, "A Tale of Two Realisms: Expanding the Institutions Debate," *Mershon International Studies Review*, 41, No. 1 (May 1997): 1–32; and see Stephen G. Brooks, "The Globalization of Production and the Changing Benefits of Conquest," *The Journal of Conflict Resolution*, 43, No. 5 (October 1999): 646–70.

[3] Students of nationalism have long stressed the rise of standardized education and its fit with the market-driven pressures for efficiency, as part of national integration and the extension of state authority which took place in the nineteenth century. For example, see Eugen Weber, *Peasants into Frenchmen: The Modernization of Rural France, 1870–1914* (Stanford: Stanford University Press, 1976); Ernest Gellner, *Nations and Nationalism* (Oxford: Basil Blackwell, 1983). On borrowing institutions of governance see Bertrand Badie, *The Imported State: The Westernization of the Political Order*, translated by Claudia Royal (Stanford: Stanford University Press, 2000), pp. 93–130.

[4] Ben Rosamond, "Globalization, European Integration and the Discursive Construction of Economic Imperatives," *Journal of European Public Policy*, 6, No. 4 (April 2002): 147–67.

accoutrements of state[5] to showy development projects[6] – as part of an endless bid to establish something that is always in danger of melting away. This differs from the notion of legitimacy as a taken-for-granted sense of what is worthwhile or *appropriate*. In this sense, absorption arguably has to do with the attractiveness of certain ideas on a principled level, as actors (especially elites and activists within powerful states) negotiate shared understandings of what constitutes "civilized" conduct.[7] In either case, however, norm propagation and diffusion take place through international organizations and transnational networks, all of which foster the adoption of desirable standards of behavior.[8] In particular, scholars associated with the "world polity" school have asserted the existence of a pervasive ideology or global institutional culture (revolving around notions of universalism, individualism, rational voluntaristic authority, progress-as-justice, and world citizenship), which contributes to the isomorphic reproduction of dominant organizational forms.[9] From a cultural standpoint, then, regardless of whether instrumental or strictly normative explanations are invoked, legitimacy is constituted by the absorption of modernity.

As if the problem of explaining absorption were not formidable enough, however, hybridization also involves a complementary quest for collective identity in the form of assertion and rejection. Again, a massive amount of scholarly effort has been devoted to addressing these issues. According to one broad approach, assertion and rejection reflect inherent characteristics of human sociality, which are merely intensified in response to

[5] As Jowitt observes, "In order to establish their claims for political survival, economic aid, and prestige, weak countries must first be intelligible in an institutional sense to powerful countries in a position to recognize or ignore them. For this reason, adoption of the organizational and ideological idiom of the dominant powers becomes situationally necessary." Ken Jowitt, *The Leninist Response to National Dependency* (Berkeley: Institute of International Studies, University of California, 1978), p. 23.

[6] For instance, in post-colonial Venezuela the state has sought to bolster its power and deflect criticism by linking itself with material accomplishments in a series of dazzling public displays. See Fernando Coronil, *The Magical State: Nature, Money, and Modernity in Venezuela* (Chicago: Chicago University Press, 1997).

[7] Gerrit W. Gong, *The Standard of "Civilization" in International Society* (New York: Oxford University Press, 1984). See also, e.g., Martha Finnemore, *National Interests in International Society* (Ithaca: Cornell University Press, 1996); also Robert H. Jackson, "The Weight of Ideas in Decolonization," in Judith Goldstein and Robert O. Keohane, eds., *Ideas & Foreign Policy: Beliefs, Institutions and Political Change* (Ithaca: Cornell University Press, 1993), pp. 111–38.

[8] While the literature in this area is vast, a useful overview is Andrew Cortell and James Davis, "Understanding the Domestic Impact of Norms: A Research Agenda," *International Studies Review*, 2, No. 1 (Spring 2000): 65–87.

[9] A general statement is John W. Meyer, John Boli, George M. Thomas, and Franscisco Ramirez, "World Society and the Nation-State," *American Journal of Sociology*, 103, No. 1 (July 1997): 144–81. See also Boli and Thomas, eds., *Constructing World Culture*.

globalization. Thus, nations – which like all groups fashion themselves in contradistinction to Others – *normally* react to alien cultural flows that challenge their self-understandings by articulating narratives of difference as well as certain other narratives of ("traditional") in-group belonging.[10] Alternatively, rejection and assertion may be viewed as stemming from the state's institutional interests (and, for that matter, the interests of its caretakers in the national bureaucracy). From this perspective the immensity of these combined cultural, informational, financial, and other flows constitute a threat to the state's viability and autonomy – and thus to its authority – semi-regardless of their particular content. Accordingly, states find themselves overwhelmed in ways that threaten their abilities to play their authorized roles as sovereign actors.[11] They respond in ways calculated to reassert sovereignty, not only through measured delegation and re-regulation, but also by underscoring the "national" dimension of the nation-state model.[12]

Nor is it necessary to treat distinct explanations for absorption and assertion as stark alternatives; synthetic or complementary explanations suggest themselves as well. An example is the well-known case of the elimination of footbinding in China, which seems to offer a vivid case of combined motivations for absorption. As Keck and Sikkink observe, criticism of footbinding was originally introduced by Westerners, but was championed domestically by a broad coalition of reformist intellectuals, entrepreneurs hoping for expanded markets, and political elites seeking efficient social mobilization.[13] Christena Turner draws a similar conclusion: "The cessation of footbinding practices was integral not just to women's emancipation but to the conceptualization of a new

---

[10] The same point holds whether or not exclusivist forms of collective identity are inherent in society. For an ecologically based argument of self–other cultural differentiation see Fredrik Barth, "Introduction," in Barth, ed., *Ethnic Groups and Boundaries: The Social Organization of Cultural Difference* (Boston: Little, Brown, and Co., 1969), pp. 9–38. A Durkheimian approach is Iver B. Neumann, *The Uses of the Other: "The East" in European Identity Formation* (Minneapolis: University of Minnesota Press, 1999).

[11] Steven K. Vogel, *Freer Markets, More Rules: Regulatory Regimes in Advanced Industrial Countries* (Ithaca: Cornell University Press, 1996); Kanishka Jayasuriya, "Globalization and the Changing Architecture of the State: The Politics of the Regulatory State and the Politics of Negative Co-ordination," *Journal of European Public Policy*, 8, No. 1 (February 2001): 101–23.

[12] As Sheila Croucher observes, states whose autonomy and sovereignty are beleaguered under globalization "turn, in defense, to their role as representatives and defenders of nations." Sheila Croucher, *Globalization and Belonging: The Politics of Identity in a Changing World* (Lanham, MD: Rowman and Littlefield, 2004), p. 110, and see pp. 103–12.

[13] Margaret Keck and Kathryn Sikkink, *Activists Beyond Borders: Advocacy Networks in International Politics* (Ithaca: Cornell University Press, 1998), pp. 60–66.

economic and political order."[14] Ultimately this included a demand for new mentalities and gender roles geared to integrating technology as part of the transition to a modern society. In this case, then, absorption seems to have served the goals of functional efficiency as well as national and international legitimacy.

Similarly, assertive and rejectionist responses to globalization may also arise from more than one source. As Ulf Hedetoft puts it, globalization "makes [nation-states] into reactors to transnational processes more than the shapers of those processes, and in the same vein makes nation-states and national/cultural identities into defensive, dependent bastions of communication, organization and 'domesticity'."[15] Social and institutional logics are both applicable here. In addition, as we will see with regard to the process of mediating globalization, state and society interact closely in negotiations over national identity and what role each should play in its reproduction. For all of these reasons it seems misguided to reduce identity attachments to structural, political, or essentialist cultural factors.[16] Anthony Smith, though often accused of the cardinal sin of primordialism, expresses this insight well: "The images and traditions that go into the making of nations are not the artificial creations of intelligentsias, cultural chefs or engineers, but the product of a complex interplay between these creators, their social conditions and the ethnic heritages of their chosen populations."[17]

Understanding hybridization

Power, governance, legitimacy, and institutional interests are key motivations which are always in play to one extent or another. It seems pointless

---

[14] Christena Turner, "Locating Footbinding: Variations across Class and Space in Nineteenth and Early Twentieth Century China," *Journal of Historical Sociology*, 10, No. 4 (December 1997), p. 471.

[15] Ulf Hedetoft, "The Nation-State Meets the World: National Identities in the Context of Transnationality and Cultural Globalization," *European Journal of Social Theory*, 2, No. 1 (February 1999), p. 89. Rosenau makes the same point: "As people and organizations experience the losses of autonomy and authority that accompany globalization, so do they seek to protect their interests and achieve psychic comfort by reverting to the more close-at-hand groups with which they are affiliated." James Rosenau, *Along the Domestic–Foreign Frontier: Exploring Governance in a Turbulent World* (Cambridge and New York: Cambridge University Press, 1997), p. 112. See also Ang, "Desperately Guarding Borders," in Souchou, ed., *House of Glass*, pp. 27–45.

[16] As Melucci observes, "Collective identity is never entirely negotiable because participation in collective action is endowed with meaning which cannot be reduced to cost–benefit calculation and always mobilizes emotions as well." Alberto Melucci, *Challenging Codes: Collective Action in the Information Age* (Cambridge: Cambridge University Press, 1996), pp. 70–1.

[17] Anthony D. Smith, *Myths and Memories of the Nation* (New York: Oxford University Press, 1999), p. 171.

to debate which of these factors are truly preeminent in such a large and central undertaking as the shaping of national identity. Nevertheless, arguments about macrohistorical processes such as institutional convergence and nationalism devolve again and again into predictable camp divides, none of which seem amenable to resolution on a metatheoretical level. (Indeed, the very fact that realist and constructivist arguments over foundational political problems have raged for over two decades, with very little narrowing of the opposing positions, in itself suggests that the debate cannot be resolved on the terms in which it is conducted.) It is tempting to seek a relativistic escape, and to conclude that such arguments simply reflect differing, yet perhaps equally legitimate, philosophical interpretations of social reality. Alternatively, however, it may be useful to explicitly adopt an agnostic stance, and instead to proceed analytically from the assumption that the observable patterns are co-determined at some deeper level of causality. Again, the problem from this perspective is not so much the existence of an underlying ontological schism, nor the complexity of the issue at hand (and thus the practical difficulties of testing propositions about hybridization). Rather, the key problem has to do with the likelihood that the constituent elements of hybridization are intrinsically interrelated. That is, absorption, rejection, and assertion do not merely coincide, but affect one another causally. This, in turn, is a function of an even more fundamental issue, which is that hybridization emerges so consistently because it is heavily over-determined by a number of factors – material-instrumental, organizational, and ideational – the interaction of which produces a mutually reinforcing dynamic. As a result, the discourse and practice of national identity formation almost always reflect a concern for functional efficiency, stable governance, and legitimacy; these are not necessarily competing, but rather are complementary objectives for states and mass publics alike.

Seen in this light, instrumental and identity-based arguments may both be equally valid and at the same time equally limited. The task, therefore, is not to determine which is correct, but instead to understand how, under what circumstances, for what reasons each comes into play. Consequently, rather than seeking to explain hybridization in positivist terms – i.e., by demonstrating covariation between certain conditions and outcomes, consistent with covering laws – it may be more useful to explore the reasons associated with its occurrence.[18] In other words, as Fierke puts it, because "the subjects of analysis are actors who generate meaning that is constitutive of action and interaction," fully *understanding* hybridization

---

[18] On the difference between causes and reasons see Friedrich Kratochwil and John Ruggie, "International Organization: A State of the Art or an Art of the State?" *International Organization*, 40, No. 4 (Autumn 1986): 753–75.

requires investigating the discursive milieu of the actors and observers involved.[19] This book therefore addresses a proximate, yet compelling question: how is globalization mediated?

Locating the social process of the nation

It has become a commonplace to say that the state is intimately involved not only in producing the nation but also in posing as its chief defender, at least in part as a way of justifying its own existence. This symbiotic relationship between state building and nation building has a long pedigree, reaching back to the period of the French Revolution.[20] Long removed from its ideological and institutional origins, however, it becomes less clear why such historical arrangements persist, and how collective identities associated with those arrangements are reproduced. Unsatisfied with accepting national identity as a self-perpetuating legacy, or treating the nation-state complex as an historical "given," scholars have become increasingly interested in problematizing the state's role in fostering categories of domesticity and myths of belonging. Accordingly, a number of scholars have begun to explore how state and nation are reproduced in everyday practice, by examining particular sites of state-led identity formation. These include public festivals and national holidays, in addition to the various institutions occupied with official historiography, military policy and training, educational policy, and public-monument building. To take one obvious example, the museum helps reproduce national identity by delineating boundaries of group membership and propounding shared traditions and symbols.[21] At the same time, the museum furnishes a "contact zone" suitable for allowing foreign visitors to distinguish themselves from their hosts, and vice versa.[22] The apparently objective status of the nation-state is also reproduced by means of territorial demarcation

[19] Karin M. Fierke, "Links Across the Abyss: Language and Logic in International Relations," *International Studies Quarterly*, 46, No. 3 (September 2002), p. 351.

[20] Otto Hintze, "The Formation of States and Constitutional Development: A Study in History and Politics," in Felix Gilbert, ed., *The Historical Essays of Otto Hintze* (New York: Oxford University Press, 1975), pp. 159–77.

[21] Sharon Macdonald and Gordon Fyfe, eds., *Theorizing Museums: Representing Identity and Diversity in a Changing World* (Cambridge, MA: Blackwell, 1996); Steven Cooke and Fiona McLean, "Picturing the Nation: The Celtic Periphery as Discursive Other in the Archaeological Displays of the Museum of Scotland," *Scottish Geographical Journal*, 118, No. 4 (2002): 283–98; Eric Davis, "The Museum and the Politics of Social Control in Modern Iraq," in John Gillis, ed., *Commemorations: The Politics of National Identity* (Princeton: Princeton University Press, 1994), pp. 90–104.

[22] James Clifford, *Routes: Travel and Translation in the Late-Twentieth Century* (Cambridge: Harvard University Press, 1997), especially pp. 188–219.

and cartography, thereby connecting common cultural traits with shared borders and political authority.[23]

While they capture a key part of the identity formation process, however, such "top–down" modes of identity construction remain incomplete insofar as they overlook the other side of the nation-state coin: i.e., the nation itself, and the bottom–up demand for belonging. This is perhaps especially true in the context of globalization, which generates mass opposition to what is feared to be an impending loss of collective identity. Today, therefore, in addition to official nationalism, one also finds everywhere a corollary *popular* nationalism, expressing what Robertson refers to as "willful nostalgia."[24] This popular and quotidian aspect of nationalism is often overlooked, even by scholars who reject elite-driven models, but who nevertheless tend to treat mass social involvement as taking place in exceptional, spasmodic moments of upheaval.[25]

While emphasizing nationalism's broad appeal, it is also important to recognize that this cannot be simply ascribed to an underlying class hegemony. Of course, tracing the evolution of the national idea clearly reveals class interests at work. There is no doubt that the nationalist movement fully emerged under specific historical conditions, in which the bourgeoisie utilized the idea of the nation as a way of overturning aristocratic control and establishing market institutions.[26] Yet while this element was important, it seems arbitrary to explain nationalism as merely an instrumental class movement. On the contrary, in order to craft compelling representations of collective identity, elites often had to rely on the zeal of cultural activists who were enamored with nationalism, *per se*. In this sense a real intellectual fervor of collective identification dovetailed with the institutional and mobilizational goals of the new statist bourgeoisie.[27]

---

[23] Westwood and Radcliffe, *Remaking the Nation*, pp. 62–7; Coronil, *Magical State*; Anssi Paasi, "The Political Geography of Boundaries at the End of the Millennium: Challenges of the De-territorializing World," in Heikki Eskelinen, Ilkka Liikanen, and Jukka Oksa, eds., *Curtains of Iron and Gold: Reconstructing Borders and Scales of Interaction* (Aldershot: Ashgate, 1999), pp. 9–24.

[24] Robertson, *Globalization: Social Theory and Global Culture*, pp. 155–62.

[25] For example, Beissinger tends to relegate social agency to episodic, "noisy" events in which the masses take to the streets. Mark Beissinger, *Nationalist Mobilization and the Collapse of the Soviet State* (Cambridge: Cambridge University Press, 2002).

[26] Miroslav Hroch, *Social Preconditions of National Revival in Europe* (Cambridge: Cambridge University Press, 1985).

[27] On the role of cultural activists in this process, see Jusdanis, *Necessary Nation*; also Michael Herzfeld, *Ours Once More: Folklore, Ideology and the Making of Modern Greece* (Austin: University of Texas Press, 1982); and also Anne-Marie Thiesse and Catherine Bertho-Lavenir, "Folk Culture and the Construction of European National Identities between the Eighteenth and Twentieth Centuries," in Alain Dieckhoff and Natividad Gutierrez, eds., *Modern Roots: Studies of National Identity* (Aldershot: Ashgate, 2001), pp. 118–29.

Moreover, nationalism did ultimately succeed in gathering truly broad-based social momentum. Over the course of the century following the French Revolution, popular involvement became more active and exuberant, and state elites increasingly sought to harness the raw, emotive nationalism they had helped to create.[28] Thus, although there was no innate or spontaneous outburst of enthusiasm for belonging to the nation, precisely this kind of passionate attachment eventually captured the popular mind. At this point, nationalism is as much sought by the masses as it is instilled in them by elites.[29]

In sum, what we find in considering the development of state and nation is a mutual attraction between them, one which largely transcends class attachments. The result is an intimate, ongoing link between nation building and state building. Indeed, as demonstrated by cases as far-flung as Japan, Australia, America, and Fiji, already by the twentieth century the state and the nation had become so intertwined that each derived its legitimacy, in part, by reproducing the other.[30] In this sense, as Roy argues, imagining oneself as national almost necessarily involves imagining oneself as a subject of the state.[31] While to some extent this continues to be due to the intentional work of the state in presenting itself as guardian of the nation, it is also important to note that the idea of the nation-state has become normalized – indeed, so much so that the nation is often considered incomplete without its own apparatus of state.

Against this historical background, when we shift to the present and consider the process of nation building in most countries of the former USSR, we cannot help being struck by the outpouring of nationalist demands – first within and then against the Soviet regime. The

---

[28] On the emergence of "the state as an ideal," including the fusion of governance with nationalism, see Martin Van Creveld, *The Rise and Decline of the State* (Cambridge: Cambridge University Press, 1999), pp. 189–205; also Benedict Anderson, *Imagined Communities: Reflections on the Origin and Spread of Nationalism* (London and New York: Verso, 1991), pp. 83–111.

[29] As Walker Connor has argued, the recent wave of nationalism reflects broad, nearly unquestioning popular devotion to the ideal of the nation itself. Walker Connor, *Ethnonationalism: The Quest for Understanding* (Princeton: Princeton University Press, 1994).

[30] As evidenced by popular involvement in national campaigns: see Sheldon Garon, *Molding Japanese Minds: The State in Everyday Life* (Princeton: Princeton University Press, 1997), pp. 106–14; Lyn Spillman, *Nation and Commemoration: Creating National Identities in the United States and Australia* (Cambridge and New York: Cambridge University Press, 1997), esp. pp. 62–9, 106–11; Claus Bossen, "Festival Mania, Tourism and Nation-Building in Fiji: The Case of the Hibiscus Festival, 1956–1970," *The Contemporary Pacific*, 12, No. 1 (Spring 2000): 123–54.

[31] Srirupa Roy, "Nation and Institution: Commemorating the Fiftieth Anniversary of Indian Independence," *Interventions: The International Journal of Postcolonial Studies*, 3, No. 2 (July 2001): 251–65.

national idea, which was instilled during the very inception of Bolshevik rule and incorporated into its constitutional forms, swiftly became universally embraced as a model of post-Soviet social organization.[32] Although intellectuals were indeed mobilized for the purpose of reinventing national identity, and although other activists then stepped into the fray, the masses also – almost immediately – latched onto the idea of the nation, and championed its cause with a fervor surpassing any simple instrumental purpose. This was true not only during the initial bloom of nationalism at the end of the Soviet period, but also during the prolonged process of nation building, and indeed it continues to be true today. Obviously, actual (as opposed to purely cosmetic) popular involvement in nation building requires at least some degree of civil society organization and freedom of expression. Where this is lacking, as for example in Turkmenistan, one finds an overwhelmingly top–down process of cultural mobilization.[33] Elsewhere, however, the process typically features a combination of state-led nation building – in which elites use identity discourse for political ends – and nation- (or ethnic-) led state building, in which decentralized popular actors galvanized by cultural identity seek to affirm order and meaning.[34] While the thrust of this book deals with identity formation processes in the former Soviet Union, therefore, there is nothing unique about the salience of nationalism in that part of the world. Rather, the evolution of mass attitudes between the early nineteenth century and the present reflects the fact that nationalism – as an institution – has become globally accepted as normal, and even indispensable, for collective well-being.

Yet although the above insights about the historical fusion of state and nation help elucidate the basic building blocks of identity formation, they fail to entirely explain this development as an ongoing *social process* under conditions of globalization. That is, they fail to clarify how and why particular national identity narratives are organized and articulated, as well as through what social mechanisms and discursive frameworks they are reproduced. To what extent is the process of nation building

---

[32] Ronald Suny, *The Revenge of the Past: Nationalism, Revolution, and the Collapse of the Soviet Union* (Stanford: Stanford University Press, 1994); Edward W. Walker, *Dissolution: Sovereignty and the Breakup of the Soviet Union* (Lanham, MD: Rowman and Littlefield, 2003).

[33] Ahmet Kuru, "Between the State and Cultural Zones: Nation Building in Turkmenistan," *Central Asian Survey*, 21, No. 1 (March 2002): 71–90.

[34] As Anderson observes with respect to the post-colonial process, "so often in the nation-building policies of the new states one sees both a genuine, popular nationalist enthusiasm and a systematic, even Machiavellian, instilling of nationalist ideology through the mass media, the education system, administrative regulations, and so forth." Anderson, *Imagined Communities*, pp. 113–14.

contentious? In other words, to what extent are national identities best understood as compromise platforms capable of reconciling competing group interests?[35] Or, does identity formation instead reveal a fundamental commonality of purpose linking state and society?

In pursuing this line of analysis, the focus increasingly shifts to the liminal space where state blends into society. That is, we closely examine the social processes of strategic action, including the planning, organization, and public production of identity.[36] In doing so it is helpful to borrow Joel Migdal's "state-in-society" perspective, which he employs to understand how the state becomes "naturalized" through its association with mundane practices of social identity formation, including law, public ritual, and informal behavior in the public sphere.[37] Specifically, in calling for an anthropology of the state, Migdal differentiates between top levels of political organization, central agencies, "dispersed field offices," and "the trenches" (the latter refers to officials "mandated to apply state rules and regulations directly").[38] The upshot is that in order to comprehend state–society relations as an ongoing process, it is necessary to consider not only the top echelons of government but also the full continuum of decentralized state actors, especially as they engage society in an effort to shape identities and practices.[39] Such actors are not merely passive recipients and executors of central governmental decisions. Nor, in most cases, are they able to preside over policy implementation while standing aloof from the social conditions in which they operate. Instead, local officials may be thought of as social intermediaries who interpret, prioritize, contest, and selectively implement central policy directives.[40]

---

[35] As is consistent with Breuilly's instrumental-mobilizational theory of nationalism. John Breuilly, *Nationalism and the State*, 2nd edition (Chicago: University of Chicago Press, 1994). See also Phillip M. Rawkins, "An Approach to the Political Sociology of the Welsh Nationalist Movement," *Political Studies*, 27, No. 3 (September 1979): 440–57.

[36] Andrew Thompson, "Nations, National Identities and Human Agency: Putting People Back into Nations," *Sociological Review*, 49, No. 1 (February 2001): 18–32.

[37] Joel S. Migdal, *State in Society: Studying How States and Societies Transform and Constitute One Another* (Cambridge and New York: Cambridge University Press, 2001), p. 150 and see 135–69.

[38] Migdal, *State in Society*, pp. 116–24.

[39] Hannerz calls this the "cultural apparatus," consisting of all actors and agencies involved in the production and dissemination of shared culture and identity. This includes educational authorities in the broadest sense, as well as the creators and managers of public performances and exhibitions, and those who participate in reporting on or critiquing their content. Hannerz, *Cultural Complexity*, pp. 81–84.

[40] The result may be a greater or lesser degree of decentralization, depending on locally prevailing norms as well as relations between political and social organizations. For an informative case study see Diana Rhoten, "Education Decentralization in Argentina: A 'Global-Local Conditions of Possibility' Approach to State, Market, and Society Change," *Journal of Education Policy*, 15, No. 6 (November–December 2000): 593–619.

In sum, thinking about why hybridization occurs – whether at the level of state interests or cultural dynamics – may be facilitated by inquiring into the microprocesses involved, i.e., the connections between institutional outcomes, social negotiation, and popular discourse. This requires asking who undertakes hybrid identity constructions, how are they framed and justified, and in what institutional settings such action unfolds. It also requires analyzing and interpreting the discourse around which national identity is constructed. Attending to these questions ought to shed light on how, and why, globalization is mediated in national and sub-national settings.

Methodological matters

Before tackling these more intrinsically interesting questions of state–society relations and national identity formation, we first need to choose a defensible methodology. Accordingly, this section briefly provides working definitions for culture, identity, and social discourse, and offers an epistemological approach for applying these concepts empirically and analytically.

For the sake of clarity it is convenient to begin with a few brisk definitions and stated assumptions. Without wading into a morass of scholarly disputation over the concept of culture, I start by understanding culture as a system of symbols invested with meaning, along with narratives and norms which construct the world as an intelligible and orderly place.[41] At the same time, culture is hardly static or abstract; it includes patterns of semiotic practice which both produce and potentially shift meaning, even while it retains essential elements of continuity through its own "cultural logic."[42] In other words, as I use it here, culture creates an intersubjective frame of reference for relevant social actors, by making imaginable – or precluding from imagination – a given action or utterance.[43] In this

---

[41] As in Clifford Geertz, *The Interpretation of Cultures* (New York: Basic Books, 1973), pp. 3–30.

[42] Lisa Wedeen, "Conceptualizing Culture: Possibilities for Political Science," *American Political Science Review*, 96, No. 4 (December 2002): 713–28; William H. Sewell, Jr., "The Concept(s) of Culture," in Victoria E. Bonnell and Lynn Hunt, eds., *Beyond The Cultural Turn: New Directions in the Study of Society and Culture* (Berkeley: University of California Press, 1999), pp. 35–61. On cultural logic as the stabilizing quality of coherent yet evolving systems of thought, see Edward F. Fischer, "Cultural Logic and Maya Identity," *Current Anthropology*, 40, No. 4 (August–October 1999): 473–99.

[43] In this sense culture generates what Bourdieu refers to as the habitus, or the pervasive and routinized understandings which produce a subconscious orientation to the world. Pierre Bourdieu, *The Logic of Practice*, translated by Richard Nice (Stanford: Stanford University Press, 1990), pp. 52–65.

respect, as Yee has argued with respect to intersubjective beliefs in general, culture may be thought of as having "quasi-causal" significance.[44]

And yet, the analysis of ideas remains truncated unless we consider the social and political conditions for thought and action, including relations of power and interest. In other words, while accepting that outcomes are in some sense ultimately contingent on social constructions, there is no benefit in replacing "vulgar" materialism with an equally vulgar form of idealism. Instead, I wish to emphasize the reciprocal nature of the interaction between ideas, institutions, and agents. Just as practice feeds back on the "web of meanings" within which it occurs, so too, configurations of power and organized interest arising within cultural systems exert effects on those systems.[45] While relaxing the strongest claims for cultural autonomy, then, we may consider culture as something *semi-autonomous*: i.e., developing within structured social and political contexts but also acquiring its own coherence – both generative of and sensitive to publicly articulated ideas.[46]

Cultural systems make possible the formation of collective identity, which I understand as a constellation of self-referential values and qualities held by (or ascribed to) members of groups. As such, identities make meanings personal and practical by opening up avenues for legitimate action. This is never a finished process, since identities are always in motion, evolving along with changing social conditions and claims.[47] The role of discourse is crucial here, understood as the linguistic process whereby cultural conditions become crystallized and explicitly formulated, and through which practice may be interpreted as legitimate and replicable.[48] Discourse thus distills and reproduces abstract cultural symbols, identities, and other representations of social life in the form

---

[44] Albert S. Yee, "The Causal Effects of Ideas on Policies," *International Organization*, 50, No. 1 (Winter 1996), pp. 96–8. See also Alexander Wendt, "On Constitution and Causation in International Relations," *Review of International Studies*, 24, No. 5 (December 1998): 101–17.

[45] Again, Wedeen's discussion is helpful on this point. "Conceptualizing Culture." See also Ronald Grigor Suny, "Back and Beyond: Reversing the Cultural Turn?" *American Historical Review*, 107, No. 5 (December 2002): 1476–99.

[46] The strong case for culture is laid out by Jeffrey C. Alexander, *The Meanings of Social Life* (New York: Oxford University Press, 2003), esp. pp. 3–26.

[47] Yosef Lapid, "Culture's Ship: Returns and Departures in International Relations Theory," in Yosef Lapid and Friedrich Krachtowil, eds., *The Return of Culture and Identity in International Relations* (London: Lynne Reinner, 1996), pp. 3–20. See also T. K. Fitzgerald, *Metaphors of Identity* (Albany: State University of New York Press, 1993).

[48] I accept Neumann's distinction between "narrative discourse," which constitutes the conceptual context within which concrete social action takes place, and "practices" or social action itself. Iver Neumann, "Returning Practice to the Linguistic Turn: The Case of Diplomacy," *Millennium: Journal of International Studies*, 31, No. 3 (2002): 627–51.

of narratives, or stories which encapsulate shared meanings.[49] In doing so, moreover, discourse functions as a key bridging mechanism within the public realm, serving to connect state and society by linking together conceptions and practices constitutive of social order. We therefore need to be concerned not only with the subjective understandings of individual actors, but also with the broad discursive terrain within which social identities arise and find their expression.[50]

The link between discourse and identity formation has received extensive scholarly attention in recent years. While the complexity and nuance of this literature is immense, one consistent thread within it has been to emphasize the importance of difference. From this perspective the emergence and reproduction of subject positions proceeds by way of drawing distinctions between the collective self and salient Others.[51] Yet while much of the available work on identity formation accentuates its relational and exclusionary aspects, national identity also includes embedded and inclusive features; that is, it involves understandings of legitimacy with respect to idealized values and practices. Therefore, in addition to self–Other differentiation, we are also concerned with ideas which are propounded as constitutive of virtue, including social morality and "good citizenship."

This additional, inclusive dimension of identity may be understood as providing the particular content for characterizations of appropriateness. Most importantly for our purposes, this includes claims about moral reliability, which as Stinchcombe argues is perhaps the single most pervasive category of society's deep moral order.[52] In exploring interventions and prescriptions relevant to youth identity formation, therefore, I consider claims about both the distinctiveness and inherent legitimacy of the ideal national subject.

[49] See Donald E. Polkinghorne, *Narrative Knowing and the Human Sciences* (Albany: State University of New York Press, 1988), esp. pp. 13–36; Margaret R. Somers, "The Narrative Constitution of Identity: A Relational and Network Approach," *Theory and Society*, 23, No. 5 (October 1994): 605–49.

[50] As Cruz usefully conceptualizes it, identity may be thought of as a set of subject positions which arise within a discursively constructed "collective field of imaginable possibilities." Consuelo Cruz, "Identity and Persuasion: How Nations Remember Their Pasts and Make Their Futures," *World Politics*, 52, No. 3 (April 2000), p. 276.

[51] Paul A. Kowert, "National Identity: Inside and Out," *Security Studies*, 8, No. 2/3, (Winter 1998/99–Spring 1999): 1–34; Neumann, *Uses of the Other*; William A. Callahan, "Beyond Cosmopolitanism and Nationalism: Diasporic Chinese and Neo-Nationalism in China and Thailand," *International Organization*, 57, No. 3 (Summer 2003): 481–517.

[52] Stinchcombe refers to "the category that distinguishes those people who can be trusted to form reliable parts for the moral constructions we make to run our lives. . . ." Arthur Stinchcombe, "The Deep Structure of Moral Categories: Eighteenth-Century French Stratification and the Revolution," in Eno Rossi, ed., *Structural Sociology* (New York: Columbia University Press, 1982), p. 69.

In doing so I focus on public discourse, which is distinguished by virtue of being openly negotiated and often highly contested, as opposed to the relatively non-negotiated and unselfconscious discourse of the private sphere. Claims and categorizations made publicly also tend to hold weight presumptively, and are influential in ways that private utterances cannot be. This is not to suggest that private understandings and actions are irrelevant from the standpoint of social order, but merely that public discourse and practice tend to be especially and immediately consequential for producing intersubjective knowledge and its statist effects. This is hardly accidental, since the purpose of public discourse is strategic: it is intended not merely to promote shared understandings *per se*, but either to fix or change such understandings.[53]

The latter point highlights the crucial dynamic quality of discourse. In part, this is simply due to the contingency of discursive reproduction, since different actors and contexts always inflect meanings differently.[54] Precisely because of this inevitable variability, slippage tends to occur in transmission. By reproducing cultural symbols and identities, discourse potentially alters their meanings; by explaining actions, it potentially suggests and justifies new patterns of action. But of course, change also occurs by design. Thus, as Smith and Alexander persuasively argue, culture is both internalized and at the same time susceptible to discursive manipulation by strategic actors.[55] We can therefore conceptualize a mutually constitutive interaction between culture and discursively informed agency, in which "agents" are shaped by culture, but shape it as well.[56] From this perspective, agency consists of the intentional use

[53] A lucid discussion is Andrew Chadwick, "Studying Political Ideas: A Public Political Discourse Approach," *Political Studies*, 48, No. 2 (Special Issue, 2000): 283–301; also M. Lane Bruner, "Rhetorics of the State: The Public Negotiation of Political Character in Germany, Russia, and Quebec," *National Identities*, 2, No. 2 (July 2000): 159–75. In this vein, Steven Lukes criticizes neo-Durkheimian approaches to public ritual for assuming that ritual unproblematically creates social integration and value cohesion. Lukes argues instead that rituals *attempt* to generate either integration or opposition, and should therefore be understood as partisan claims. Steven Lukes, *Essays in Social Theory* (New York: Columbia University Press, 1977), pp. 52–73.

[54] See Jennifer Milliken, "Discourse Study: Bringing Rigor to Critical Theory," in Karin Fierke and Knud Jorgensen, eds., *Constructing International Relations: The Next Generation* (Armonk, NY, and London: M. E. Sharpe, 2001), pp. 136–59.

[55] See Jeffrey C. Alexander and Philip Smith, "The Discourse of American Civil Society: A New Proposal for Cultural Studies," *Theory and Society*, 22, No. 2 (April 1993): 151–207. For a discussion of culturally embedded versus individualistic approaches to agency, see Carl Ratner, "Agency and Culture," *Journal for the Theory of Social Behaviour*, 30, No. 4 (September 2000): 413–34.

[56] Heather Rae, *State Identities and the Homogenisation of Peoples* (Cambridge: Cambridge University Press, 2002), pp. 44–47. See also Michael Barnett, "Culture, Strategy and Foreign Policy Change: Israel's Road to Oslo," *European Journal of International Relations*, 5, No. 1 (1999): 5–36.

of available, inherently ambiguous discursive resources, so as to devise and legitimate specific claims within the opportunity structures presented by culture.[57] Taking this position side-steps an essentially irreconcilable, chicken-and-egg debate about the primacy of agents versus structures,[58] and provides a useful standard for evaluating the significance of social action; that is, it allows us to grasp not only relatively constrained forms of entrepreneurship, but also more creative and generative forms. Borrowing loosely from Bourdieu, we may conceptualize this entrepreneurial capacity as "virtuosity," understood both as the ability to improvise within a set of established rules, and to wield discursive and/or symbolic power in innovative ways.[59]

Moving beyond this insight requires addressing some key analytical problems. In particular, it requires thinking about how, and under what conditions, actors produce or resist change. Some useful suggestions along these lines have been made by Sonya Rose, in her discussion of continuity and change in discursive patterns of socialization. Rose argues that a key stratagem whereby actors attempt to shift or anchor discourse involves the invocation of moral standards which lie at the very foundation of social structure.[60] Demonstrating that fundamental moral standards have been transgressed implies the need for rectification, and thereby authorizes action for this purpose. Furthermore, Rose argues that moral discourses intensify under certain social circumstances, marked by unusually high levels of open contestation, in which established assumptions and collective identity constructs are called into question.[61]

---

[57] A useful discussion of this point is Patrick Thaddeus Jackson, "Hegel's House, Or 'People Are States Too'," *Review of International Studies*, 30, No. 2 (April 2004): 281–87.

[58] For example, see Colin Hay, "What Place for Ideas in The Structure–Agency Debate? Globalisation as a 'Process Without A Subject'," *First Press: Writing in the Critical Social Sciences* (2001), available online at: http://www.theglobalsite.ac.uk/press/. I wish to avoid rehearsing this long-sterile debate. My own position is essentially similar to Stuart McAnulla, "Structure and Agency," in David Marsh and Gerry Stoker, eds., *Theory and Methods in Political Science* (London: Palgrave, 2002), pp. 271–91.

[59] The first, more restricted conceptualization of virtuosity is from Bourdieu, *Logic of Practice*, pp. 66–7. On enlarging this notion of virtuosity in order to escape from structural deterministic tendencies in Bourdieu's thought, see Anthony King, "Thinking with Bourdieu Against Bourdieu: A 'Practical' Critique of the Habitus," *Sociological Theory*, 18, No. 3 (November 2000): 417–33. Bourdieu himself ultimately acknowledged the ambiguity of his thinking with regard to symbolic capital and the possibility of agency. Pierre Bourdieu, "Scattered Remarks," *European Journal of Social Theory*, 2, No. 3 (August 1999): 334–40.

[60] Sonya Rose, "Cultural Analysis and Moral Discourses: Episodes, Continuities, and Transformations," in Bonnell and Hunt, eds., *Beyond the Cultural Turn*, pp. 217–38.

[61] *Ibid.* As Pollner observes, the tendency in such situations is to affirm the validity of one normatively acceptable, "objective" reality while the other is characterized as deviant and flawed. Melvin Pollner, *Mundane Reason: Reality in Everyday and Sociological Discourse* (Cambridge: Cambridge University Press, 1987), pp. 69–86.

Such a coincidence of dislocation and moral claims is strikingly similar to the dynamic of globalization and social contestation, which forms the subject of this book. Examining the discourse of hybridization reveals profound distress and stridently moralistic claims about legitimate social identity. Cultural globalization thus poses, in Calhoun's words, "the modern challenge of deciding how to fit into projects of collective and individual identity that presuppose inscription in a multiplicity of often incommensurable identity schemes."[62] The problem is how to make such schemes appear commensurable and socially acceptable – including how to be modern and traditional, or global and national – at the same time. Herein lies the social challenge of hybridization.

The process follows a predictable pattern. First, while specific (and presumably inimical) foreign influences are easily detected, the totality of globalization often passes unnoticed, at least at the start. Gradually, however, the absorption of alien values – such as efficiency or individualism – leads to a widening range of normative and organizational shifts, which in turn generate increasing dissonance. Ultimately it becomes impossible to embrace such values and identity constructs piecemeal, without them jostling uncomfortably against established beliefs and behaviors. Mike Featherstone makes this point well in explaining modern (or "global") culture as "the sense of heaps, congeries and aggregates of cultural particularities juxtaposed together on the same field . . . in which the fact that they are different and do not fit together, or want to fit together, becomes noticeable and a source of practical problems."[63]

Eventually the stakes become apparent to all. At this point, language becomes overtly (de)legitimative, as commonly accepted social facts are disputed and generally unnoticed "background" understandings are thrust forward and questioned.[64] In this context too, discourse consists of claims and counter-claims through which various actors attempt to fix social identities and values. Quite aside from whether such efforts actually achieve their desired ends, exploring them is illuminating because of the significant consequences they have for society.

Examining the contentious social and political dynamic of hybridization requires delving into the microprocesses of national youth identity formation. In particular, it requires examining the actors engaged in these processes, which thus raises the need to distinguish among various

---

[62] Craig Calhoun, "Social Theory and the Politics of Identity," in Calhoun, ed., *Social Theory and the Politics of Identity* (Oxford: Blackwell, 1994), p. 12.

[63] Mike Featherstone, *Undoing Culture: Globalization, Postmodernism and Identity* (London: Sage Publications, 1995), pp. 123–24.

[64] On social facts and background understandings see John Searle, *The Construction of Social Reality* (New York: Free Press, 1995), pp. 23–28 and 137–47.

types of actors regarding their abilities to engage in and influence public discourse. Without denying the significance of charismatic personal
qualities, by and large this ability derives from position; that is, from
the institutionally defined power to authoritatively delineate difference,
and/or to assert standards of morality and virtue. I therefore focus on several categories of actors, which I categorize as "state," "sub-state," and
"non-state," with reference to the institutional resources at their disposal.
More so than the public at large, these actors are capable of inflecting
discourse – and for that matter, shaping social practice as well – in ways
calculated to influence young people's identities and patterns of conduct.

Undertaking this work also involves extensive discourse analysis. In
particular, I consider two categories of public discourse. First, in keeping
with the above comments, elite discourse (on the part of actors able to
draw upon privileged symbolic and material resources) shows how, and
for what reasons, certain identities may be systematically mobilized and
institutionalized. The cultural and symbolic aspects of globalization are
therefore mediated through different discursive channels. While the vast
majority of people partake "only" in ambient social discourse, cultural
entrepreneurs are affected by additional, relatively rarified flows of ideas
related to national identity formation. Second, social (or "popular") discourse in the public sphere constitutes the range of available identities in
the former Soviet cities and tells us where boundaries are uncertain, under
negotiation, or in the process of being redrawn. As Hopf cogently argues,
inasmuch as decision-makers partake in the social cognitive structures
that make up discourses and identities, their own self-understandings are
also constituted through these structures.[65] Thus, while privileged with
respect to power, elite discourse and action – including state policymaking – are nevertheless grounded in a broader social discourse.

For reasons already discussed, within the universe of social discourse,
public utterances have particular salience and potential import. I therefore examine public discourse in order to infer prevailing social understandings relevant to national identity formation. Of course, determining
what counts as prevailing discourse is itself an important interpretive and
empirical task. I attempt to do so by being sensitive to the centrality and
recurrence of various themes, as they are expressed within highly visi-
ble media organs, rather than by reducing this question to the officially

---

[65] Ted Hopf, *Social Construction of International Politics: Identities and Foreign Policies,
Moscow, 1955 and 1999* (Ithaca and London: Cornell University Press, 2002), p. 20.
Hopf further defines social cognitive structure as "a sociotemporal historical site within
which there is a collection of intersubjective meanings to the discursive practices of its
members," p. 21.

articulated position of the state or any narrow group of elites.[66] In addition, rather than imposing specific analytical categories on this data, I let the values and concerns expressed therein emerge by themselves, inductively. This in turn requires making the assumption that individuals who participate in debates and strategic interventions relevant to national identity are aware of the ideas they express, and that these ideas (and the practices predicated on them) are in fact consequential in their own right, as opposed to being effectively determined by material and/or institutional structures.[67] Thus, while I remain cognizant of the domestic and international distribution of power as well as state institutions, the focus of my interpretation is on explicit and evident (rather than implicit and inferred) connections between discourse, values, and intentional acts.[68] In particular, I attend to questions of modernity, development, and legitimacy, including moral judgments as well as claims about the substance and form of national identity.

Data selection

As noted in the introduction, this study examines the social response to cultural globalization in three cities of the former Soviet Union: Astrakhan (Russia), Almaty (Kazakhstan), and Baku (Azerbaijan). The reason for selecting these cities is that, as significant metropolitan centers, they each encountered massive flows of foreign culture in the decade following the fall of the USSR. This of course makes them unrepresentative of their countries as a whole, which, in rural areas and smaller towns, continue to experience relatively low levels of cultural globalization (this is especially true of Kazakhstan and Azerbaijan). And yet clearly the three cities are not entirely alike. In certain respects Almaty and Baku are different from Astrakhan, since the former two are national capitals while the latter is only a regional capital. The population of Almaty is estimated at about 1,300,000, while Baku is officially home to 1,800,000 (although unofficial estimates put the number closer to three million). In contrast, Astrakhan is a city of "only" about half a million inhabitants, and with less bustling intensity than a national hub. The volume of international capital, goods, services, and people flowing through Almaty and Baku

---

[66] For a related discussion see Jacqueline Stevens, "Ideology and Social Structure: A Review Article," *Comparative Studies in History and Society*, 39, No. 2 (April 1997): 401–09.

[67] Robert Wuthnow, *Meaning and Moral Order: Explorations in Cultural Analysis* (Berkeley and Los Angeles: University of California Press, 1987), pp. 299–330.

[68] See Ruth Wodak, Rudolf de Cillia, Martin Reisigl, and Karin Liebhart, *The Discursive Construction of National Identity*, translated by Angelika Hirsch and Richard Mitten (Edinburgh: Edinburgh University Press, 1999).

substantially exceeds that flowing through Astrakhan. Nevertheless, even in Astrakhan the shift relative to Soviet times is enormous. And most importantly, specifically with respect to cultural flows – including youth culture – there is no perceptible difference among the three cities. Strictly for the purposes of this study, therefore, they seem roughly comparable.

I could have selected a number of other national capitals with equal justification, such as Bishkek (Kyrgyzstan), Tbilisi (Georgia), or Kiev (Ukraine). In Russia, I might have chosen other regional centers, especially those located in European Russia, such as Nizhnii Novgorod, Saratov, or Samara. I should note, however, that I decided not to study Moscow and St. Petersburg, because I regarded them as categorically different from any of the cities I ultimately selected. First, both had long been exposed to a higher degree of foreign influence than anywhere else in the former USSR. Moreover, by 1999, Moscow and St. Petersburg were already too far along with regard to cultural globalization: they had been swiftly inundated by foreign culture, and the first wave of social response had already crystallized. I wanted to observe this process unfolding, as close as possible to the peak of its initial cultural impact and public reaction. (Indeed, as it worked out the timing was ideal in each of the three cities selected.)

In conducting discourse analysis for this study I used four kinds of sources, each for a different purpose. First, as a way of gauging the structure of prevailing social attitudes I read hundreds of public texts. Second, in order to explore elite attitudes – that is, the attitudes of those in positions of authority or influence, who act to influence youth identity formation – I conducted numerous personal interviews. Third, as a brief point of comparison regarding youth attitudes, I conducted focus groups for young people themselves. Fourth, to gauge state policy goals and approaches I consulted official state doctrines, decrees, and programs, as well as related legislation enunciating state policy toward youth and youth identity formation. It is worth briefly discussing the nature of these sources and my criteria for selecting them.

In order to tap into social discourse at large I examined newspapers having a wide circulation in each of the three cities, looking for discussions of modernization, culture, and youth. For Almaty I used *Kazakhstanskaia pravda* (the main government organ), *Karavan*, *Panorama* (the latter two were controlled by President Nazarbaev's family network), and *Ekspress-K* (an independent paper at the time). All of these sources are in Russian, which continues to be widely spoken in Almaty. For Baku I relied extensively on media translation services, including Habarlar-L, which provides items from a range of local (as well as international) outlets. In addition I used *Zerkalo* and *Ekho*, both of which are independent

Russian language daily newspapers. While Russian is rapidly becoming a minor language in Baku, it remains spoken or at least understood by a large section of the population. In any case, as my findings attest, with regard to basic questions of national identity there is no difference in content between Russian language and Azeri newspapers. For Astrakhan I was limited to two sources: *Astrakhanskie vedomosti*, the official organ, and *Volga*, a nominally though not entirely independent paper. In addition, in each city I picked up a smattering of magazines available to the public at newsstands. The key criterion in selecting any of these texts was precisely their ready availability and (presumably) not insignificant readership. My assumption is that such attributes make them, collectively, reliable indicators of prevailing social discourse on the cultural themes in question. Finally, my strategy for perusing these media sources was to do so haphazardly: I read widely but without following any set pattern of selection with regard to dates or frequency, for the period 1999–2005. The intended result was to produce a completely random sample of the media.

Within these sources, the content of relevant discourse might involve partisan endorsement of an official ideal, acclaim or puzzlement over the meaning of a given practice, or debate over norms emerging from domestic or international sources. I see the media as neither entirely popular nor entirely organized from above. Obviously, reactions and views expressed in the officially sanctioned media (such as *Kazakhstanskaia pravda*) tend to be broadly influenced by, and responsive to, state agencies. At the same time they are not systematically subordinated to the state by censorship, nor are they wholly subsumed within the state-building agenda. On the contrary, even in such organs alternative viewpoints appear. More fundamentally, in the post-Soviet setting no single, orthodox position exists with regard to many of the central issues raised by cultural globalization. Instead, social contestation emerges, precisely because of the complexity and ambiguity attending many of the issues involved.

In order to explore entrepreneurial discourse and practice I conducted depth interviews with state officials and bureaucrats, librarians, youth center directors, school principals and teachers, and youth group leaders. The reason for selecting such people is that they are all, in various capacities, directly involved in attempting to shape national youth identity. As such they are also intimately caught up in the process of mediating cultural globalization and constructing hybrid identity templates. A total of ninety-four structured, personal interviews were conducted in the three cities between June 1999 and July 2003. This included thirty-five in Almaty, twenty-six in Baku, and thirty-three in Astrakhan, as well as one set of interviews in Moscow at the Committee on Youth Policy under the Ministry of Education. In addition, I more briefly interviewed many young (teenage and early twenties) as well as older-age citizens, outside of a structured format, about the general issues of concern to us here. Finally, in a number of cases I was able to conduct a more ethnographically informed discourse analysis by observing organized interactions between cultural activists engaged in socializing young people, as well as between such activists and young people themselves.

By way of interview strategy, I inquired about broad themes designed to elicit general perceptions of youth culture as well as factors imping- ing on it, yet without biasing responses by preloading any specific fac- tors or values. I began by asking participants to describe their work with young people, including the goals of their work. Next, interviewees were asked whether they had observed a significant influx of foreign culture since the fall of the USSR. After follow-up probing about the forms of this cultural influx, participants were asked how they personally encoun- tered such foreign culture, what influence they believed it had on society (including young people), and their personal opinions about it. Analyti- cally, the goal is to discern how, and why, perceived foreign influences are related to the programs and messages offered to young people by cultural entrepreneurs. Finally, interviewees were asked about their awareness of, and possible interactions with, other state and non-state actors involved in working with youth.

I also conducted (or, in one case, supervised) eight focus groups, in order to provide a cursory gauge of youth attitudes.[69] While youth attitudes and youth culture *per se* are not the focus of this book, it is

---

[69] Specifically, three focus groups were conducted in Almaty during June and July 2003. One, which included seven young women and eleven young men, aged fourteen to sev- enteen, was conducted in Kazakh (by Elvira Ayapova) at a summer camp. The other two were conducted by the author, in Russian. The first was held at KIMEP (Kazakhstan Institute of Management, Economics and Strategic Research), an elite educational insti- tution, in which nine young women and four young men participated, aged eighteen to twenty-two. The second was conducted at the Kazh-Zhol hotel for menial staff mem- bers, including eight young men and three young women, aged eighteen to twenty. Two focus groups were run in Baku in June 2003. The first was held at Khazar Univer- sity, including members of a class on international politics, and was led in English by the author. Participants included twenty-one students, eight young women and thirteen young men, aged eighteen to twenty-two. A second group was held at a coffee house, and was conducted by the author in Russian (with assistance from other members regarding certain responses of two participants, who spoke poor Russian). All eleven participants were males aged seventeen to twenty-two. In Astrakhan three groups were conducted by the author, in Russian, between June 2002 and May 2003. Two were held at Astrakhan State University, for students aged eighteen to twenty-four. The first comprised students in an extra-curricular Economics Club, including seven young women and ten young men. The second was drawn randomly from an introductory class on Political Science, and included twenty young women and thirteen young men. The third group was held at a local restaurant and included ten young women aged sixteen to nineteen, all of whom frequented Liudmila's modeling club, a young women's group that encourages its members to "model" propriety and national identity in addition to beauty.

nevertheless important to gain a sense of whether young people's views diverge radically from prevailing social attitudes. The data from these focus groups therefore serves to complement published survey sources (which are mainly available for Russia). These data suggest that although young people's views may diverge from those held by adults on certain issues (such as premarital sex), on the whole their attitudes are quite similar, and in fact reproduce the central elements of hybrid national identity structure. For all focus groups, participants were invited to an open discussion about globalization and foreign culture. (Having worked professionally for nine years in marketing research, and having conducted thousands of live group discussions, I am quite familiar with the theories and strategies associated with this method.) In each case, the strategy was similar to that followed for personal interviews: groups were asked general, open-ended questions about the influence of foreign culture, and were later probed regarding the range of opinions expressed. In addition, participants were asked whether they took part in, or were aware of, various cultural programs and youth groups.

The final category of sources I used consists of programmatic texts, which are useful in revealing official attitudes and goals relevant to nation building. As such they are indicative of the strategies pursued by state actors, either alone or in conjunction with other actors outside the formal institutional bounds of the state, at the junction of state and society.[70] Official texts are therefore useful not only in their own right as substantive indicators of preferred (by the state) national identity, but also as methodological checks on inferences about the values and constructs contained in elite discourse. Indeed, in examining official texts I pose essentially the same "questions" about perceptions, goals, strategies, and values.

Empirically, across all of these sources I see a great deal of interest in the maintenance or management of collective identity, articulated as puzzlement, pride, vexation, and other (often highly emotional) responses to perceived Westernization and youth cultural change.[71] *What* is attended to is often as important as *how*. Not surprisingly, innovations and stark juxtapositions of new and old are especially likely to provoke public comment. I attempt to unpack the conceptions and values revealed in this

---

[70] On the need for such an analytical focus in order to fully comprehend the state and state–society relations see Joel Migdal, "The State in Society: An Approach to Struggles for Domination," in Joel Migdal, Atul Kohli, and Vivienne Shue, eds., *State Power and Social Forces: Domination and Transformation in the Third World* (Cambridge: Cambridge University Press, 1994), pp. 7–34.

[71] On the importance of "sentiment" in determining the resonance of a discourse, see Bruce Lincoln, *Discourse and the Construction of Society: Comparative Studies of Myth, Ritual, and Classification* (New York: Oxford University Press, 1989), p. 8.

discourse, and consider what insights they yield into the relationship between cultural globalization and the construction of national youth identity.

With these general guidelines in mind, at this point it is possible to begin the empirical investigation of narratives and practices relevant to the construction of national youth identity. The following chapter does so by exploring how youth identity is perceived and addressed in the social discourse of Almaty, Astrakhan, and Baku.

3 The discourse of globalization and youth culture

In the former Soviet Union, one finds a veritable preoccupation with cultural globalization. Many people – like Volkov, the Astrakhan official we met in the Introduction – tend to experience it as Westernization (or, often, as "Americanization"), which is widely understood as conveying a massive pressure for homogeneity. This in turn generates a powerful mix of emotions: excitement, pride, anxiety, and disgust. After all, the perceived trend of homogenization is perceived to carry with it a range of potentially positive and negative effects, both with regard to national integrity and autonomy as well as pedestrian, everyday matters. Left unmediated to intermingle with locally produced ideas and practices, therefore, global influences beckon with opportunity, but also with danger. As a result, strikingly ambivalent attitudes percolate up into social discourse, in the form of an intense engagement with globalization. In a variety of public forums people in all walks of life struggle to come to terms with the influx of foreign ideas, groping for their underlying significance and spinning out narratives of the future, upon which they project their hopes and fears for the nation. And naturally, such hopes and fears are especially vivid where they surface in the discourse of youth culture.

Disentangling the strands of social discourse

As the following sections describe, what we find in this discourse is a typical pattern of hybridization: selective absorption, rejection, and assertion of national identity constructs. Before moving on to consider the active mediation efforts of state officials and non-state cultural entrepreneurs, we need to understand the texture of this discourse, including the meanings and reasons for action which are articulated within it. So as to avoid redundancy, in many instances I provide representative examples of the key ideas which emerge, without systematically demonstrating the presence of similar ideas in the other cities. However, one of the key empirical findings of this study is that the discourses in all three cities are remarkably alike. Except where noted, therefore, readers may assume an essential equivalence in discursive terrain relevant to the themes discussed below.

Absorption

Western culture is carried by multiple vectors,[1] including popular music, films, television, tourism, and migration. As such, diffusion takes place through broadly dispersed social and technological channels, which frequently circumvent state institutions and affect mass publics directly. In its most obvious forms the diffusion of pop culture in each city takes place in typical fashion, as young people are inundated by global media flows and then imitate Western styles of dress, music, and behavior.[2] While it is possible to detect variations and subcultures,[3] in urban settings the general tendency is to absorb superficial styles uncritically (and at times even unwittingly). Much of this is purely a matter of fashion and image, as youth respondents in a focus group freely admitted: "In the West they will do something because they want to. Here they will do it, like, 'I'm doing something Western.' It has prestige."[4]

As such, the ability to parrot Western lifestyles successfully is often a matter of pride. For example, a story on "international pop stars"

[1] On vectors in the formation and transportation of culture, see Leslie White, *The Concept of Cultural Systems: A Key to Understanding Tribes and Nations* (New York: Columbia University Press, 1975), pp. 59–69.

[2] For an overview of similarities in Russian youth culture, see Hilary Pilkington, "Youth and Popular Culture: The Common Denominator?" in Russel Bova, ed., *Russia and Western Civilization: Cultural and Historical Encounters* (New York: M.E. Sharpe, 2003), pp. 319–50; Irina Poluekhtova, "Amerikanskie filmy kak factor sotsializatsii molodezhi v Rossii 90-kh godov," in Vladimir S. Magun, ed., *Sotsialnye izmeneniia v Rossii i molodezh* (Moscow: Moscow Social Science Foundation, 1997), pp. 57–81; Anna Stetsenko, "Adolescents in Russia: Surviving the Turmoil and Creating a Brighter Future," in B. Bradford Brown, Reed W. Larson, and T.S. Saraswathi, eds., *The World's Youth: Adolescence in Eight Regions of the Globe* (New York: Cambridge University Press, 2002), pp. 243–75. For typical examples elsewhere, see the snapshots presented in Marat Yermukanov, "Kazakhstan after a Decade of Independence," *Central Asia – Caucasus Analyst*, December 18, 2002, available online at www.cacianalyst.org; "Bindis becoming popular in Russia," *Times of India*, August 6, 2002, available online at http://timesofindia.indiatimes.com/; and Laura Hruby, "A Rapper in Baku: Coolio Gives Concert at Heidar Aliyev Palace," *EurasiaNet*, April 9, 2004, available online at www.eurasianet.org. On the antecedents of cultural westernization during the Soviet period, see Ball, *Imagining America*, esp. pp. 177–205.

[3] In Russia (and to a lesser extent in Baku and Almaty) imitation is especially common among average youth ("normals"), compared with "progressives" who are more likely to depart from direct borrowing of Western styles. See Hilary Pilkington (with Elena Starkova), "'Progressives' and 'Normals': Strategies for Glocal Living," pp. 101–32; and Pilkington, "Reconfiguring 'the West'" pp. 165–200, both in Pilkington, ed., *Looking West*. On exposure to global youth culture generally see also Markowitz, *Coming of Age in Post-Soviet Russia*, esp. pp. 123–41.

[4] Focus group, Almaty, June 2003.

appearing in Baku concluded: "The concert has demonstrated that Baku, located on the crossroads of West and East, is recognized as musical capital of the Silk Route. . . ."[5] In this context, the ability to reproduce Western popular culture is far more important than achieving some sort of national authenticity. As one writer claimed, in a bubbly review of a local DJ challenge: "Night time Almaty is no less interesting than daytime, and if you think that, say, night time London or Berlin are cooler, then you are badly, badly mistaken. Well, what don't we have, that they do?"[6]

Thus, what is actually imitative may become so thoroughly naturalized that it is perceived to be essentially indigenous. For example, students at Astrakhan State University tended to argue that although current Russian rock music obviously bore some degree of Western influence, it also contained specifically Russian features. According to one focus group participant, "You have to know it to see this. [Russian rock] has a lot of references to Russian poetry and novels, things like that . . . It has idioms and sounds that they don't have in the West."[7] As a result, young people frequently appear to regard themselves as participating equally in a transnational youth culture, rather than as merely passive recipients or borrowers of something created outside.[8]

Nevertheless, among the population at large, there is a widespread tendency to regard Western sensibilities as constituting the very essence of fashion. Thus, the announcement of a new "Parisian-style" modeling agency (run by a Turkish businessman) in Baku promised clients a course of training that included not only modeling but also English language and "general culture."[9] The same infatuation applies to material goods as markers of taste, sophistication, and wealth.[10] Especially during the immediate pre- and post-Soviet period, Western goods served to

---

[5] "Baku – Silk Route Musical Capital," AssA-Irada News, January 10–12, 2000, in *Habarlar-L Digest*, January 12, 2000, as translated.

[6] "Bitva di-dzheevf: oboshlos bez zhertv," *Karavan*, July 17, 1998.

[7] Focus group, Astrakhan State University.

[8] For example, a graffiti artist in Astrakhan presented "standard," global patterns of this art form alongside local innovations. Interview with graffiti artist, Youth Exhibition, Astrakhan, April 2003.

[9] "V Baku otkrylas Parizhskaia shkola manekenshchits," *Zerkalo*, July 1, 2000.

[10] Sigrid Rausin, "Signs of the New Nation: Gift Exchange, Consumption and Aid on a Former Collective farm in North-West Estonia," in Daniel Miller, ed., *Material Cultures: Why Some Things Matter* (Chicago: Chicago University Press, 1998), pp. 189–213; Olga Shevchenko, "'Between the Holes: Emerging Identities and Hybrid Patterns of Consumption in Post-socialist Russia," *Europe-Asia Studies*, 54, No. 6 (September 2002): 841–66. At the same time, Soviet kitsch provides an element of camp, irony, or nostalgia. Theresa Sabonis-Chafee, "Communism as Kitsch: Soviet Symbols in Post-Soviet Society," in Adele Marie Barker, ed., *Consuming Russia: Popular Culture, Sex, and Society Since Gorbachev* (Durham: Duke University Press, 1999), pp. 362–82.

signify separation from the Soviet mentality. High technology goods have made rapid inroads, especially among the younger generation, where they combine practical as well as status benefits.[11]

More interesting for our purposes, however, the appropriation of material culture provides symbolic functions for collective identity, which are analogous to those it provides for individual identity. Some of this is clearly related to efficiency concerns. Yet the quest for efficiency itself is to a significant extent fetishistic, and cannot be understood simply as a rational program for increasing power, development, or any other political or economic objective. Thus, in describing the renovation of the library at Abaia University in Almaty, the author rhapsodizes, "With the support of TACIS, in partnership with Holland and Italy the automation and computerization of the university library is being completed – it thus becomes completely modern in terms of the instant accessibility of any essential piece of information in the arsenal of knowledge."[12]

The quest for modernity leads not only to the replication of urban infrastructural models, but also to the reflexive embrace of neoliberal ideas underpinning the market. In the words of an architect from Baku:

An independent country with a new governmental structure and a new privatized market economy requires a service sector, including banking, insurance, transportation, shipping, airports, terminals, business and commercial projects, housing and mixed-use developments. This infrastructure requires many new buildings: hotels and restaurants for the tourism industry, shopping centers, business centers, communication centers, sports facilities, conference centers . . . This is a determining moment in Azerbaijan's history. So many changes are going on that the transformation seems quite overwhelming. Baku was not designed to handle this much growth. At the same time, it cannot inhibit growth, nor should it.[13]

The same attitude is manifested in civic pride over the construction of a shopping mall in downtown Astrakhan, or the proclamation that a new cinema in Almaty is "up to world standards."[14] Indeed, much of

---

[11] Already by 2003, 22 percent of Azerbaijanis had access to cell phones compared to 13 percent of Russians; 13 percent of Azerbaijanis had access to e-mail compared to 18 percent of Russians; 5 percent of Azerbaijanis had access to a computer compared to 10 percent of Russians. 5 percent of Russians and 8 percent of Azerbaijanis used computers as a form of entertainment. Nadia Diuk, "Pervoe svobodnoe pokolenie: Molodezh, politika i identichnosti v Rossii, Ukraine i Azerbaidzhane," *Polit.ru*, December 27, 2003, available online at www.Polit.ru.

[12] "Kliuchi 1000-letiia," *Kazakhstanskaia pravda*, December 4, 1999, and see also "Kompiuter – drug i pomoshchnik," *Kazakhstanskaia pravda*, August 13, 2004.

[13] Pirouz Khanlou, "The Metamorphosis of Architecture and Urban Development in Azerbaijan," *Azerbaijan International*, 6, No. 4 (Winter 1998), www.azer.com.

[14] My statement about civic pride in Astrakhan's shopping mall is based on numerous discussions with local residents. On meeting world standards in cinema construction, see

the borrowing and transplantation appears superfluous, at least from the standpoint of efficiency, as in the mimicry of parking lots, advertising styles, and street signs.[15] While the goal of participating in an objectively utilitarian development process is obviously relevant here, being modern per se is also a palpable wish, one which in part reflects the internalization of a new, materialistic standard of "civilization." As a leader of the Astrakhan branch of the Edinstvo Party youth wing remarked, "It is necessary to think about the future. Otherwise you are not a modern person."[16] And for most people, young and old, this is an increasingly unthinkable option.[17]

Beyond the relatively superficial features of popular and material culture, there is also enormous interest in acquiring the ideological underpinnings of Western life. Thus in adopting the prevailing market-based development model, the prevailing discourse extols individual rationality and initiative, both of which are widely conflated with freedom. Also extolled are international integration and foreign investment, which are considered equally desirable and inevitable. In the opinion of Nursultan Karimbaev, Head of the Youth Program section of the Department of Youth Policy within the Kazakhstan Ministry of Culture,

Today you can hardly find a person who would dare to argue with the fact that the idea of democracy and the free market have become dominant in world politics and economics, they have attained victory in the minds of millions. A clear confirmation of this is the countries of Western Europe and the USA. The Soviet Union fell victim to its own non-competitiveness. Today we have become eye-witnesses to globalization, which signifies a single world market, universal values. . . .[18]

"Moi gorod: moia bol, liubov, nadezhda," *Kazakhstanskaia pravda*, June 17, 2000. Similarly, an Azerbaijani example is the proclaimed intention to repair Nakhchivan City University buildings "in conformity to European standards." *AzadInform*, April 20, 1999, in *Habarlar-L Digest*, April 20, 1999, as translated.

15   Representative examples from 1999 include "Americans Propose to Build Parking Lots in Baku," *Azernews-Azerkhabar*, February 24–March 2, 1999, Part 2, in *Habarlar-L Digest*, March 4, 1999; on road construction in Astrakhan based on projected increases in traffic load, see "Stroitelstvo obezdnoi avtomobilnoi dorogi," accessed at the official Astrakhan Oblast website: www.adm.astranet.ru/invest.htm; "Azeri Advertizers To Attend 'Sign Expo-99' Exhibition," *AzerNews-AzerKhabar*, April 21–27, 1999, Part 2, in *Habarlar-L Digest*, April 27, 1999; "The Eurasian Advertising Association to Emerge in Baku," *Azer-Press*, September 25, 1999, in *Habarlar-L Digest*, September 29, 1999.

16   Interview, Edinstvo youth wing, Astrakhan.

17   For example, when participants in a focus group in Baku were asked what, if anything, they considered positive about Western influence, their responses included statements like, "It is good that people are becoming modern," or "It is positive that people have modern styles."

18   Echoing President Nazarbaev's question as to whether Kazakhstan will "attain success in the exhausting and difficult process of world competition" the author suggested that "in large measure this question is addressed to the rising generation." Nursultan Karimbaev, "Molodezh gotova konkurirovat i pobezhdat," *Kazakhstanskaia pravda*, April 2, 2004.

While Karimbaev's official position is rather exalted, his opinion (including his social perception) is entirely ordinary in the three cities being explored here. In the widely echoed words of a member of the Economics Club at Astrakhan Technical Institute, "You can't stop globalization. It's impossible."[19]

At the same time, there is also a fairly common wish to avoid the harshest aspects of economic integration. Even many of its strongest advocates tend to voice concern over "excessive" competition and its resulting extreme social stratification. Thus, according to a leader of the Youth Enlightened Organization of Azerbaijan, an unrestricted marketplace leads to a "loss of flexibility," and as a result "it becomes impossible to be humane in work relations."[20] Or, in the words of another activist, "An unfavorable aspect of globalization is the lack of personal connection. There is no empathy in the workplace. Workers can be fired, or they are not supported in case of medical need."[21] Such opposition notwithstanding, however, the more telling point is that serious critiques of neoliberalism are relegated to the margins; even those who reject slavish adherence to this model tend to accept its key underlying premises and institutional pillars, including individualism, the market, and technologically driven progress. And this makes it seemingly imperative to foster "desirable" qualities such as personal responsibility and entrepreneurial creativity, thus furthering the state's developmental and efficiency-seeking orientation.

Again, such views transcend generation. Young people strongly endorse the key values associated with economic liberalization.[22] Focus group respondents repeatedly made similar statements: "The market

---

[19] Focus group, Economics Club, Astrakhan Technical Institute. Other members of the club voiced agreement with this statement.

[20] Interview, Youth Enlightened Organization of Azerbaijan, Baku. Economic integration and the IGOs associated with it are also at times perceived to be coercively hegemonic. For example, see "Knuty i prianiki vsemirnogo banka," *Nedelia* (Baku), No. 27, July 27, 2000. For further evidence from Russia see Aleksander Buzgalin, "Russia's Generation XXI: Caught Between Pragmatism, Radicalism And . . . Antiglobalism?" Jamestown Foundation, *Russia and Eurasia Review*, 1, No. 9 (October 8, 2002).

[21] Interview, Guliya Akhmedova, president of the National Children's Organization, Baku.

[22] In each city, focus group participants said that they respected values of "individualism," "personal discipline," "being goal oriented," and "having responsibility." For data showing that Russian youth are attracted to values of individualism, personal initiative, and responsibility, see Natalia Zorkaia and Nadia Diuk, "Tsennosti i ustanovki rossiiskoi molodezhi," *Polit.ru*, August 21, 2003, available online at www.Polit.ru. As Diuk notes elsewhere, however, Russian youth also wish for a greater degree of state paternalism. Nadia Diuk, "The Next Generation," *Journal of Democracy*, 15, No. 3 (July 2004): 59–66. For a similar picture emerging from Kyrgyzstan, see Kathleen Kuehnast, "From Pioneers to Entrepreneurs: Young Women, Consumerism, and the 'World Picture' in Kyrgyzstan," *Central Asian Survey*, 17, No. 4 (December 1998): 639–54.

is dynamic"; "We must build up the market economy, so we can be developed"; "We have to adapt to the market system." Moreover, young people appear overwhelmingly to approve of the personal attributes associated with liberalization.

While there is far more ambivalence among the older generation, here too one finds overall agreement.[23] In every sphere of life one encounters statements to the effect that adopting "Western," "American," or "international" standards is crucial for efficiency and national development, including in areas where such concerns are not immediately obvious. For example, the director of tourism for the Almaty city government said that his office had "adopted the American approach to organizing the tourist industry. This is being done everywhere in Kazakhstan." The director regarded such influence as having been thoroughly positive, including the construction of a convention bureau and tourism center, and establishing links with NGOs.[24]

Indeed, becoming socialized for the market is a common theme in everyday discourse. An important marker of such socialization is Western professional demeanor, which is often slavishly copied. An example is the "need" to act Western for success in business. For example, a newspaper article entitled "Do Not Knit Your Brow – It is Not Businesslike," offered a cautionary tale. "Upon meeting her, Natasha appeared extremely businesslike, with some even negative shades of this businesslike-ness. Too strict and fierce, with an aggressive look. Probably this is exactly how she pictured the figure of a modern businesswoman."[25] Not surprisingly, Natasha failed in her efforts at first. But having changed her demeanor, she became "a charming and smiling young woman," and very successful. The lesson was unmistakable:

The peculiarities of the socialist past gave rise among us to a pile of all sorts of complexes. Until recent times directors of enterprises perceived themselves as robotic leaders, without evincing any human weakness. It was acceptable to be interested in the health of co-workers or the results of the latest match only during an exceptionally good mood. Today practice has shown that having not only professional knowledge but also a culture of interpersonal relations, the director is able to achieve better results.[26]

---

[23] As an orphanage director opined, "We have to socialize young people for the market. This system is inevitable." Interview with Anzhela Karasaeva, Director, Orphanage Number 2, Almaty. Another typical statement is that education must "meet modern demands." Interview, Education Center for Youth (NGO), Baku.

[24] Interview with Zhanabai Kaseinov, Director, Department of Tourism, City Akimat, Almaty.

[25] "Ne xmurte brovi C eto ne po-delovomu," *Kazakhstanskaia pravda*, February 3, 2001.

[26] *Ibid.*

A related theme is praise for "democracy," including its institutional contours and individual freedoms. But strikingly, arguments in favor of democracy tend to be couched in neoliberal terms, as being inseparable from the market and individualist values. According to a typical sentiment,

Individualism is a very positive thing. You can make your own decisions, you can have your own life. Maybe you will move away from family, if you want to. No one decides anything for you. Before, you would have to do what your father did, or what your father wanted. Now you can choose your own career . . . This is freedom.[27]

Thus, more often than not the intrinsic merit of free thought takes a back seat to its perceived pragmatic value for national economic development. A member of the youth wing of President Nazarbaev's Otan party in Kazakhstan put the same point in negative terms: "Censorship is impossible. If we have censorship we will lag behind the entire world again."[28]

And yet, rational instrumentalism is not the only perspective in play. Alongside it we find strictly normative arguments, according to which national identity, standardized state institutions, and even neoliberalism are accepted unquestioningly on the grounds that they contribute to a legitimate social identity. Even explicit justifications, when provided at all, tend to hinge on the notion that these are simply "normal" patterns of conduct which were needlessly forbidden for so many years.[29] Beneath the surface, then, much of the tendency for absorption seems to express a repudiation of Soviet values through their inversion. As one youth center director remarked, "In the Soviet times there was plenty of extremism; now we want to avoid too much single-mindedness."[30]

In sum, one cannot help but be struck by the extent to which institutional and infrastructural changes have been enacted since the fall of the Soviet Union, and along with them the rise of attitudes conducive to marketization. At face value, and within the ambit of globalization read

---

[27] Focus group, Khazar University, Baku.

[28] Interview with Timur Bakiev, member of central staff, Otan (President Nazarbaev's Political Party), Almaty.

[29] This is consistent with the tendency to view Western culture as the norm. On this point see Elena Omelchenko and Uliana Bliudina, "On the Outside Looking In? The Place of Youth in Russia's New Media and Information Space," in Pilkington, ed., *Looking West*, pp. 41–48.

[30] Interview with Akmara Pazilova, Director, Almatynskii raion Youth Center, Almaty. Often practical and normative arguments for openness are blurred. Thus according to Akram Abdullaev, president of the state-backed youth umbrella group NAYORA, "Independent thinking is good, integration is good. We need more exchange, more science and technology." Interview, Baku.

as convergence, this in itself would seem to imply a steamrolling trend of deep cultural uniformity on the heels of capital and commodity flows.

Rejection

Nevertheless, within mainstream social discourse there is also a powerful element of backlash. This should not be confused with a radical refusal to embrace international flows per se. Although it is possible to locate expressions of virulent anti-Westernism and xenophobia,[31] such attitudes are far from the typical form of rejectionism, which is aimed merely at preventing the unrestricted influx of Western culture. In the eyes of many adults, such an influx threatens to damage national identity and, quite possibly, to destroy it completely.

Protestant values, the subculture of city blocks of American megalopolises come to us in highly attractive packaging, and are easily accessible – one has only to turn on the television, radio or computer. An ever wider audience of various ages gives its preferences to forms of Western culture, losing their own national identity. Little kids easily reproduce "Jingle Bells" instead of "In the Forest Grew a Fir," sing "Happy Birthday To You" on a birthday. Older children imitate the heroes of children's serials, and young people seriously prepare to celebrate St. Valentine's Day, only a few years ago completely unknown. In other words, the destruction of national identity which accompanies the process of globalization may one day lead to the American anthem, many times repeated in popular films, at some point becoming even better known than our own. Folk customs, music, traditions are beginning to seem anachronistic and at best are used for stylizing or adapting to Western models. Half-naked girls performing Kazakh folk songs already does not seem like something out of the ordinary, even though in itself such an interpretation contradicts the canon of behavior of Kazakh women which has existed for centuries.[32]

The implication here seems to be that with the gradual erosion of identity, the nation will simply cease to exist in any meaningful terms, and the country itself may effectively lose sovereignty in the process. Of course, for a minority, especially the more intellectually inclined critics, the entire barrage of Western-style popular culture is intrinsically offensive due to its superficiality and glitzy materialism.[33] As we have already seen, this

---

[31] In addition to Islamists, such sentiments are also articulated by various "national-patriots" and, especially in Russia, skinheads or die-hard Communists. See Stephen Shenfield, *Russian Fascism: Traditions, Tendencies, Movements* (Armonk, NY: M. E. Sharpe, 2001); also Aleksandr Neklessa, "Konets tsivilizatsii, ili Zigzag istorii," *Znamia*, No. 1 (1998): 165–79.

[32] Maksim Levchenko, "Nash shans," *Vremia* (Almaty), January 9, 2003.

[33] Thus in the view of Boris Kagarlitsky, director of the Institute of Globalization Studies, the purpose of global media broadcasting is "to make us consumption junkies." See Boris

is far from being the case for most people, and still less so among the younger generation. Yet even young people are concerned about what they regard as excessive Westernization. For many, the spread of delinquent behavior is a particularly objectionable form of Western influence. According to one young man, himself a guitar player in a group called "Death Track,"

> Western influence is an objective process. There are a lot of good things that come with it. The music is good, there are good films, and so on. But it is too much. . . . Especially the American films, they are propagandistic. You know, sex, thrillers. They show kids using narcotics. This kind of thing appeals to ignorant and uneducated people.[34]

Uncritically and exclusively aping Western styles is thus often viewed as revealing a lack of national pride or an absence of refinement and sophistication; becoming completely Westernized, especially at the lowest-common-denominator level of popular culture, is simply déclassé. Participants in a focus group conducted in Astrakhan agreed with the idea (expressed by one young man) that there was a "cultural invasion" taking place, which ought to be resisted. Similarly, according to a youth group leader in Baku,

> Western oriented kids who respect themselves and respect globalization and their own reputation go to the standard discos at the Europa [hotel] or the Hyatt. If they went to the regular night bars they could lose their reputation . . . Both are Western, but the night bars have the negative Western values. The discos are more civilized.[35]

More concretely, there is also a pervasive sense of anxiety over an impending moral and social collapse, which is often perceived to be a result of over-exposure to Western values. Naturally, the potential effects on young people are the source of greatest concern for people in all walks of life. In the words of Moscow mayor Yurii Luzhkov,

> The globalization of culture is capable of overwhelming our distinctive culture, the globalization of culture today, in essence, has conquered our youth . . . I am afraid to let my daughters near the television screen. At any moment there is

---

Kagarlitsky, "Hooked on the New Paganism," *Moscow Times*, December 25, 2003. On the culture of advertising as based on individualist indulgence and eroticization of the female form, see also Tatiana Cherednichenko, *Rossiia 90-kh: Aktualnyi leksikon istorii kultury* (Moscow: Novoe Literaturnoe Obozrenie, 1999), e.g. pp. 115–19 and 133. On similar fears among the Azerbaijani elite, see Ceylan Tokluoglu, "Definitions of National Identity, Nationalism and Ethnicity in Post-Soviet Azerbaijan in the 1990s," *Ethnic Racial Studies*, 28, No. 4 (July 2005): 722–58.

[34] Interview with Max Saklakov, Almaty.
[35] Interview with Nabil Seidov, president of Reliable Future, Baku.

everything: sex, violence, vandalism, brutality, blood, death. There is nothing of ours there. . . .[36]

Not coincidentally, indignation over the loss of propriety among the youth and its unsettling social impact is at times expressed in ways strikingly reminiscent of reactions to Sixties counterculture in the West.[37] Likewise, an Almaty cultural official disdainfully referred to the problems caused by "hippies, rap, rock, and narcotics."[38] The danger is often spelled out in highly alarmist terms. According to a participant at a public seminar on "The Social Ecology of Azerbaijan," the nation was being exposed to a new phenomenon of "psychological pollution":

. . . the frenzied influx of shoddy advertisements, hidden propaganda for amoral values, almost daily advertisement of consumer relations in all spheres of life and other mass production of dubious quality. [Imported TV shows] dismantle national culture, tradition, ethnic customs and rituals, [and] are contradictory to the notion of "family" in general and education as a whole.[39]

The ultimate concern, then, is that corrosive cultural influences will weaken the moral fibers that hold the social fabric together. This in turn leads to decadence and depravity, since the individual devoid of social attachments is vulnerable to the allure of the senses. Sexual promiscuity is seen as an abundant temptation in which the mindless aping of Western behavior leads to especially unrewarding results, bringing shame and disease in its wake.[40]

Inevitably, moral factors come into play, as reflected in the Russian Ministry of Education's efforts to ban Barbie dolls[41] – although some of the anxiety about promiscuous sex is also related to fears of an HIV

---

[36] Transcript of meeting of the State Council, "Prioritety razvitiia rossiiskoi kultury," June 16, 2003, online at: www.kremlin.ru.

[37] In the words of an Almaty police sergeant, "Their crazy looks and behavior annoy me . . . If I had my way, I would put those lowlifes away, cut their hair and goatees, dress them in normal clothes, and make them go get a job." Quoted in Erbol Jumagulov and Eduard Poletaev, "Kazak Cops Hammer Counter-Culture," Institute of War and Peace Reporting, *Reporting Central Asia*, No. 62 (July 27, 2001), available online at: www.iwpr.net/.

[38] Interview, Department of Youth Affairs, Division of Culture, Information and Social Accord, City Akimat, Almaty.

[39] "Otkrovennaia poshlost zagriazniaet nashe soznanie," *Zerkalo*, August 3, 2000.

[40] E.g., Igor Kon, "Kak zerkalo seksualnoi revoliutsii," *Samarskoe obozrenie*, September 8, 1997.

[41] "'Provotsiruiut agressiiu, strakh, prezhdevremennye seksualnye proiavleniia': Minobrazovaniia protiv vrednykh igrushek," *Gazeta*, November 5, 2002, available online at: www.gzt.ru/. This is not to be confused with the anti-globalization and anti-materialist campaign against the "Barbie" image associated with the Russian Miss Universe contest, in which a relatively unglamorous young woman became a popular symbol of protest. Kevin O'Flynn, "Anti-Barbie Wins Hearts," *The Moscow Times*, April 13, 2004.

epidemic. Sex, however, is the only subject on which discursive positions differ substantially among the three cities, and is therefore worth treating in more comparative detail. Thus at one end of the spectrum is Baku, where Islamic attitudes toward sexuality exert considerable influence.[42] As an orphanage director exclaimed, with regard to Western values of sexuality, "This is Azerbaijan. This is Islam. Of course this is a civilized country, but there is still a need for decency. This is not the West."[43]

Of course, for Islamic radicals all expressions of stylized modernity are objectionable. Islamists have expressed particular opposition to the new fad of beauty pageants and their sensual representation of women.[44] Yet even among professed Muslims who oppose such extremist views and favor liberal gender relations, the perceived trend in youth culture is considered offensive. To cite a typical comment, "Western influence is negative in many ways. . . . Girls are smoking, there is more vulgar behavior of both sexes, especially girls, like kissing in public, [there are] shorter skirts and more revealing dress in general, [and] pornography."[45]

Such views are obviously changing among the younger generation in Baku, although here too there remains substantial resistance to unrestrained sexuality, again often attributed to Islam. Thus, while most expressed traditional views about sex, a number of participants in focus groups expressed quite liberal attitudes, without this evoking surprise, disgust, or censure from others.[46] Nonetheless, among young people in Baku there is a widespread awareness of Islam as a social and normative constraint. As one young man put it (to the nods of many others), "This is an Islamic country. We are not like hippies and skinheads."[47]

---

[42] A broad survey of people in Islamic states – including Azerbaijan – conducted by Norris and Inglehart found that young people generally had traditional attitudes toward gender and sexual freedom. Pippa Norris and Ronald Inglehart, "Islamic Culture and Democracy: Testing the 'Clash of Civilizations' Thesis," *Comparative Sociology*, 1, Nos. 3/4 (August 2002): 235–63.

[43] Interview with Ms. Makhbuba, Orphanage Number 3, Akhmed Li, Baku.

[44] In the words of one press report, "Chairman of the Azerbaijan Islamic Party Haji Muzaffar thinks democracy does not envision denial of faith and national traditions. According to him, organizers of the contest will be held accountable for this on the doomsday." "Beauty Beats Islamists," *AssA-Irada News*, December 27–30, 1999, in *Habarlar-L Digest*, January 1, 2000, as translated.

[45] Interview with Parvana Kazymzade, First Deputy Director, Division of Youth, Sport and Tourism, City Administration, Baku. Likewise, Sevda Mamedalieva, the Deputy Minister of Culture of Azerbaijan, complained that Western movies were wearing away traditional taboos, as sex was depicted as "something horrible, primitive, on the level of physiology." Interview.

[46] This observation was confirmed in an interview with staff members at the National Debate Center in Baku.

[47] Focus group, Baku.

In contrast, attitudes in Almaty are substantially more relaxed than in Baku, particularly among young people. This was abundantly evident in focus groups. For example, in one interesting exchange, a young man stated that he was opposed to sex before marriage. Immediately he was teased by others in the mixed gender group, who pointed out that he was "still young" and should relax and enjoy life.[48] Still, concerns about lax sexuality as well as porous gender boundaries are expressed even among the youth. For example, an Almaty newspaper forum on "whether girls today are losing face" drew a number of letters from young people answering in the affirmative. Most made the connection between individualism and self-indulgence, on the one hand, and the loss of traditional aspects of feminine dignity on the other.

There are no rules. Everyone does whatever they feel like, using freedom [as a justification] . . . Secondly, foreign films and pornographic pictures have a negative influence.

I have to admit that girls haven't changed for the better . . . Many rush to savor all the "pleasures" of youth. They just want to party, dress well, and hang out.

It's a shame to see girls with unattractive behavior. I think girls should think not only about themselves, but also about their parents.

Even those who wrote apologetically acknowledged the existence of a problem and prescribed a solution:

Smoking is not evil, it's a fashion. The weakness of girls is due to immaturity. I think if you want to raise a healthy and mentally well-developed generation, you have to start when they're little.[49]

On this point Astrakhan offers a major contrast to Baku and even to Almaty. For example, at a staff meeting of one youth-run NGO, the women in the group (with the author present) began casually discussing the bitter taste of ejaculate. Similarly, young women at a modeling club agreed that sex before marriage was perfectly acceptable (although smoking was "unladylike"). Nor is this difference simply a function of generation; the ambient discourse on youth sexuality is simply far more relaxed in Astrakhan. This was evident in the opinions of the Deputy Mayor, who, when asked whether subsidization of the Top Model youth club might inadvertently contribute to hyper-sexualization, replied, "It's

---

[48] The young man in question acknowledged that his "traditional" views were out of step with those of his peers. Focus groups (two conducted by the author in Russian, one conducted by Elvira Ayapova in Kazakh), Almaty, June–July 2003.

[49] "Kak reagiruete na mnenie: 'Kazakhskie devushki teriaiut svoe litso'?" *Karavan*, February 5, 1999.

better than prostitution. Otherwise they would read journals [about sex] anyway. What's the difference?"[50]

Despite such differences on the issue of sexuality, the social discourse in each city – to repeat a point already made – is quite similar on the general topic of youthful hedonism and its larger social dimensions. This includes a perceived connection between the decline of morality and a general drift toward alienation, asocial behavior and crime.[51] The escalating pattern of juvenile drug use in each city (and country generally) occasions a great deal of anxiety, which is often addressed in the media. For example, at a meeting on issues affecting young people held in Astrakhan in 2003, it was noted that 6,500 people were officially registered as narcotics users, including 3,000 who "have fallen into powerful dependence, from which it is already almost impossible to save them (they have become addicts)."[52] In part such fears are linked to the sharing of hypodermic needles and resulting HIV transmission.[53] Unlike the early post-Soviet years, already by 2000 observers were sophisticated in their ability to differentiate among various drugs, including the threat of addiction and other health dangers they posed. They were also nearly unanimous in sounding the alarm about the implications of narcotics use for the future:

Drug addiction is one of the worst tragedies that may happen to a person. It is a life-long trouble. Only facing it directly, [can] one realize its seriousness. [The] human personality degrades and death threat increases . . . Reasons include unemployment among young people, corruption of the state law enforcement bodies, and decaying of general moral standards . . . [As a result] we are losing an entire generation of people.[54]

[50] Interview, Vadim Monin, Deputy Mayor, Astrakhan.
[51] For example, *Polozhenie molodezhi v Rossii: Analyticheskii doklad* (Moscow: Mashmir, 2005), http://stat.edu.ru.
[52] Natalia Tokhonova, "Oblastnye vlasti izuchili obraz zhizni molodykh astrakhantsev," RIA Avers, October 30, 2003, www.astrakhan.net. By 2004 there were 17,187 registered addicts in Azerbaijan, leading one expert to suggest that the actual number was probably 300,000. "Survey Shows Azerbaijan Has Over 300,000 Drug Addicts – Campaigner," *BBC Monitoring*, February 25, 2004, available via ISI Emerging Markets. According to the office of the Kazakhstan Ministry of Internal Affairs, between 1999 and 2003 the number of drug addicts increased from 37,492 to 47,924. Website of the Ministry of Internal Affairs, www.mvd.kz.
[53] "Chislo VICh-infitsirovannykh v Azerbaidzhane rastet," *Zerkalo*, May 1, 2000; "Kazakhstan ozhidaet novaia volna epidemii VICh-infektsii, osnovnym faktorom kotoroi budet narkomaniia," *Panorama*, No. 45 (November 2000); L. S. Kolesova, "Adolescents as a Group That Is Vulnerable to Narcotics Addiction and HIV Infection," *Russian Education and Society*, 45, No. 4 (April 2003): 39–53, translated from the Russian original published in *Pedagogika*, No. 1 (January 2002): 34–41. On these and related social problems affecting youth, see International Crisis Group, *Youth in Central Asia: Losing the New Generation*, Asia Report No. 66 (October 31, 2003), available online at www.crisisweb.org/.
[54] Nygmet Ibadildin, "Drug Addicts: People, Doses and Deaths," *Vremia Po Grinvichu* (Almaty), June 26, 2001, available ISI Emerging Markets, online at www.securities.com;

Not entirely unrelated to the perception of rampant illegal drug use is the well-founded perception that youth criminality is rising sharply.[55] This in turn appears to be linked to the view that the global media features too much violence. A widely held opinion is that overexposure to media violence may have harmful spillover effects on social behavior. In a common complaint, one local administrator blamed Hollywood. "American films," he said, "like the ones with Schwarzenegger, are so fierce and warlike . . . They have too much influence on kids. They lose their shock over death."[56]

As already discussed, the underlying individualist content of the new ideas is lauded in many respects. At the same time, the prevailing social discourse objects to Western pop culture for what is perceived to be its *excessive* individualism: too aloof and alone; too unconcerned with social effects; breeding social atomization and a lack of respect for elders and betters – indeed, for all others. This social dimension is always implicit in discussions of Western culture, since the rise of extreme individualism might undermine the essential integrative function of identity. In the words of one teacher, "There has been a loss of ideals. This came after the fall of the Pioneers and the Komsomol. There was a loss of collectivism, which unfortunately has been replaced by egoism."[57]

The emergence of a "cult of individualism" is therefore unfavorably contrasted with one or another variant of social or collective identity. As the head of a state-sponsored youth umbrella organization in Almaty observed, "Kids want to be not just free, but absolutely free. And in this gap there is a great danger of negative ideological influence."[58] These views are echoed at the official level,[59] which has important consequences

---

see also T. Iakusheva, "Narkomania: bolezn bezdelnikov," Foundation for Public Opinion, available online at http://bd.fom.ru/report/map/d021230.

[55] Examples are, "Juvenile Delinquency Facts Become More Frequent in Baku," AssA-Irada News, October 12–14, 1999, in Habarlar-L Digest, October 14, 1999; Anton Dosybiev, "Kazakhstan: School Gang Violence On the Rise," Institute of War and Peace Reporting, *Reporting Central Asia*, No. 253 (December 16, 2003), available online at www.iwpr.net/.

[56] Interview, Trusovskii district administration, Division of Youth Affairs, Astrakhan. Again, even young people in Russia tend to view Western culture as being excessively violent, at least as conveyed by the media. Elena Omelchenko and Moya Flynn, "Through Their Own Eyes: Young People's Images of 'the West'," in Pilkington, ed., *Looking West*, pp. 77–100. See also "Moscow Is Tired Of Sex, Violence On Television," RFE/RL *Newsline*, 6, No. 201, Part I, October 24, 2002.

[57] Interview with Lida, teacher, State Pedagogical College, Almaty.

[58] Interview with Arman Kudaibergenov, then president of the State Foundation for the Development of Youth Policy (Talapker), Almaty.

[59] Gulia Karsybekova, Head of the Department of Education, Science and Culture in the Almaty City Akimat, "There used to be Komsomol and Pioneers. Homo-Sovieticus was more inclined to collectivism." Interview.

for organizational efforts among the youth. The implication is clear: left on their own, the youth lack direction and tend to develop hedonistic, selfish attitudes. The resulting pathologies are said to be everywhere. According to one young woman in Almaty, "Men were trained to respect women. Boys had to stand up on the bus. But now you can see the guys sitting there in black glasses and not paying attention to the disabled woman."[60] Strikingly, young people also tend to agree with the notion that one can have too much freedom, or that freedom can be taken too far. As one focus group member stated, "Of course there is a lot more freedom now . . . It is a good thing, if you can handle it."[61]

One last category of cultural rejection concerns the malaise of computer addiction. While young people consider the Internet to be useful and enjoyable, and often discount its influence on their general outlook, older people tend to hold strikingly different views.[62] In each city there is profound anxiety that the youth is becoming preoccupied with virtual realities: computer games, chat rooms, and unsavory websites. The addiction is bad enough in its own right. In addition, popular anxiety appears to be based largely on the nature of the medium itself, including its psychologically alienating effect, quite aside from the specific content of games or websites young people might visit.

Use of the Internet depends on cultural factors. This needs to be taught to children. It is a form of narcotic; a virtual reality. Books are artistic, for the soul, but the Internet is a deeper penetration into the subconscious. The Internet should be only a means of getting information. It changes not only psychology, but the *psyche* – he enters into a virtual reality and everything is experienced in this way, instead of real feeling and real performances.[63]

The pattern of seeking abnormal forms of diversion while sitting in front of computer screens is also translated to the booming craze for gambling machines, most of which use similar video or computer-based technology. Here again, the emphasis is on the underlying psychopathology and its potentially disruptive social effects.

Three thousand Muscovites, including teenagers and adults, are suffering from psychological abuse of gambling machines and houses. The Health Ministry's chief psychiatrist and head of the Medical Stress-Induced Injury

[60] Interview with Samira Allahverdiyeva, UN Volunteers Program, Youth Volunteer Management Unit, Baku.
[61] Focus group, Almaty.
[62] Anzhela Indzhigolian, "O sotsializiruiushchem vozdeistvii Internet (na primere rossi-iskikh i kazakhstanskikh studentov)," unpublished paper prepared for the Second Russian Congress of Sociologists, Moscow, 2003. I am indebted to the author for helpful personal communication regarding this paper.
[63] Interview, National Children's Library, Almaty.

Rehabilitation Center, Vladimir Voloshin gave the information at [a] press-conference on Wednesday. Besides, psychiatrists point to the parents' increasing anxiety about their children's passion for [the] computer. Today the psychiatrists even have a special term "computer syndrome," according to Mr. Voloshin. The psychiatrists unambiguously consider the passion as disease, and that it is hard to be cured for [sic].[64]

In these ways, computer gaming among the youth is widely associated with asocial and even anti-social conduct. As such it becomes linked in popular discourse with other forms of normative decay, with all of the same disturbing implications for social order. What is more, the craze for computer games is perceived to come at the direct expense of literacy. In part this is seen to have detrimental effects on general psychological development. In addition, a certain aesthetic and moral sensibility is often considered to be at stake here, as is evident in discussions about the sad state of libraries and the fact that young people rarely frequent their carrels.

Once upon a time we called ourselves the most literate people in the world. . . . Today in the times of videocassettes and computers interest in reading has died down, especially among the youth. How to revive it, how to compel (in the best sense of the word) people to go to the library?[65]

The importance of this change in behavior goes well beyond the mere failure to acquire knowledge; what is at stake is respect for socially accumulated wisdom and established values. Observers from the older generation in each city bemoaned the decline of reading and the loss of its beneficial effect on psychological development. This is lamented because the very act of taking out an old book is viewed as embodying the stable transmission of ideas, and as encouraging a more refined and reflective approach to life than that transmitted by modern popular culture.[66] According to one music teacher,

[Kids] used to read, but now they use computers, or they just don't read. And so we have this degradation, slang, loss of a grammatical literate language. And

---

[64] "300,000 Muscovites Suffer from Psychological Gambling Abuse," RIA Oreanda – Economic and Political Press Review, March 12, 2004, translated from the original in Trud, available ISI Emerging Markets, online at: www.securities.com. See also Erbol Jumagulov, "Kazaks Despair at Childrens' Gambling," Institute of War and Peace Reporting, *Reporting Central Asia*, No. 210 (June 11, 2003), available online at www.iwpr.net/.

[65] "A ty zapisalsia v biblioteku?" *Kazakhstanskaia pravda*, December 9, 1999. In a follow-up article, the director of the main library in Uralsk bemoaned, "Young people have begun to read noticeably less, the level of culture has declined." "Neopalimaia kupina," *Kazakhstanskaia pravda*, December 11, 1999.

[66] I base this on interviews at State Pedagogical College, Almaty; National Youth Library, Almaty; Oblast Children's Library, Astrakhan; and Children's Library, Baku.

with this comes a loss of sharing a [refined] culture. Because reading provides these things: it provides a higher status, it provides symbols. It is more spiritual and soulful. . . . So the problem is not just the Western culture coming in, but the decline of our own culture, our cultural standard of living.[67]

The end result, then, is a popular perception of negative Western influences coalescing in the form of a syndrome. Combining a broad range of negative cultural manifestations, this syndrome is seen as threatening to block both the absorption of positive qualities and the acquisition of distinctive national identity traits. In contrast, a ubiquitous phrase in the public and private discourse of cultural agents is "a healthy way of life," which refers to the entire panoply of desirable values. References to "a healthy way of life" are thus constantly invoked in opposition to various hazardous influences, and on behalf of state- and nation-building efforts in all three locales.

Assertion

Alongside the influx of Western culture and the partial backlash against it, we also find a conscious, officially endorsed effort to ground modernity in an indigenous narrative or "tradition." This represents a bid to reconstruct social identity in ways calculated to stabilize social order and legitimate the role of the state. Moreover, in these globalizing post-Soviet cities retraditionalization is deeply embedded in social discourse. It is not, therefore, simply reducible to elite calculations or political brokerage, but is instead a reflection of available structures of meaning and the uses made of them by social actors at large.[68] Consider the following appeal in an Almaty newspaper:

Metaphorically speaking, Kazakhstan stands before a choice: either to become completely westernized under the powerful ideological influence of the West, or to try to preserve and breathe life into its culture, but not in terms of "local exotics" or a certain "national picturesque," but on the level of one of the important components of world culture.[69]

Globalization is seen as the obvious culprit. According to this viewpoint, the electronic media was creating such a blur of cultural exchange

---

[67] Interview with Natasha, teacher at a private Arts Academy, Almaty.
[68] For further discussion of this point with reference to Central Asia see Andrew Phillips and Paul James, "National Identity between Tradition and Reflexive Modernization: The Contradictions of Central Asia," *National Identities*, 3, No. 1 (March 2001): 23–35. For a review of Russian public opinion regarding the West which reaches this same conclusion, see Boris Dubin, "'Protivoves': symvolika Zapada v Rossiia poslednykh let," *Pro et Contra*, 8, No. 3 (April 2004): 23–35.
[69] Maksim Levchenko, "Nash shans," *Vremia* (Almaty), January 9, 2003.

and imitative consumption that national identity was becoming eroded, insidiously.

In all times the authentic production of art had strong national roots, was fed by folk poetry, music, philosophy. This is natural. However what is occurring everywhere now carries the world away to total unification. Thanks to scientific-technical progress the process of cultural interaction has become so intensive and extreme that we simply do not manage, during all of these changes, to think through their consequences and avoid unjustified losses.[70]

Similar points have been frequently made in each country, to the effect that support for national cinema is necessary to safeguard the "spiritual-moral health of the people" and prevent society from being utterly corrupted by global popular culture.[71] For the same reason it is considered urgent to arrange television content which would be fit for impressionable eyes, as discussed at a festival of programming for children and youth in Astrakhan. According to one participant, "Television possesses enormous attractive force, capable of exerting a powerful educational influence on the younger generation, of putting healthy forces in motion, of enriching the world of feelings of a young person, and of promoting the idea of peace and national reconciliation."[72]

Another objective of national identity assertion is fostering inter-ethnic harmony, notwithstanding the inconsistencies in implementing a truly inclusive civic nationalist policy. This is obviously a sore subject in Baku, where memories of the 1990 pogroms against Armenians are still vivid, and where the unresolved Nagorno-Karabakh conflict continues to inflame ethnic resentments. Nevertheless, in each locale, one finds both official and informal attempts to construct a synthetic national identity – which, paradoxically, often goes hand in hand with pandering to majoritarian forms of nationalism. A typical sentiment along these lines was expressed by an official at the Almaty city Department of Youth Affairs, who proudly noted various efforts to foster knowledge of Kazakh language and culture. When asked whether this marginalized Russians and other ethnic groups living in Almaty, his response was that no contradiction

---

[70] The author therefore praised the French for introducing a cultural exception in trade policy. Sapargali Suleimenov, "Taina talantlivogo kino," *Kazakhstanskaia pravda*, September 30, 2000.

[71] Bauyrzhan Nogerbek, "Gerostrat: zabyt ili pomnit?" *Kazakhstanskaia pravda*, November 23, 1999. Similarly, Rustam Ibrahimbeyov, "Editorial-Cinema: Can it be Revived?" *Azerbaijan International*, 5, No. 3 (Autumn 1997), available online at www.azer.com/. On problems faced by the Russian film industry as well as efforts (outlined by Culture Minister Shvydkoi) to support domestic cinematography, see "U kultury est problemy i bez kino," *Vedomosti*, April 12, 2001; and "Stimul ili kormushka?" *Vremia novosti*, July 19, 2002.

[72] Interviews conducted at Astrakhan programming festival, July 1999.

existed between promoting a specifically Kazakh identity alongside an inclusive, pan-national identity. On the contrary, the goal was to "make all languages balanced," while at the same time ensuring that "everyone must understand that this is Kazakhstan."[73] Despite the obvious tensions involved in taking such a position, the common hope is to overcome ethnic particularism and thereby quell the danger of conflict.

In addition, as we have seen, the prevailing discourse is bound up with an encounter between national identity and the otherwise unopposed forces of globalization. Neotraditionalism is therefore considered necessary to counter the threat of cultural homogenization along Western lines. Were such identity convergence to take place, the state's ability to govern, and even to manage the functional aspects of international integration, would be severely undermined. Indeed, the official national symbols of Kazakhstan (as presented in the national flag, emblem, and anthem), which feature various natural and folk motifs, have been explicitly justified as a bulwark of collective identity against the homogenizing trends of globalization.[74] But the same general idea holds true in each locale: retraditionalization serves not only to promote a sense of pride in national aesthetics, but also as a hedge against harmful influences. In its most naive form, the hope is that traditional elements will somehow expunge the negative aspects of Western pop culture:

The loss of national traditions, the oblivion of the culture leads to a collapse of the moral level of society . . . Today the enliveners of culture in the country, as in the city, counteract the rise of drug addiction, criminalization of consciousness, lack of trust and disillusionment with authorities and reform, social backwardness of the impoverished population. . . .[75]

Importantly, such views are often voiced by those who endorse neoliberal values. The focus on native-traditional culture is therefore not intended to promote insularity among the younger generation. On the contrary traditionalism is often regarded, somewhat counter-intuitively, as useful for facilitating international economic and political integration. As one young woman in Baku argued, "It is important to consider integration and the national mentality. We need to retain our own values . . . [And yet] integration into the West is good for economic development, for thinking for oneself . . . Therefore it can be said that preservation of our national mentality *allows* integration."[76]

[73] Interview with Dauren Umeshev, Department of Youth Affairs, City Akimat, Almaty.
[74] "Den simvolov strany," *Kazakhstanskaia pravda*, June 4, 2002.
[75] "'Zhivi, glubinka Astrakhanskaia!' Khrani nas ot bespamiatstva i bed!" *Volga*, February 8, 2000.
[76] Interview with Rugiya Yusifova, Youth Enlightened Organization of Azerbaijan, Baku.

In other words, consolidation of a distinct national identity makes it possible to encourage globalization and integration without risking the loss of social cohesion.

Appeals to "ancient folk wisdom" frequently surface as an antidote for the stress of modernity, or as a way of allowing integration without sacrificing a uniquely national quality of life in the bargain. One example is an ode to "not forgetting folk traditions," in which the author rhapsodized about the soothing effect of native customs: "long drawn-out women's songs in combination with handicrafts save one from the mad rhythm of contemporary life. Unhurried knitting, embroidery, a needle in the hands of women dressed in antique costumes, give a basis for thinking that folk traditions are not being forgotten."[77] Similar, conscious efforts to mobilize folklore so as to enact national identity, while also fending off the evils of globalization, are often encountered in these three post-Soviet regions.[78]

Another effort to manage the transition to global interconnectedness involves portraying neoliberal practices as consonant with native traditions (much like the manipulation of "Confucian values" by the Asian development state, as discussed earlier). An example is the argument that the market system is not only "civilized" but is also grounded in pre-revolutionary Russian history. Thus, according to an Astrakhan newspaper article, "this is a rebirth of the good tradition of Russian merchantry and a rebirth of faith in Russia as a great power."[79] Similarly, although the absorption of Western political institutions has generally been rather superficial in post-Soviet states, there have also been efforts to appeal to the past in order to promote certain desirable practices. For example, Kazakh nomadism is often claimed by nationalists to be a natural precursor of democracy due to its historical independence from the centralizing state. Therefore, according to its defenders, Kazakhstan's nomadic traditions make it uniquely well-suited to democratic institutionalization.[80]

In addition to facilitating cultural absorption, the discourse of national assertion also works to cement social bonds by propagating "traditional" norms to replace archaic Soviet ones. To underscore the prevalence of this theme, it should be emphasized that – as is the case with absorption

[77] "Ne zabyvaia narodnye traditsii," *Kazakhstanskaia pravda*, June 28, 2000.
[78] See Laura J. Olson, *Performing Russia: Folk Revival and Russian Identity* (New York: Routledge-Curzon, 2004), esp. pp. 106–37 and 204–20.
[79] "Ot bazara k tsivilizovannomu rynku," *Volga*, February 2, 2000. This resembles the argument, made by cultural entrepreneurs, that Novgorod has an historical tradition of democracy. Nicolai N. Petro, *Crafting Democracy: How Novgorod Has Coped With Rapid Social Change* (Ithaca: Cornell University Press, 2004).
[80] Cengiz Surucu, "Modernity, Nationalism, Resistance: Identity Politics in Post-Soviet Kazakhstan," *Central Asian Survey*, 21, No. 4 (December 2002): 385–402.

and rejection – the values underlying national assertion are shared not only by adults, but also by many young people. A common thread in personal interviews and focus groups was the demand for a national identity, including receptivity to traditional culture, which is widely understood as not only intrinsically valuable but also symbolic of collective attachment. Thus, according to a focus group participant, "I need to know my national culture. First I must understand myself, and then I can understand other cultures."[81]

Of course, this prevailing discourse does not preclude the existence of outlying views. A small minority ridicules the artificiality of reinventing traditions. For example, as one teacher at a Western-oriented business school complained, "There are people who try to turn the clock back, to revive old customs . . . They say, 'Let's have some Dombra [traditional instrument], more old Dombra.' Everyday we are struggling about this."[82] Conversely, in rare cases assertion takes extreme forms, verging on national chauvinism. An example is the establishment of a Russian Association in Astrakhan, which blends economic nationalism (especially geared to the revival of domestic industry) with revival of spirituality and Russian Orthodoxy.[83] The mainstream attitude, however, is geared towards the revival of tradition along with a carefully circumscribed absorption of international (especially Western) culture. As one young woman in Astrakhan stated,

Copying the West is not good. We are starting to get our own beliefs, and our own pride. There are very negative and positive aspects, and it is important and possible to choose. The thing is how to be Russian, despite globalization . . . [This can mean] little things, like being hospitable or giving presents.[84]

A related aspect of national assertion is "spirituality," albeit often of a rather secular nature. Obviously, as already mentioned, the pursuit of spirituality may take overtly religious forms. Yet in general, within this discourse spirituality refers to an attachment to non-material values, especially values related to national culture. While not displacing the quest for wealth and efficiency, the idea is to embed youth culture within a transcendent moral foundation of social connectedness, and to thereby offset the egoistic and profligate tendencies introduced along with modernization. In the words of an Astrakhan librarian, "The priority directions

---

[81] Khazar University, Baku, June 2003.
[82] Interview with Balzhan Suzhikova, International Business Institute, Almaty.
[83] "Russkoe obshchestvo sozdaetsia s pomoshchiiu russkoi partii," *Astrakhanskie vedomosti*, October 14, 1999.
[84] Interview, member of NGO "We Are Youth," Astrakhan (I translate the word Rossiiskii here as "Russian"). Similar views were expressed by other focus group participants in each locale.

in the work of the library have become the moral and economic education [related to] the rebirth of national traditions, family life and regional
enlightenment . . . Only in this way is it possible to regenerate the spiritual
wealth of our people."[85] One of the key functions of spirituality in this
context is its ability to provide a basis for differentiation: between sublime
national culture and vulgar materialist Western culture. And at the same
time, such ideas serve to bound individualism and underscore broader
collective meanings.

Naturally, all such discussions of youth morality have an important
political dimension as well. Thus not only does tradition impart a sense
of connectedness and identification with national purpose, it also fosters
state control in more practical terms. As one librarian stated, "They [kids]
must learn history – their own history. They need their own unique history . . . This is fundamental, moral. Otherwise there can be no optimism
or love of country."[86] Or, in the view of a member of the youth wing of
Kazakhstan's ruling Otan political party, "If you take an average kid, they
are unlikely to be national patriots. If you ask them what they are ready
to do for their country, they'll say 'I don't want to.'"[87] Here again, the
assertion of both neotraditionalism and spirituality serves to complement
the discourse of rejection, by laying down a shared cultural foundation
for governance.

A final issue that emerges from popular discourse is the general tendency to look to the state. Rather than assuming that such matters are
best left to parents or teachers, social commentators frequently demand
that the state do more to mediate globalization and shepherd the youth.
A typical call for government action is the following:

What is needed is an organization of broad social, ethical, aesthetic, ecological
upbringing, medical education, able to convincingly show the social, physiological
and genetic harm from the use of psychoactive substances. . . . In this connection
arises a general government task of elevating the level of the culture of health of
the entire Russian society, of forming a demand for a healthy way of life.[88]

As the following several chapters will discuss, this attitude has immense
implications for structuring official policy as well as sustaining collaborative interventions designed to shape youth identity.

[85] As an indication of state and social interest in such matters, this was named Library
of the Year. "Bibliotekar goda – iz sela Obraztsogo," *Volga*, January 11, 2000. See also
"Shkola: pora podumat o dukhovnom," *Kazakhstanskaia pravda*, August 22, 2000.
[86] Interview with librarian, National Children's Library, Almaty.
[87] Interview with Timur Bakiev, Youth Wing, Otan, Almaty.
[88] Aleksandr Arafev, "Pokolenie, kotoroe teriaet Rossiia," *Polit.ru*, December 6, 2002,
www.polit.ru.

Ambivalence

The upshot of such powerful wishes to both embrace and eschew Westernization is a marked ambivalence. It is worth exploring this ambivalence in our three globalizing cities of Eurasia, due to the insight we gain into the conflicts associated with simultaneously pursuing absorption and rejection. The key point to be made here is that ambivalence occurs not only in the obvious and unremarkable sense that both wishes coexist within society as a whole, but also in the more subtle sense that both wishes often coexist on the part of an individual actor. The latter form is particularly dynamic inasmuch as it practically requires some form of resolution, which, as we will see, takes place in part through the assertion of unique identity markers and values. Of course, it is difficult to gauge such personal ambivalence from aggregate data.[89] However, glimpses of intense personal ambivalence are sometimes available in social discourse (and as we will see later, it is unmistakably clear in the statements of actors involved in mediating globalization). An Astrakhan commentary gives a vivid portrait of this feeling:

Not everything is changing for the worse. With every generation new things are introduced in the technical world. The appearance of computers, notebooks, the Internet, and robots shows that the mind of man swiftly develops, that society progresses.

[89] However, some suggestive data are available from Russian sources which dovetail with this impression. First, Kolsto's 2000 survey data reveals that 72 percent of respondents favored a state ideology, of which 41 percent favored a combination of "universal values and traditional Russian values." Pal Kolsto, "Epilogue," in Pal Kolsto and Helge Blakkisrud, eds., *Nation-Building and Common Values in Russia* (Lanham, MD: Rowman and Littlefield, 2004), pp. 327–39. Second, according to an opinion poll conducted by the Moscow-based Foundation for Public Opinion in December 2000, 84 percent of those surveyed felt that too many Western films were shown on Russian television while nearly 60 percent believed that Western culture and values were having a negative effect on the arts in Russia. However, close to 60 percent said that Western culture and values were having a positive influence on Russian knowledge and learning. As a result, respondents were split almost evenly between those who assessed Western influence positively versus negatively overall. The single largest group, about 40 percent, indicated that Western influence was both positive in some ways and negative in others. "Zapadnaia kultura i Rossiia," available online at http://bd.fom.ru/cat/societas/culture. Moreover, some Russian evidence suggests that the ratio between perceived positive versus negative changes has been shifting towards the latter, which may imply an increasingly powerful ambivalence. Two surveys conducted by VTSIOM in 1994 and 1999 are relevant here. Respondents were asked about changes since the fall of the USSR, including whether convergence with the West had been positive or negative. In 1994, 47 percent of responses were positive and 19 percent negative, whereas in 1999 only 38 percent were positive versus 23 percent negative. A summary is "'Chelovek sovetskii' desiat let spustia: 1989–1999: Predvaritelnye itogi sravnitelnogo issledovaniia," *Polit.ru*, January 17, 2001, available online at www.Polit.ru.

On the other hand:

Someone who doesn't smoke, doesn't drink, and doesn't take drugs is already a great rarity. Who asked him to start drinking, smoking, and shooting up – nobody. He wanted to look cool . . . As for sexual life, here there is already nothing forbidden.[90]

As we have already seen, a common concern in these locales is that too much borrowing is a bad thing regardless of content, since the ultimate outcome is derivative thinking and value decay. But it is hard to know where to draw the line. Consider the exciting break dance competition in Almaty. On the one hand, a newspaper reporter seemed to shake his finger at the imitative nature of local youth culture: "The love of our youth for anything Western in the spirit of 'Oh, no, they killed (you know who) [South Park's Kenny],' allowed breakdancing to establish itself firmly in the souls of local 'progressive' teenagers."[91] On the other hand, an unmistakable note of pride is injected: "By the way, the presence of certain traditions of Almaty region 'break' quite positively influence the professional level of the dancers." Therefore, the author concludes, "This, perhaps, is one of those rare occasions when it is not necessary, while blushing deeply, to say, 'Well, this . . . we, of course, are not Moscow'."[92] Likewise, the fascination with hip-hop and rap music soon arrived in Baku, where some attempted to interpret it as a form of fusion with traditional, rhythmic Meykhana poetry.[93] In each case, the proficiency of local performers as well as the purported resonance with native traditions marks imitation as something both embarrassing and praiseworthy.

Another aspect of ambivalence has to do with incorporating Western notions of beauty, something which is felt especially acutely in Azerbaijan and Kazakhstan, where native ethnic features obviously differ. Evidence comes from the "top model" competition conducted for the French agency "Metropolitan" in Baku. The jury for the competition included figures from the fashion world and representatives from the magazines *Elle* and *Cosmopolitan*, but no Azerbaijanis. According to the article, many beautiful young women were turned away flatly. According to a newspaper report, "The furious parents of those who did not advance nearly broke down the doors, demanding that their children be let go and 'not deceived anymore'." The young woman who was eventually chosen,

[90] "Kto my? Kakie my?" *Volga*, August 10, 2001.
[91] "Ia by v breikery poshel," *Karavan*, September 17, 1999.   [92] *Ibid.*
[93] Narmina Rustamova, "Dayirman: Combining Rap, Tradition, and Frustration in Azerbaijan," *Central Asia – Caucasus Analyst*, February 25, 2004, available online at www.cacianalyst.org.

in the view of most local observers, did not typify Azerbaijani beauty. The Metropolitan agency representative, one Mr. Montlere, was asked to explain: "Your choice seems rather strange: all the beautiful girls, according to our understanding, you have swept aside . . ." Montlere responded by saying that the selection was based on "objective parameters: height and figure," as well as subjective considerations developed by the agency. "What do you mean by the words 'pretty girl'? There are, of course, different conceptions of beauty in France and Azerbaijan."[94]

Similarly, in reporting on the Miss Azerbaijan contest held at the fashionable Hyatt Regency in Baku, the news commentator acknowledged, "This year, not unlike several previous ones, a non-Azerbaijani girl becomes winner" (a Slavic woman, Inna Pupikina, won instead). In the words of the judge, himself an Azeri, "We were not determining the beauty of Azerbaijan or Baku, but were selecting the seven most beautiful contestants." Inevitably, though, this raised questions about whether making such choices was in itself a form of self-loathing. The commentator hurried to soothe any such doubts: "This, however, does not at all mean that Azeri girls are any less beautiful. A lot depends on the mentality, as not every Azeri girl would agree to appear on the stage in a bathing suit, which is a requirement of such competitions."[95] It remained unclear what conclusions to draw from this unsettling event. For many young women, however, the general conundrum is managed (however unsatisfactorily) by absorbing Western ideals, and then struggling with the conflicting feelings and social commentary that come in its wake.[96]

Again, the fundamentally contested issue is individualism; as globalization accelerates, there is an increasing appreciation for the double-edged nature of individualist self-perceptions and values. In the words of one cultural official from Astrakhan, "There should be some individualism. This contributes to self-sufficiency, which is very positive. But it is bad for traditions, for common understanding and decision-making, for [a shared] Orthodox identity."[97]

---

[94] "Sostoialsia pervyi kasting s uchastiem spetsialista 'Metropolitan'," *Zerkalo*, October 4, 2000.

[95] "Beauty Beats Islamists," *AssA-Irada News*, December 27–30, 1999, in *Habarlar-L Digest* 1282, January 1, 2000, as translated.

[96] Consider the Azeri television star Aigun Kazimova, who went to Israel for plastic surgery. "As a result of the plastic surgery, the singer's breast's size has reduced to 3. It turned out that her nose has also shortened . . . [She also lost weight.] And now Azeri Madonna is going to return home in her new image." "A Plastic Surgery," ANS-ChM Cultural News, November 16, 1999, in *Habarlar-L Digest*, November 17, 1999, as translated.

[97] Interview with Leonid Volkov, Head of Division of Youth, Tourism, and International Linkages, Astrakhan Oblast Administration, June 2000.

Once grasped at this level, the inherent indeterminacy of individualism makes it difficult to evaluate and respond to. A similar confusion about whether to praise or condemn specific expressions of individualism is often mirrored in media commentaries about social events. For example, in reporting on the highly sexualized imagery of the music group "Ekstazy" and its flamboyant lead singer Ramaz, the author of a newspaper article noted his "extravagant behavior" and "irritating manner" of "arrogance." But this did not yield an entirely negative conclusion: "However, it must be admitted that with the appearance of his group Ekstazy in Baku there arises the possibility of choice in popular stage dance."[98]

Even less ostentatious expressions of individualism are problematic. Thus while considered normal and desirable, it is also widely viewed as suspect, because potentially asocial – perhaps especially in contrast to lingering Soviet collectivist norms.[99] The influx of impersonal, contractual forms of individualism is therefore welcomed but at the same time lamented as undermining the socially supportive, Soviet-era practice of minding other people's business. Distress over this disturbing trend was clearly implied by the author of a newspaper article, in an interview with the director of an Azerbaijani modeling agency. The director was asked about rumors that her models were engaged in promiscuity or overt prostitution:

[Director:] Actually there are girls whose moral character leaves something to be desired. . . .[But] what my girls do after work, I don't know and don't want to know. I have my own understanding of work. If a person comes to work on time, is disciplined, and clearly and professionally does their job, I don't need anything else from that person.

[Interviewer:] And you don't think it's worth it to look after their behavior, in order to protect the reputation of your agency?

---

[98] Similar ambivalence about tolerance of sexual deviation was also evident, as the author asked Ramaz whether he had an "unordinary" sexual orientation and then quoted his reply without editorializing: "It's not even an unordinary, but a normal orientation today. Maybe for Azerbaijan it is an unordinary orientation. [However] the whole world is bisexual . . . The Azerbaijani mentality does not allow openness, uninhibitedness." In contrast, "In Georgia [his native country] it is rather different. I'm not saying that Georgia relates to this like in Europe. But today Georgia is strongly Europeanized." "'Ves mir biseksualen, i ia ne iskliucheniie,' govorit Ramaz B direktor i solist gruppy 'Ekstazy'," *Zerkalo*, July 8, 2000.

[99] In Pilkington's words, Russian youth "envisage an enviable 'calm' resulting from the abundance and stability of life in the West, but see this as going hand in hand with a coldness, lack of genuine spirituality, and extreme individualism." "Youth and Popular Culture," pp. 333–34. This precisely parallels my findings as well.

[Director:] What, don't they have parents? . . . I have a contract . . . but it's not written there, "You don't have a right to have a lover, or to come home after eight in the evening."[100]

Of course, when individualist conduct concerns sexuality one might expect especially powerful negative responses, and as we have seen promiscuous behavior comes in for its share of potent rejection. Yet even here one encounters intriguing signs of ambivalence, which suggest that to some extent confident sexual assertiveness may also be considered an admirable expression of personal freedom. Thus an article about the proliferation of tattoos among the younger generation in Baku duly noted its insidious carnality: "it has not yet progressed to the lower parts of the body, breast, etc., but. . . ." In other words, this was simply a matter of time. And yet the author also observed that wearing a tattoo requires "bravery and independent judgment," aspects of the new individualism clearly deserving of praise.[101]

A final, vivid example – in which I draw on my personal experience as unobtrusive ethnographer – concerns Nabil Seidov of the Baku NGO "Reliable Future." In an interview, Seidov expressed himself in a manner entirely consistent with prevailing discourse, in arguing the need for selective borrowing from the West on all matters, including not only market behavior but also moral issues like sexuality. He favored open sex education, but deplored the tendency toward promiscuity and shameless public displays. On the whole, he suggested, things were loosening up but within definite limits: there was a more casual attitude toward sex, but "still no kissing in public." The next day, by coincidence, as I wandered through the central square of Baku, I passed the McDonald's, which (perhaps tellingly?) has become a standard meeting place, much like the clock at New York's Grand Central station. Who was there but Seidov. At that very moment his girlfriend arrived, and, smiling broadly, he took her into his arms and kissed her in public.

Ultimately, then, no amount of finessing and rationalizing can obscure the fundamental tension between the twin values of modernization and retraditionalization, and between subjective morality and established standards of decency. The ensuing ambivalence is as evident in post-Soviet space as anywhere else in the world, as we see by the mixture of

---

[100] "V teatre mody Galiny Buldyk, vopreki slukham, ne prodaiut," *Zerkalo*, November 20, 1999.

[101] "Natelnye izobrazheniia," *Zerkalo*, August 3, 2000. See also Nancy Condee, "Body Graphics: Tabooing the Fall of Communism," in Barker, ed., *Consuming Russia*, pp. 339–61.

disgust, excitement, and admiration which marks the social discourse on cultural globalization.

In sum, a nearly uniform discourse associated with state and nation building is evident in these three globalizing cities of Russia, Kazakhstan, and Azerbaijan. On one hand, the general embrace of Western-style modernity would suggest that economic and institutional convergence is gathering pace, and with it the essential hallmarks of rational individualism. And yet, as we have seen, this discourse vigorously rejects problematic manifestations of these same trends, while also assiduously promoting cultural traditionalism.

It is of course possible to detect certain differences among the specific local discourses in these places. In Baku, not surprisingly, considerable emphasis is placed on Islam as an anchoring feature of national youth identity. In contrast, in Almaty the role of Islam is less pronounced (and more secularized), while in Astrakhan it is not at all a prominent feature of public discourse.[102] In Astrakhan one also finds a somewhat greater affinity for Western values, as part of an ambivalent tendency to see Russia as both *sui generis* and part of the West. As a result there is relatively less emphasis on rejecting Western cultural trends than on supplementing them through the assertion of uniquely national ones. Finally, Azerbaijan and Kazakhstan share some degree of pan-Turkish identity. The Turkish government has made an effort to promote such identification since the fall of the USSR, by providing scholarships for students to study in Turkey as well as opening Turkish schools and language centers in both countries.[103] This Turkish identity is especially salient in Azerbaijan, where the pan-Turkish aspect of national identity is officially propounded, something which is not true of Kazakhstan.[104] Nevertheless, one is left with an overwhelming impression of the essential unity of national identity discourse in these cities, marked by selective absorption and rejection of Western culture, as well as the assertion of supposedly

---

[102] Azade-Ayse Rorlich, "Islam, Identity and Politics: Kazakhstan, 1990–2000," *Nationalities Papers*, 31, No. 2 (June 2003): 157–76.

[103] Lerna K. Yanik, "The politics of educational exchange: Turkish Education in Eurasia," *Europe-Asia Studies*, 56, No. 2 (March 2004): 293–307.

[104] In Baku one finds events such as a Turkish Youth Festival, which are attended by Azerbaijani prominent cultural and political figures, as well as officially endorsed ties between youth organizations. "S'ezd Tiurkskoi molodezhi mira," *Zerkalo*, August 24, 2000; "Youth Associations of Azerbaijan and Turkey Sign Cooperation Protocol," *Trend – Daily News*, April 27, 2006. In addition, Turkish cultural-philanthropic organizations have a high profile in Baku, unlike in Astrakhan or Almaty. The most prominent example is "The Fund of Aid for Youth," which has a network of offices and volunteers throughout the city.

national narratives and symbols. We have also seen that unmistakable signs of ambivalence emerge from this discourse, as actors at various levels of society wrestle with seemingly contradictory values, and try to resolve the tensions between them.

Of course – from a strictly social scientific perspective – such discursive similarity is really not a very interesting finding. That is, there is nothing surprising about it; in fact, as discussed in chapter 1, it follows essentially the same pattern that we find in other sites of globalization all over the world. However, a close analysis of this discourse is valuable in two crucial respects.

First, by examining discourse more closely we are indeed able to grasp the meanings of, and reasons for, each of the elements of hybridization. This includes pragmatic as well as purely normative calls for adapting to international market pressures and promoting rational development goals. It also involves an appeal to shore up social stability, especially insofar as this is challenged by globalization (including the fall of the USSR and the rise of marketization), through an ongoing dialogue aimed at strengthening the consensual foundations of morality. We find not only official statements, but also highly personal demands for a national identity, as something both inherently legitimate as well as instrumental in facilitating an orderly transition to a modern polity which is integrated into international life. As a potentially stable and stabilizing social process, then, national identity formation has to work at a number of different levels – practical as well as normative – in order to gain institutionalized expression. In short, by inquiring into discourse we uncover a logic of identity formation, consisting of intertwined threads of meaning arising from local and international contexts.

Second, we place ourselves in position to understand key "how" questions associated with the *process* of mediating globalization: how arguments in favor of hybridization are made, and by whom, in concrete social settings. In this way it becomes clear that society as a whole is engaged in wrestling with questions of national identity, including the status of the younger generation, and that certain institutions as well as entrepreneurs of collective meaning become intimately involved in this process. Exploring these questions, in turn, makes it possible to comprehend hybridization at a deeper level of political and social complexity, thereby shedding light on the evolving nature of state–society relations. This requires examining three sites of identity formation: 1) the state, including formal legislation as well as the actions of individual state officials at both high and low levels of centralization; 2) cultural activists operating "below" the state; and 3) the juncture of state and society, particularly with regard to the intentional and often systematic interactions between state and non-state actors. Accordingly, the following chapters will explore post-Soviet nation building as a process both reproducing and disrupting the state–society divide, as actors situated at different levels of social and political organization attempt to selectively appropriate, contest, and accommodate cultural flows in an effort to institutionalize, and then inculcate, a stable national identity for the youth.

4   National youth identity policy

The goal of this chapter is to explore the evolution of official policy regarding national youth identity in Russia, Kazakhstan, and Azerbaijan. After all, official policy represents one important aspect of collective identity formation, and serves as the framework for local negotiations and interventions concerning such matters. I begin with a brief discussion of the key features of "indigenous nationalism," including myths of origin and officially propounded constellations of social values and norms. Beyond describing such idealized constructs, however, my main concern is to examine how the formal process of state building is implicated in efforts to articulate and enact an official national identity. As we will see, youth policy is inextricably bound up with nation building, given the importance of youth identity for the prospects of coherent nationhood. This requires not only an apparatus for formulating policy, but also a vision of governance, including desirable modes of institutionalizing the processes of youth socialization and politicization. I therefore consider, first, the development of official policymaking in each country. Next, I review the nature of the official policy statements which have resulted, and compare them to the analytical categories of hybridization examined in the previous chapter. Finally, I assess the prevailing perspectives, in each state, on how to manage relations between central governing structures and youth organizations.

Nation building

Since the collapse of the USSR, the post-Soviet states have attempted to establish their legitimacy through the process of nation-building, involving the creation of new systems of social meaning and order.[1] In

[1] Rogers Brubaker, *Nationalism Reframed: Nationhood and the National Question in the New Europe* (Cambridge: Cambridge University Press, 1996), pp. 23–54; Olivier Roy, *The New Central Asia: The Creation of Nations* (New York: New York University Press, 2000), pp. 161–89; John Glenn, *The Soviet Legacy in Central Asia* (New York: St. Martin's, 1999), pp. 136–41.

Kazakhstan and Azerbaijan (and to a lesser extent in Russia) this process has followed a somewhat contradictory pattern, of favoring the titular ethnic group while at the same time formally articulating inclusive
civic nationalism. This includes promoting the indigenous titular language as well as reinventing national histories, cultural narratives and
symbols, often drawing heavily on Soviet ethnography.[2] These tendencies are also apparent in standard approaches to teaching history, and in
many widely used history textbooks themselves.[3] In practice, the embrace
of titular ethnicity has also meant allowing (with some flagrant exceptions such as the Armenians in Azerbaijan and Chechens in Russia) the
phenomenon of "re-ethnification" more generally, as local ethnic-based
groups seek to mobilize cultural attachments for purposes of small-scale
social organization. The goal is to reconcile such potentially centrifu-
gal forms of ethnicity with an overarching, non-ethnic identity.[4] This
offsetting project of social integration is an urgent one, since recollec-
tions of the Soviet period tend to fragment diverse groups (especially
Russians and non-Russians) rather than bring them together.[5] In these
ways national official policy resonates strongly with social discourse at
the local level.

Azerbaijan features an official national identity based on an improbable
blend of Turkism, Zoroastrianism, moderate Islam, as well as its historical
function as "bridge" between Asia and Europe along the Silk Road.[6] In
actuality there has been little historical basis for national identity formation among Azeri elites, who were significantly affected by Russification

---

[2] On the role of Soviet ethnography in facilitating ethnic particularism see Yuri Slezkine,
"The USSR as a Communal Apartment, or How a Socialist State Promoted Ethnic
Particularism," *Slavic Review*, 53, No. 2 (Summer 1994): 414–52.

[3] Carolyn Kissane, "History Education in Transit: Where To for Kazakhstan?" *Comparative Education*, 41, No. 1 (February 2005): 45–69; Gulnara Khasanova, "Nation-Building
and Values in Russian Textbooks," in Pal Kolsto and Helge Blakkisrud, eds., *Nation-
Building and Common Values in Russia* (Lanham, MD: Rowman and Littlefield, 2004),
pp. 269–99; Gerlind Schmidt," New Paradigms of National Education in Multi-Ethnic
Russia," in Stephen Webber and Ilkka Liikanen, eds., *Education and Civic Culture in Post-
Communist Countries* (New York: Palgrave, 2001), pp. 94–105; Il'gam Abbasov, "Uchebniki istorii epokhi nezavisimosti," *Azerbaidzhan v Mire*, 1, No. 3 (2006), available online
at www.realazer.com/mag.

[4] On this process in Kazakhstan see Jorn Holm-Hansen, "Political Integration in Kazakhstan," in Pal Kolsto, ed., *Nation-Building and Ethnic Integration in Post-Soviet Societies:
An Investigation of Latvia and Kazakstan* (Boulder, CO: Westview, 1999), pp. 153–226,
and on this phenomenon in Central Asia more broadly see Phillips and James, "National
Identity between Tradition and Reflexive Modernization."

[5] Pal Kolsto makes this point in "Bipolar Societies?" in Kolsto, ed., *Nation-Building and
Ethnic Integration*, pp. 39–41.

[6] Elin Suleymanov, "Azerbaijan, Azerbaijanis and the Search for Identity," *Analysis of Current Events*, 13, No. 1 (February 2001).

and have been generally lukewarm in their expression of pan-Turkism.[7] In addition, there remain strong local allegiances and ethnic distinctions, including submerged tensions between Azeris, Russians, Lezgins, and Talysh, as well as stubborn religious cleavages: roughly 80 percent of the Islamic population is Shiite, twenty percent Sunni.[8] Official nationalism thus attempts to surmount particularist cleavages among Azeris while also accommodating the basic interests of minority populations. Perhaps the most powerful source of social cohesion and state legitimacy is the war in Nagorno-Karabakh, which has generated a collective identity as victim of Armenian aggression.[9] In addition, however, language policy has been a powerful source of ethnic cohesion and nation building. Azeri is spoken by an extremely high percentage of the population, and not only is it promoted as the official language (this was already true of the 1978 Constitution), but since August 2001 all official and business documents are required to use Latin characters instead of Cyrillic.[10]

Much like Azerbaijani identity, Kazakh identity has been constructed from a combination of Soviet and pre-Soviet sources. In this case the national identity narrative focuses on a genealogical register of clan networks (*zhuzes*), which were compiled by Kazakhs as an expression of resistance during the first decades of Soviet rule.[11] Thus on the one hand, President Nursultan Nazarbaev's regime has worked hard to construct a national identity for the titular group through the familiar pattern of promoting the indigenous language and creating cultural narratives and symbols.[12] On the other hand, given the fact that Kazakhs make up only

---

[7] Ronald Grigor Suny, "Provisional Stabilities: The Politics of Identities in Post-Soviet Eurasia," *International Security*, 24, No. 3 (Winter 1999/2000): 139–79; Tadeusz Swietochowski, "Azerbaijan: Perspectives from the Crossroads," *Central Asian Survey*, 18, No. 4 (December 1999): 419–35. On the availability of various historical narratives in Azerbaijan, see Charles Van Der Leeuw, *Azerbaijan: A Quest for Identity* (New York: St. Martins, 2000).

[8] Mehran Kamrava, "State-Building in Azerbaijan: The Search for Consolidation," *Middle East Journal*, 55, No. 2 (Spring 2001): 216–37; Audrey Altstadt, "Azerbaijan's Struggle Toward Democracy," in Karen Dawisha and Bruce Parrott, eds., *Conflict, Cleavage, and Change in Central Asia and the Caucasus* (Cambridge: Cambridge University Press, 1997), pp. 110–55; Swietochowski, "Azerbaijan: Perspectives from the Crossroads."

[9] Svante Cornell, *Small Nations and Great Powers: A Study of Ethnopolitical Conflict in the Caucasus* (Richmond: Curzon Press, 2001), pp. 78–125.

[10] For background on language policy and law in Azerbaijan see Jacob M. Landau and Barbara Kellner-Heinkele, *Politics of Language in the Ex-Soviet Muslim States* (Ann Arbor: University of Michigan Press, 2001), esp. pp. 77–80 and 114–15.

[11] Saulesh Esenova, "Soviet Nationality, Identity, and Ethnicity in Central Asia: Historic Narratives and Kazakh Ethnic Identity," *Journal of Muslim Minority Affairs*, 22, No. 1 (April 2002): 11–38.

[12] On the salience of Kazakh ethnicity over competing identities and the basic cleavage between Kazakh and Russian ethnicities in national identity, see Kolsto, "Bipolar Societies?" An example is the state's use of Novruz as an ethnicized Kazakh symbol of

about 53 percent of the population as compared to roughly 30 percent ethnic Russians, not surprisingly considerable emphasis has been placed on constructing a unifying civic-national identity.[13] Also, a far smaller proportion of the population speaks Kazakh, as compared to the proportion of Azerbaijanis who speak Azeri. Even so, despite constitutional safeguards of equal treatment, in practice "Kazakhification" has taken place in the spheres of government employment and culture, including language policy.[14] To some extent this has been driven by local political processes. After the fall of the USSR, a massive influx into the cities pitted originally rural, traditionally oriented and clan-based Kazakhs against both ethnic Russians and cosmopolitan-urban, Russian-speaking Kazakhs.[15] This resulted in an artificial "ethnification" of politics as a reflection of the competition for scarce resources. The bottom line is that the Russian population in particular has been somewhat marginalized within the political and administrative elite.[16]

Nation building in Azerbaijan and Kazakhstan also shares several features which are absent in Russia. One is that in constructing the nation a new cadre of titulars has used ethnic markers as part of a strategy to displace Russian as well as Soviet era, "russified titulars" from positions of power, employing a combination of instrumental and primordialist strategies.[17] In addition, the idea of a shared Turkic heritage has featured in the

unification which, however, is also a secular alternative to Islamic symbols and holidays. Hilda Eitzen, "Nawriz in Kazakhstan: Scenarios for Managing Diversity," in Ingvar Svanberg, ed., *Contemporary Kazakhs: Cultural and Social Perspectives* (New York: St. Martin's, 1999), pp. 73–101.

[13] Ermukhamet Ertysbaev, "Natsionalnyi dialog: barometr i kompas soglasiia," *Kazakhstanskaia pravda*, June 24, 2000; these points were made repeatedly by Nursultan Nazarbaev in his *Strategiia-2030: poslanie Prezidenta strany narodu Kazakhstana* (Almaty: Bilim, 1997). The 1995 Constitution, which enshrines Kazakh as the official state language, also designates Russian as an "official language." Glenn, *Soviet Legacy in Central Asia*, p. 6.

[14] Azamat Sarsembayev, "Imagined Communities: Kazak Nationalism and Kazakification in the 1990s," *Central Asian Survey*, 18, No. 3 (September 1999): 319–46; Erlan Karin and Andrei Chebotarov, "The Policy of Kazakhization in State and Government Institutions in Kazakhstan," in Natsuko Oka, ed., *The Nationalities Question in Post-Soviet Kazakhstan* (Chiba, Japan: Institute of Developing Economies, Japan External Trade Organization, 2002), pp. 69–108. On language policy and law in Kazakhstan see Landau and Kellner-Heinkele, *Politics of Language*, esp. pp. 73–76, 83–92, and 116–19.

[15] Surucu, "Modernity, Nationalism, Resistance." On unintended tribal identity effects of delegating this process to local actors, see Edward Schatz, "The Politics of Multiple Identities: Lineage and Ethnicity in Kazakhstan," *Europe-Asia Studies*, 52, No. 3 (2000): 489–506.

[16] Martha Brill Olcott, *Kazakhstan: Unfulfilled Promise* (Washington, DC: Carnegie Endowment for International Peace, 2002), pp. 174–83; Taras Kuzio, "Kazakhstan Grapples with Cultural Revival Dilemmas," *EurasiaNet*, January 17, 2002, available online at www.eurasianet.org/.

[17] For the origins of this policy see Philip G. Roeder, "Soviet Federalism and Ethnic Mobilization," *World Politics*, 43, No. 2 (January 1991): 196–232.

official historiography of Azerbaijan and Kazakhstan as part of the effort to establish myths of origin and descent.[18] Similar observations might be made about Islam in both countries: that is, it provides a cultural vehicle for the state in its claim to represent an indigenous national identity.[19] However, as public symbolism and as private religious practice, Islam has a far larger role in Baku than in Almaty.

In Russia, by comparison, the fact that sovereignty was not accompanied by any such ethnically based, social and political displacement has obviously had important implications for the official discourse of nationalism. Although it has been necessary to construct new ideologies and narratives of belonging, these have generally not come at the expense of any single out-group. Thus although Russian discourse often demonizes Chechens and other swarthy Caucasians, its overall thrust – especially in official discourse and policymaking – has been to embrace civic nationalism, at least more consistently than has been the case in Kazakhstan or Azerbaijan.[20] Nevertheless, exclusivist ethnic-based themes can also be discerned, including a self-image of Russia as the embodiment of transcendent truth or goodness which is frequently linked to Orthodox Christianity.[21] Moreover, while no definitive answer has yet emerged in

---

[18] Viktor Shnirelman, "National Identity and Myths of Ethnogenesis in Transcaucasia," in Graham Smith, Edward Allworth, and Vivien Law, eds., *Nation-Building in the Post-Soviet Borderlands: The Politics of National Identities* (Cambridge: Cambridge University Press, 1998), pp. 48–66; Edward Allworth, "History and Group Identity in Central Asia," in Smith, Allworth and Law, eds., *Nation-Building*, pp. 67–90.

[19] Graham Smith, *The Post-Soviet States: Mapping the Politics of Transition* (New York: Oxford University Press, 1999), chapter 4. Despite official use of Islamic symbols, the Azeri elite has been from the outset overwhelmingly secular in orientation. See Tadeusz Swietochowski, *Russia and Azerbaijan: A Borderland in Transition* (New York: Columbia University Press, 1995), pp. 193–220; also Anar Valiyev and Yusif Valiyev, "Islamic Extremism in Azerbaijan: Reality and Myth," *Central Asia-Caucasus Analyst*, July 17, 2002, available online at www.cacianalyst.org/. See also Rorlich, "Islam, Identity and Politics."

[20] Valery Tishkov, *Ethnicity, Nationalism and Conflict in and After the Soviet Union: The Mind Aflame* (London: Sage Publications, 1997), esp. pp. 259–71; Vera Tolz, "Forging the Nation: National Identity and Nation Building in Post-Communist Russia," *Europe-Asia Studies*, 50, No. 6 (1998), 993–1022; J. Martin Daughtry, "Russia's New Anthem and the Negotiation of National Identity," *Ethnomusicology*, 47, No. 1 (Winter 2003): 42–67.

[21] See Timo Piirainen, "The Fall of an Empire, the Birth of a Nation: Perceptions of the New Russian National Identity," in Chris Chulos and Timo Piirainen, eds., *The Fall of an Empire, the Birth of a Nation: National Identities in Russia* (Burlington, VT: Ashgate, 2000), pp. 161–96. On the increasing role of Orthodoxy see Nikolas Gvosdev, "The New Party Card? Orthodoxy and the Search for Post-Soviet Russian Identity," *Problems of Post-Communism*, 47, No. 6 (November–December 2000): 29–38; and for an historical perspective see Tim McDaniel, *The Agony of the Russian Idea* (Princeton: Princeton University Press, 1996), pp. 22–55. A review of relevant Russian scholarship is Andrei P. Tsygankov and Pavel A. Tsygankov, "New Directions in Russian International Studies: Pluralization, Westernization, and Isolationism," *Communist and Post-Communist Studies*, 37, No. 1 (March 2004): 1–17.

the quest to define a unifying "Russian idea," we find here (as elsewhere in the world) the same efforts to construct the nation and its past in ostensibly unique, indigenized terms.[22]

These attempts to establish a unifying national identity in Russia, Kazakhstan, and Azerbaijan have been closely connected with state building. In particular, there has been a wide recognition within policymaking circles that the prospects for successful nation building depend on enlisting not only the loyalty, but also the active participation, of young people in achieving newly defined national goals. The result, in each case, is a project designed to create an integrated set of policies for managing problems of the younger generation, while also inculcating a modern, moral, and thoroughly national identity. The following section examines how these projects have unfolded, including the nature of the youth policy frameworks which have emerged in these countries since the fall of the USSR.

National youth policy

The situation affecting youth – and its immense implications – were quickly recognized by authorities in the newly independent states. However, in the early years after the fall of the USSR, essentially no one was minding the shop. The fledgling state structures were overwhelmed with the requirements of establishing sovereignty and managing crises in virtually all areas of governance. Youth policy was in abeyance, consisting of a mixture of archaic or incoherent legislation which was hastily thrown together at the time of the Soviet collapse. Lacking a systematic, integrated legal foundation and institutional underpinning, these early post-Soviet policies were at best temporary measures, and in fact existed mainly on paper. Meanwhile, the previous system of institutional oversight and social welfare provision had disintegrated, leaving the younger generation unsupervised and adrift.[23] Bolat Baikadamov, deputy head of the Social-Political Department of the presidential apparatus under Nazarbaev, acknowledged the resulting situation: "It must be admitted that in recent years the state organs have paid insufficient attention to the problems of youth. . . . Established forms of work with them at home and

---

[22] A stimulating and accessible discussion is James H. Billington, *Russia in Search of Itself* (Baltimore and London: Johns Hopkins University Press, 2003). See also Kathleen E. Smith, *Mythmaking in the New Russia: Politics and Memory During the Yeltsin Era* (Ithaca: Cornell University Press, 2002), esp. pp. 158–84.

[23] A good snapshot analysis is Jakob Rigi, "Conditions of Post-Soviet Youth and Work in Almaty, Kazakhstan," *Critique of Anthropology*, 23, No. 1 (March 2003): 35–49.

outside of school have been somewhat lost, and the results have quickly made themselves known."[24]

The potential consequences of this trend were dire indeed. Increasingly, it dawned on authorities that the problems of youth combined several key features: material impoverishment and a lack of concrete prospects rooted in the post-Soviet economic collapse, a rapid increase in deviant behaviors linked to rising Western influence and media exposure, and growing alienation from the essential values and development imperatives pursued by the state. In the words of another influential document:

In contemporary youth sub-culture, especially in the sphere of leisure, consumption prevails over creativity, passive forms of consumption over active forms of independent cultural-creative activities. Essential, often shocking detachment and isolation of youth subculture from the cultural values of older generations and from national traditions and mentality, carries the potential to shake loose the fundamental culture of society.[25]

Russia, with its profusion of relevant documentation, provides abundant evidence of official perceptions. Again and again, authoritative statements as well as comments by policymakers in various official venues reflect the same concern: i.e., that cultural globalization threatened to undermine the prospect for constructing a coherent national identity, especially by hijacking the values and allegiances of young people. According to one typical report, nothing less than the very fate of Russia was at stake, inasmuch as the younger generation "grows within itself the shape of the future," and yet is also especially likely to make "erroneous choices."[26] This inherently problematic situation was said to be exacerbated in post-Soviet reality by globalization and the accompanying shift in youth attitudes:

The changes which have occurred in the structure of value orientations [of youth] reflect contradictions arising between spiritual and rational values. Family, general culture, honesty and principled behavior have noticeably relinquished their position. . . . [Thus] the process of spiritual development of youth takes place through a conflict of two layers of consciousness: traditional and contemporary.[27]

What was needed, then, was the establishment of a stable, well-conceived legal basis to address the full range of practical and cultural

---

[24] "Ved zhizn na meste ne stoit . . . ," *Kazakhstanskaia pravda*, August 5, 2000.
[25] "Initsiativa molodykh – budushchee Rossii," July 16, 2002, p. 94, available on-line at: www.gov.ru/main/ministry/isp-vlast47.html.
[26] "Doktrina Molodezhi Rossii," article 1.1.
[27] *Polozhenie molodezhi i realizatsiia gosudarstvennoi molodezhnoi politiki v Rossiiskoi Federatsii: 2002 god*, report prepared by the Department of Youth Affairs of the Ministry of Education and Science (December 17, 2003), p. 22. Available online at www.ed.gov.ru/junior/news/.

problems. In part this was to be accomplished through general legislation on issues such as education, drug enforcement, cultural development, and so forth. But in addition, in each country a separate policy initiative was specifically geared toward the youth. This included ensuring long-term funding to give young people an education, create jobs, and build housing for young married couples. It also included reviving ideological work, although in the early post-Soviet context it was difficult to mention this term.

By the late 1990s the process was well under way, with the drafting of general "concept statements" and "target programs." After being debated to a greater or lesser extent within parliament and the state bureaucracy, the documents were revised to become official "doctrine" between 2002 and 2004 (and in Azerbaijan and Kazakhstan were actually signed into law). These consisted of general principles and issue-specific rules designed to mold the younger generation, and to channel its energies toward the larger nation building goals of the state. Before considering the substantive content of each, the following provides a brief overview of the policymaking process in these three post-Soviet states which underscores the differences between the policy mechanisms operating in each country.

Azerbaijan

Following his return to power, Gaidar Aliev established the Ministry of Youth and Sports (briefly named the Ministry of Youth, Sports, and Tourism from 2001 to 2006). Among other things, the ministry was tasked with overseeing the formation of youth policy, which Aliev identified as one of the state's many pressing tasks. Officials immediately began to compile information on youth organizations, including government-backed groups as well as fledgling youth NGOs, and also began to develop the foundation for youth legislation.[28]

The political process of approving the new policy was relatively straightforward, as national legislation was effectively mandated by the strongman in power. Reflecting Aliev's virtually unchallenged position, the president's personal understandings provided the foundation for policymaking. Aliev personally oversaw the outlines of national youth policy

---

[28] At the same time, in order to accelerate the process of drafting the new policy, Aliev created a Center of Scientific Research of Youth Problems under the Ministry of Youth and Sports. Additional information on the broader context of youth policy is available in UNICEF (in coordination with Mery Gardashkhanova, Azerbaijan State Statistical Committee), *Youth at Transition Period in Azerbaijan Republic* (Florence: UNICEFs 2000), available online at www.unicef-icdc.org/.

development beginning in 1996, culminating in the idiosyncratic, pseudo-historical edict "On the Realization of State Youth Policy" in July 1999.[29]

The ensuing draft law was submitted to parliament, although – given the latter's compliant nature – this step was merely *pro forma*.[30] The predictable end result was a slim packet of legislation entitled "On Youth Policy," which was published in April, 2002, and officially endorsed by Aliev the following month.[31] Compared with Russia and Kazakhstan, then, the policy development process in Azerbaijan was highly streamlined. In addition, as another reflection of the essentially dictatorial nature of Aliev's regime, the legislation on youth policy is sparse and relatively amorphous, removing juridical accountability and leaving a great deal of latitude to central and local officials. Neither the legislation nor the policy mechanisms associated with it have changed since Ilham Aliev succeeded his father in October 2003.

Kazakhstan

As in Azerbaijan, the president's ideas constituted the basis for youth policy development in Kazakhstan. The general blueprint for national development was articulated by President Nazarbaev in 1997 in his landmark address to the nation, "Kazakhstan – 2030," in which he clearly indicated an awareness of the enormous pressures of globalization, including its possible benefits and pitfalls. Consistently, however, globalization was portrayed as an imperative to which the country was forced to adapt.[32]

Nazarbaev also created a bureaucracy to oversee youth policy. In order to further develop policy ideas and to coordinate inter-agency work, a Department of Youth Policy was established under the Ministry of Culture, Information, and Social Accord (which after a ministerial rearrangement in September 2003 fell under the new Ministry of Culture). This was followed in 2000 by the formation of an advisory body under the Prime Minister's office, and at around the same time a Committee on

---

[29] "O realizatsii gosudarstvennoi molodezhnoi politiki," Presidential Decree no. 169, July 29, 1999, translated by Vugar Yagubov, available online at www.infoyouth.az.

[30] The only (relatively minor) disagreements which surfaced within the Milli Mejilis concerned specific levels of funding and questions of bureaucratic control. Interview with Professor Alikram Abdullayev, Academy of Public Administration, Baku; interviews, Azerbaijan Ministry of Youth, Sports and Tourism.

[31] "O molodezhnoi politike," State Law No. 4434, April 9, 2002. Three subsequent decrees introduced slight corrections in the law, on May 6, 2002, March 25, 2003, and June 5, 2003. The specific documents are available via LexInfoSys, online at: www.cis-legal-reform.org/.

[32] "Kazakhstan – 2030" is available online at the President's official website, www.president.kz/.

Social and Cultural Development was established within the Senate with responsibilities for questions of youth policy.[33] Finally, a working group on youth affairs was created within the parliament for dialogue with the Ministry on formulating concrete legislation.[34]

Official policy statements were soon forthcoming. After a series of drafts, a government program, "Youth of Kazakhstan," was published in 2001, and was followed by the creation of a draft law, "On State Youth Policy," in 2002.[35]

At this point – quite unlike in Azerbaijan – the policymaking process in Kazakhstan suddenly became overtly contentious. This in itself is a telling reflection of differences in political culture. While a far cry from democratic (and in fact frequently punctuated by overt acts of repression), the climate in Kazakhstan is nevertheless far more open than in Azerbaijan. The brief history of post-Soviet parliamentary politics has been a tumultuous one, marked at times by organized resistance to the president's policies. Despite the fact that Nazarbaev dissolved the parliament in 1995 and effectively eliminated its power, it has never been fully compliant, especially on matters of economic policy.[36] The same holds for youth policy, as the work of drafting a new law was increasingly conducted with the active participation of youth organizations, some of which proved to be highly critical of the government's plan for its failures to guarantee services needed by young people.[37] Debate spilled over into the next session of the lower house of parliament (Mazhilis), where the new legislation was finally approved in late 2003, although only in the form of a vague compromise on the key issues.[38]

---

[33] "On the Creation of the Council for Youth Affairs," Resolution No. 1165, July 31, 2000; "Kazakh Upper House Sets Up New Culture, Youth Committee," Khabar TV, Almaty, June 8, 2000, BBC Monitoring, June 9, 2000, available via ISI Emerging Markets.

[34] "Mazhilis Speaker Zharmakhan Tuyakbay: We Failed to Progress in Solution of Problems of Young Generation for 10 Years of Independence," Khabar Information Agency, from Media Monitoring Report, June 19, 2001, available via ISI Emerging Markets.

[35] See, respectively, "Programma 'Molodezh Kazakhstana'," Government Resolution No. 249, February 17, 2001; "O gosudarstvennoi molodezhnoi politike v Respublike Kazakhstan," April 29, 2002, available on-line at www.parlam.kz. The preceding document was the 1999 "Kontseptsiia gosudarstvennoi molodezhnoi politiki Respubliki Kazakhstan," Decree of the President of the Republic of Kazakhstan, No. 73, August 28, 1999.

[36] For background see Olcott, *Kazakhstan: Unfulfilled Promise*, pp. 107–23.

[37] See Aleksandra Kazakova (a member of MISK), "Nam 'Kongress molodezhi' ne nuzhen," *Novoe Pokolenie*, November 15, 2002, available online at www.np.kz.

[38] "V Mazhilis spory o molodezhi prodolzhaetsia," *Kazakhstanskie novosti*, January 13, 2003, available via ISI Emerging Markets; "Draft Laws on NGO Activity to Be Inserted into the Parliament," Kazakh Information Agency, July 10, 2003, available via ISI Emerging Markets; "Mazhilis odobril zakonoproekt 'O gosudarstvennoi molodezhnoi politike v RK'," Kazakh Information Agency, December 12, 2003, available via ISI Emerging Markets.

The remaining details were hammered out in the Senate. However, largely as a result of the lobbying efforts of youth NGOs, discussions in the Senate focused largely on meeting the demands of the youth movement. Remarkably, this was reflected in the final law on youth policy (signed into law by Nazarbaev in July 2004), which made some concessions on funding for social services.[39] Nevertheless, despite this relatively pluralistic approach to policymaking, the essential elements of Nazarbaev's conception remained securely in place. The official youth policy of Kazakhstan is thus committed to the goal of fostering a unified national youth identity in light of the challenges posed by globalization.

Russia

The process of formulating a coherent and institutionally well-fortified youth policy in Russia slowly began to take shape under Boris Yeltsin in the early 1990s.[40] These early steps paved the way for a federal program, entitled "The Youth of Russia,"[41] which was followed by an abortive attempt to gain passage of a comprehensive law governing youth policy.[42] As a result, the only major federal laws relevant to youth policy which came out of the Yeltsin period were those setting general frameworks for dealing with youth organizations and combating juvenile crime.[43]

Following Putin's accession to power in 2000, problems of youth were accorded much higher priority, and a new structure was swiftly established for overseeing youth policy formation. Primary responsibility for developing youth policy was transferred to the Department of Youth Policy under the Ministry of Education (renamed the Ministry of Education

---

[39] The legislation is No. 581, "O gosudarstvennoi molodezhnoi politike v Respublike Kazakhstan," July 7, 2004, available online at: www.zakon.kz.

[40] "O pervoocherednykh merakh v oblasti gosudarstvennoi molodezhnoi politiki," Presidential Decree no. 1075, September 16, 1992; "Osnovnye napravleniia gosudarstvennoi molodezhnoi politiki," Resolution of the Supreme Soviet no. 5090–1, June 3, 1993; "Molodezh Rossii," Presidential Decree no. 1922, September 15, 1994.

[41] "Molodezh Rossii," Resolution of the Government of the Russian Federation, no. 746, June 18, 1997.

[42] Endorsed by the upper and lower houses of parliament, the bill was vetoed by Yeltsin in the waning months of his presidency on the grounds that it was institutionally and ideologically underdeveloped. See Federal Law, "Ob osnovakh gosudarstvennoi molodezhnoi politiki v Rossiiskoi Federatsii." The law was vetoed by Yeltsin on November 25, 1999.

[43] "O gosudarstvennoi podderzhke molodezhnykh i detskikh obshchestvennykh obedinenii," Russian State Law, no. 98-F3, June 18, 1995; "Ob osnovakh sistemy profiliaktiki beznadzornosti i pravonarushenii nesovershennoletnykh," Russian State Law, no. 120-F3, June 24, 1999.

and Science in 2004), which then led the process of drafting a new federal program.[44] Second, a State Commission for Youth Affairs was charged with responding to ideas and drafts created within the Department of Youth Policy, as well as coordinating policy relevant to youth which fell within the purview of various other ministries. Third, as an additional check on both institutions, in 2002 the State Council – an advisory body created by Putin and composed of the heads of Russia's territorial units – was tasked with commenting on proposals and drafts emanating from the State Commission on Youth Affairs and the Department of Youth Policy. With several other agencies also active in this area, the current Russian system thus includes a number of independent organs involved in formulating and systematizing new policy ideas.[45]

The creation of a new policy structure was followed by a spate of decrees and legislative acts, culminating in a draft framework, "Strategy of State Youth Policy" for the period 2006–16.[46] Yet by mid-2006 no comprehensive law on youth policy had been passed. This was due in part to opposition over the enormous expenditures requested, which reflected an effort to seriously address massive problems in health, education, employment, and living space for young people. In addition, passage was impeded by uncertainty over the nature of center–periphery relations, including responsibility for funding and implementing such measures, as reflected in the still-evolving draft Law on Local Self-Government. This unsettled state of affairs with respect to youth policy testifies to the relatively complex, contentious process of policy-making in Russia, notwithstanding the "super-presidential" system in place.

---

[44] Resolution of the Government of the Russian Federation, no. 1350, "Statute on the State Committee of the Russian Federation for Youth Policy," December 6, 1999. In addition, in June 2004 a new Federal Agency for Education was created under the Ministry of Education and Science, for the purpose of overseeing implementation.

[45] Within the State Duma there also exists a Sub-Committee on Youth Affairs (under the Committee on Physical Culture, Sports, and Youth Affairs), as well as a Youth Chamber, both of which have at times been significant participants in debating various documents and proposals.

[46] "Proekt Strategii gosudarstvennoi molodezhnoi politiki v Rossiiskoi Federatsii," June 9, 2005. For additional documentation and analysis see the Ministry of Science and Education website, at www.won.gov.ru. Previously, in 2000 a draft program entitled "Youth of Russia 2001–2005" was adopted, which devoted extensive space to center–periphery institutional linkages and outlined activities which might be undertaken at the regional level in the pursuit of youth policy goals. "O federalnoi tselevoi programme 'Molodezh Rossii (2001–2005 gody)'," no. 1015, December 27, 2000. Essentially the same goals were enshrined in the "Conception of State Youth Policy in the Russian Federation," which was approved in late 2001 by the Ministry of Education's Department of Youth Policy. "Kontseptsiia gosudarstvennoi molodezhnoi politiki v Rossiiskoi Federatsii," December 5, 2001, available on-line at www.gov.ru.

As the foregoing overview suggests, despite significant differences in the policymaking process across these three countries, the relevant doctrines reveal a number of striking similarities. Most importantly, all reflect a shared belief in the need for an official youth policy. Each doctrine also expresses a broad consensus about the state's obligation to intervene, in order to provide essential services for young people – including a solid moral foundation. In an interview, a member of the Russian Ministry of Education's Department of Youth Policy underscored this point, noting the existence of cross-cultural differences in assumptions about the desirability of drafting a national youth policy to begin with: "I understand that in America there is the idea that morality cannot be regulated. But there *must* be moral regulations. Nobody wants to have economic achievements and moral counter-achievements."[47]

The programmatic content of youth policy

The official documents of each country invariably include an analysis of current problems, designation of operational goals, and concrete plans of action. Along the way, they also clearly frame the envisioned moral compass of youth. To be sure, this is not the only concern of state policymaking. A substantial part of each document deals with practical questions, such as youth employment and the flow of finances. Furthermore, not all moral instruction is concerned with mediating global influences; considerable emphasis is given to combating religious and ethnic intolerance. Still, in each case the central concern is how to anchor youth in a stable social and moral foundation, within the overarching context of globalization. This includes the potential benefits and dangers of globalization, as well as the need to orient young people toward explicitly national values. The official youth policy statements therefore reveal a high degree of uniformity regarding the nature of desirable moral regulation for young people. That is, we repeatedly encounter essentially the same themes and analytical categories which surface time and again in popular discourse: rejection; assertion; and absorption, but absorption firmly rooted in the assertion of a national self, and buttressed by measures to preclude excessive and harmful forms of cultural borrowing.

---

[47] Interview, Committee on Youth Policy, Moscow. Similarly, according to a 2002 report from the same Department, "In striving for de-ideologization and de-statization of education the reformers of the first wave destroyed the developed system of moral instruction, which had accumulated invaluable historical experience, bringing enormous damage to the moral cast of the contemporary generation of youth." *Polozhenie molodezhi i realizatsiia gosudarstvennoi molodezhnoi politiki*, p. 17.

Rejection

The official policies of each country recognize the material and moral problems encountered by young people in their transitional societies, including rampant unemployment, disease, and substance abuse. The final versions of each national legislation are relatively terse, and generally refrain from expounding on the values and assumptions underlying their statutes. This can, however, be clearly seen in the draft documents leading up to the final versions, in which the authorities' anxieties and wishes are expressed rather freely. Particularly evident is concern over the pernicious influence of foreign popular culture. For example, in the words of the 1999 Kazakhstani "Conception":

It is necessary to recognize that the mass media, especially the electronic, vitally affects the formation of ethical and moral values of youth. The propaganda of a cult of viciousness and violence exerts massive pressure on the psychological condition of youth, forms corresponding models of behavior [and] stereotypical perceptions of life.[48]

As a reflection of its relatively unreconstructed Soviet style, Azerbaijan's law "On State Youth Policy" calls for "moral-ethical instruction of youth, reducing and liquidating crime, drug abuse and other negative manifestations among youth."[49]

Rejection of untoward foreign influences also figures prominently in Russia, as reflected by the emphasis on prevention of sexually transmitted disease, prevention of drug abuse, and generally "propagandizing a healthy way of life." While the problems afflicting youth are variously ascribed to internal and external sources, frequently the chief culprit is said to be globalization. As one Russian document observed, youth policy must be geared to countering "the unlimited pressure of artificially foisted styles of life, value-meaning and worldview constructs, which are destroying cultural-historical traditions."[50] Thus, although various agencies differed with regard to the degree of emphasis they placed on this issue,[51] there was complete agreement that rejection had to be a key element of youth policy. This resulted in a raft of specific policy guidelines

---

[48] "Kontseptsiia gosudarstvennoi molodezhnoi politiki," section IV, point 3.
[49] "O molodezhnoi politike," article 5, point 3.
[50] "Doktrina molodezhi Rossii," article 1.1.
[51] Whereas the State Council's "Doctrine" focuses on rejection, the Ministry of Education's "Initiative of Youth" criticizes an earlier policy statement (and by implication the State Council's position) for dwelling overmuch on "overcoming negative manifestations in the sphere of youth, and not on developing the positive potential of youth." "Initsiativa molodykh – budushchee Rossii," pp. 101–02.

for preventing violence and the abuse of narcotics.[52] Moreover, just as in social discourse at large, the focus of rejection was also partly directed at compensating for "excessive" individualism brought on by absorption. In the words of Sergei Mironov, the chairman of the Federation Council or upper house of parliament, "Speaking from my conscience, I do not like an arrangement in which exclusively pragmatic, wealthy young egoists should dominate in Russia. In an epoch of transitions a lot of foam always rises on the surface of social life, but it inevitably recedes, and unshakeable moral values attain strength again."[53]

Reflecting the discursive salience of the notion of a "healthy way of life," organized state programs have been launched in each city to combat dangerous Western influences, and to agitate for wholesome values and lifestyles. In each case the assumptions, language, and outreach work are practically identical. In Kazakhstan the government established eponymous regional and district Centers for this purpose (including three in Almaty); in Baku the "Healthy Way of Life" program is supported by national and city government and coordinated by UNICEF; and in Astrakhan analogous functions are provided by the Regional Social Service for Youth.[54]

In sum, as Kazakhstan's "Conception of State Youth Policy" wistfully put it, through such state-led efforts, perhaps someday, "such personal qualities as decency, integrity, patriotism, professionalism, respect for elders, [and] a sense of responsibility for oneself and close others will become prestigious."[55]

Assertion

Consistent with social discursive demands, the emerging policies in each country accentuate the importance of a nationally identified youth. For

---

[52] For example, "O merakh po preduprezhdeniiu zloupotrebleniia psikhoaktivnymi veshchami sredi nesovershennoletnykh i molodezhi v 1999–2000 godakh," Ministry of Education, Order No. 718, March 23, 1999. In addition, at the request of the Ministry of Education, the Ministry of Internal Affairs drafted its own set of guidelines. See "Metodicheskie rekomendatsii po realizatsii sotsialnykh profilakticheskikh i reabilitatsionnykh program," Resolution 15-52-521, July 27, 2003. There is also a Federal Program for War On Narcotics.

[53] "Trebuetsia molodezhnaia politika," *Tikhookeanskaia zvezda*, September 24, 2005, available via ISI Emerging Markets.

[54] Interview, Center for a Healthy Way of Life, Almaty, June 2002; and see "O kompleksnoi programme 'Zdorovyi obraz zhizni'," Resolution of the Government of Kazakhstan, No. 905, June 30, 1999; interview with Samira Allahverdiyeva, Youth Volunteer Management Unit, UN Volunteers Program, Baku; and interview with staff, Astrakhan Regional Social Service for Youth, June 2002.

[55] "Kontseptsiia gosudarstvennoi molodezhnoi politiki," section IV, point 3.

example, the Azerbaijani law "On Youth Policy" calls for "Instruction of youth on the basis of principles of patriotism, Azerbaijanism, statism, secularism, in the spirit of respect for history, cultural inheritance, habits and traditions, the state language and symbols of the Azerbaijani people, [and] national-moral and all-human values."[56] Similarly, Gaidar Aliev's 1999 and 2002 decrees on youth policy (the latter of which shortly followed passage of the state law) were devoted largely to an overview of Azerbaijan's unique cultural heritage, as it supposedly coalesced at the end of the nineteenth century.[57]

Much the same has transpired in Kazakhstan, where 2000 was declared the Year of National Culture and where an ongoing state program entitled Cultural Heritage seeks to locate a unique national and spiritual tradition. In this context President Nazarbaev has repeatedly stressed the dangers as well as the potential benefits of globalization, which "arouses in many people the fear of losing their historical roots, ethnic identity, language, cultural and religious traditions."[58] Thus although the 2004 law merely pledged to "secure conditions for the development of national culture and language among the youth," in fact substantial efforts toward this end were being made in official policy.[59]

A particular accent is placed on promoting patriotism. While in Azerbaijan this is typically linked closely with military training, in Kazakhstan and Russia the narrow military dimension of patriotism is secondary to its larger identity implications. Thus the Russian Ministry of Education has endorsed what it claimed was an increasingly widespread view, according to which patriotism is the "most important value," insofar as it "integrates not only social, but also spiritual-moral, ideological, cultural-historical and other components."[60] The result is another Federal Program, this one on "Patriotic Education for Citizens of the Russian Federation."[61]

---

[56] "On Youth Policy," article 3.2.1

[57] "O realizatsii gosudarstvennoi molodezhnoi politiki"; "O primenenii Zakona Azerbaidzhanskoi Respubliki 'O molodezhnoi politike'," May 6, 2002.

[58] "Kazakh President Sets Tasks for People's Assembly for 2004," Kazakhstan television first channel, December 23, 2003, BBC Monitoring, December 23, 2003, available via ISI Emerging Markets.

[59] "O gosudarstvennoi molodezhnoi politike," article 5, point 9.

[60] "Initsiativa molodezhi," p. 48.

[61] The current program, "Patriotic Education for Citizens of the Russian Federation, 2006–2010" is the successor to an eponymous program for 2001–2005 (see government act No. 422, July 11, 2005, "Patrioticheskoe vospitanie grazhdan Rossiiskoi Federatsii na 2006–2010." The latest program is slated to receive a total of $17.4 million from the federal budget between 2006 and 2010, for the purpose of sponsoring summer camps and other organized activities, especially emphasizing sports and military themes. This general initiative predates Putin: Presidential Decree No. 727 of May 16, 1996, had

Cultivating patriotism was thus to be a cornerstone of youth policy, and of Russian national identity as a whole. Consistent with this idea and with ongoing attacks on liberal tendencies, in January 2004 the Ministry of Education announced plans to revise all history textbooks so as to remove traces of "pseudo-liberalism" and correct unduly negative characterizations of Soviet achievements.[62] Of course, the practical benefits of patriotism also went beyond its strictly social and normative aspects, to include its implications for Russia's geopolitical status. The Ministry of Education's draft program went so far as to state that reviving patriotism was "the most important condition for the rebirth of Russia as a great power."[63]

Likewise, in the words of one member of the Kazakhstan parliamentary committee tasked with debating youth policy, "During these years [since the fall of the Soviet Union] we have not managed to learn to consistently and clearly instill in children a feeling of patriotism. . . . Now in other countries people proudly sing the hymns of their countries, [whereas] we do not know either the words or the music. We must fill the spiritual vacuum which is forming."[64] Not surprisingly, the 2004 Kazakhstan law listed the "formation of Kazakhstani patriotism" among the cardinal goals of youth policy.[65] The same attitudes are frequently expressed in Azerbaijan, too, where the government supports an ongoing program "On the Patriotic Upbringing of Youth." And in each country, the government vigorously employs media in order to achieve its goals. For example, as the Azerbaijan law on youth policy pledges, "The state will assist in preparing television and radio programs, theater presentations and films, directed at forming the worldview of youth, its moral-ethical upbringing, and also in the publication of literature and print organs."[66]

called for "state measures to support public youth organizations which provide young people with a military/patriotic education."

[62] "Uchebnik – ne propagandistskaia agitka," *Nezavisimaia gazeta*, January 30, 2004.

[63] "Initsiativa molodezhi," p. 106. The Ministry of Defense has also been directly involved in policymaking, working with other agencies to foster patriotic attachments among youth. See "O podderzhke obshchestvennykh obedinenii, vedushchikh rabotu po voenno-patrioticheskomu vospitaniiu molodezhi," Russian Ministry of Defense, Order No. 6, January 2, 2000.

[64] Serik Abdrakhmanov, "Nado vospityvat patriotov!" *Novoe Pokolenie*, September 27, 2002, available online at www.np.kz.

[65] "O gosudarstvennoi molodezhnoi politike," article 3, point 5. This was actually a slight downgrading of the priority attached to patriotism compared to the 1999 "Conception," in which the first goal of youth policy was stated to be "formation among the youth of patriotism, moral, and spiritual development." "Kontseptsiia gosudarstvennoi molodezhnoi politiki," section II, point 1.

[66] "O molodezhnoi politike," article 5, point 2.

Absorption

The theme of absorption emerges from the policy documents of each country, although it is rather muted in comparison to social discourse, and certainly far outweighed by the programmatic emphasis on molding a distinct national identity as well as barring harmful influences from the outside world.

Russian policy has consistently sought to ensure that young people were given "an education corresponding to the demands of contemporary material and spiritual productivity," so that they might develop "qualities of entrepreneurship, conscientiousness, responsibility."[67] The point was both to facilitate domestic growth and to become modern with respect to social sensibilities and norms. This was linked to the notion of trying to engineer attitudes conducive to integration into the international economy. Thus the Federal Program for the period 2001–05 stated that one goal should be "orienting individual and social groups toward values ensuring the successful modernization of Russian society."[68] More explicitly, the framework document for the following period, 2006–10, aimed to "facilitate the formation of an innovative climate, which is essential for the development of competitiveness."[69] One corollary is the state's systematic effort to create a "unified electronic information space," including increased computer access, training, and online libraries.[70]

In Kazakhstan, as already mentioned, the public positions taken by President Nazarbaev have often been the basis for subsequent policy. Indeed, in his speeches Nazarbaev has proudly stressed the thoroughly modern attributes of Kazakhstan's younger generation:

The cultural norms of the twenty-first century, its educational standards and information skills – all of this is embodied in the youth of Kazakhstan, which already knows not two, but three or four languages besides unqualified knowledge of the native language. This is a youth which is integrated into world cultural space.[71]

---

[67] "Kontseptsiia gosudarstvennoi molodezhnoi politiki," section 4.
[68] "Kultura Rossii 2001–2005," Resolution of the Government of the Russian Federation, No. 955, December 14, 2000.
[69] "Proekt Strategii gosudarstvennoi molodezhnoi politiki," program goal II.
[70] For example, see "O Federalnoi tselevoi programme 'Razvitie edinoi obrazovatelnoi informatsionnoi sredy (2001–2005)'." Available at the website of the Federal Agency for Education, www.ed.gov.ru/ntp/fp/pfzp/post-p/656/. See also "Proekt Strategii gosudarstvennoi molodezhnoi politiki," goal I.
[71] Address to the inter-ethnic forum Assembly of the People, "Dukhovno-kulturnoe razvitie naroda – osnova ukrepleniia gosudarstvennoi nezavisimosti Kazakhstana," printed in *Kazakhstanskaia pravda*, December 16, 2000.

Official Kazakhstani documents have thus been explicit in pursuing selective absorption, and in linking this to the imperatives of development under current global conditions. For example,

A highly effective system of education is one of the fundamental factors for ensuring stable growth of the economy of the country and of Kazakhstan society. The goal of the reform which is being undertaken in the system of education of our state is to ensure its qualitative transformation under conditions of a market economy, taking into account globalization.[72]

And as in Russia, so too in Kazakhstan, the imperatives of modernization are associated with "state support for entrepreneurial activities undertaken by youth."[73]

While policy in Azerbaijan has apparently been less concerned with the prospects of international integration than is the case in Russia and Kazakhstan, here too the law pledges state assistance for "professional development" and "entrepreneurial activities of youth, providing them with knowledge about the basis of a market economy."[74] Succinct to the point of being laconic, official Azerbaijani policy thus offered only barebones guidance for those working directly with youth.

Nevertheless, in practice many of the same absorptive patterns are evident in all three countries. For example, there has been a great deal of similarity in their efforts to integrate modern technocratic approaches into the educational system. Russia and Azerbaijan have signed the Bologna Accord, established by the EU to promote standardization of secondary education curricula and degree conferral among member states. Although Kazakhstan (as a non-European state) is not a potential signatory, the Ministry of Education has affirmed the validity of the Bologna principles. Leading institutions in each country have adopted the new degree conferral system, and the same trends toward standardization in curriculum, testing, and introduction of technology into the classroom are evident as well.[75] Indeed, when asked whether the Soviet or Western educational

---

[72] "Obrazovanie," Presidential decree no. 448, September 30, 2000. Almost the same wording was subsequently adopted in February 2004 in "Kontseptiia razvitiia obrazovaniia v Respublike Kazakhstan do 2015 goda," online at www.edu.gov.kz/.

[73] "O gosudarstvennoi molodezhnoi politike," article 9.

[74] "O molodezhnoi politike," article 4, point 4.

[75] For example, see "Rasskazy ministra obrazovaniia o khode modernizatsii," *Izvestiia*, October 25, 2003; "One of the Three Models Has to Be Taken as a Basis for the Reconstruction of Educational System," *AzadInform* 90, April 27, 1999, *Habarlar-L Digest* 796, April 27, 1999; "Kazgu: effektivnaia model vuza," *Kazakhstanskaia pravda*, June 28, 2000. See also David W. Chapman, John Weidman, Marc Cohen, and Malcolm Mercer, "The Search for Quality: A Five Country Study of National Strategies to Improve Educational Quality in Central Asia," *International Journal of Educational Development*,

model was preferable, Azerbaijan Minister of Education Misir Mardanov responded,

Without a doubt, Western! The Soviet system had its achievements, it is true. We must remember that it succeeded in eliminating illiteracy. The level of education in the Soviet Union was very high for its time . . . but it also had many shortcomings. It was too centralized, and much too closed to the outside world.[76]

State policy toward youth organizations

As the previous section demonstrates, there is virtually complete agreement among policymakers in each country regarding the key features of moral instruction, as well as the absolute necessity of providing such instruction to youth. However, a number of substantial disagreements exist over how to conduct this strategy, including what relations ought to be established between government authorities and youth organizations. Not surprisingly then, in official documents as well as in actual practice, a great deal of ambivalence surfaces about whether to control, coopt, cooperate with, or simply tolerate youth NGOs that demonstrate true independence. In this respect the general thrust of each state's approach to managing relations with youth organizations is broadly similar. In each case we find an effort to balance control and cooptation, while also maintaining at least a veneer of democratic accommodation. The following section discusses the substance of government policy in this area, including formal as well as informal arrangements intended to shape youth activity.

Again, a good place to begin is the official policy frameworks. In addition to structuring what might be called a loose hierarchical relationship between central and local bureaucracies, each national doctrine envisions a stable network of ties between state agencies and non-governmental youth organizations. At least on the face of it, such ties are expected to be based on mutual accommodation. Indeed, the language of the national policy documents suggests an elaborate social partnership in which young people would be accorded a significant role. The Russian draft program "Youth of Russia 2006–2010" proclaims "support for social initiatives of youth" as well as "creating conditions for . . . the development of civic activity of youth, [and] including youth in the activities of governing organs. . . ."[77] Similar ideas are also expressed in the Kazakhstan youth

---

25, No. 5 (September 2005): 514–30, which however emphasizes inadequacies in implementation.

[76] "Ministerstvo obrazovaniia nachinaet reformu," *Zerkalo*, July 1, 2000.

[77] "Molodezh Rossii na 2006–2010 gody," Article 6.2.

policy law, which calls for "attracting youth organizations . . . for consulting and coordinating activities in the areas of forming and implementing state youth policy."[78] Even the centralized tone of the Azerbaijani policy is softened on this issue, as it is noted that "The state creates conditions for the formation and development of youth organizations."[79]

To some extent this receptive approach is due to the perception that such an arrangement – or at least the image of such an arrangement – would be most acceptable to young people themselves. For example, in roundly endorsing decentralized youth NGOs, one Russian document noted that "young people prefer new forms of their participation in social life (informal groups, youth groups, realizing separate projects or programs) to the traditional youth organizations."[80] And naturally, the same close ties might afford authorities the ability to influence youth activities in a direction consistent with national policy. To quote from "Youth of Kazakhstan":

[W]orld practice shows that cooperation and the attraction of children's and youth social organizations to the resolution of actual problems of children and youth is the less expensive and most effective path. Under the conditions of partnership relations in the framework of such organizations optimal conditions are created for the socialization and self-realization of a young individual's personality.[81]

To borrow a phrase which crops up time and again in each country, youth are thus seen as a "strategic resource," potentially useful in achieving the state's goals if they can be successfully coopted. At the same time, this orientation reveals the delegitimation of the rigid Soviet-style control over social organizations, as well as the sense that such meddling will merely lead to a backlash. Thus, the very idea of forging a partnership with youth reflects a bow to the reality of an increasingly independent younger generation. In this respect it builds on lessons learned in the late Soviet period, when authorities belatedly attempted to coopt the

---

[78] See "O gosudarstvennoi molodezhnoi politike," article 14, points 1–3; also "Doktrina molodezhi Rossii," article 3.4.

[79] Funding is promised to groups whose objectives accord with national goals. "O molodezhnoi politike," articles 10.1 and 10.2. In these ways the law builds on more general provisions contained in earlier legislation on social organizations. See "O nepravitelstvennykh organizatsiiakh (obshchestvennykh obedineniiakh i fondakh)," Azerbaijan State Law no. 894, June 13, 2000.

[80] "Initsiativa molodykh – budushchee Rossii," p. 207. Similarly, according to the Kazakhstani "Conception," "it is precisely in a system of social organizations that the most favorable conditions develop for the realization of economic, innovative, creative activities of the younger generation." "Kontseptsiia gosudarstvennoi molodezhnoi politiki," section IV, point 6.

[81] Resolution of the Government of Kazakhstan No. 249, February 17, 2001, "Programma 'Molodezh Kazakhstana'," introduction to section 5. A similar orientation was evident in the previous "Kontseptsiia gosudarstvennoi molodezhnoi politiki," section I.

spreading "neformaly" youth groups instead of trying vainly to oppose them.[82] In reality, however, despite the veneer of social partnership, relations between youth organizations and central government agencies have at times been marked by considerable friction, and – especially in Kazakhstan and Russia – public debate. The key issues at stake concern the degree of autonomy to be accorded to youth organizations, as well as the extent to which the state – as opposed to youth NGOs or any other social organization – should guide the process of youth socialization.

As a result, the three states' approaches to youth organizations closely resemble each other in seeking to constrain the expression of political views within a formal, well-controlled institutional context. The ideal format is a government-run event in which delegates from "respectable" youth organizations are invited to participate. Furthermore, in an obvious institutional carry-over from the Soviet period, the state's bid for control also includes building a semi-official (or pseudo-independent) organization to oversee youth activities on the ground. The goal here is to essentially recreate the Komsomol, the pervasive institution in which all well-socialized and ambitious Soviet youth were expected to participate. Not only was the Komsomol a near-obligatory proving ground for aspiring party members and upwardly mobile professionals, it also represented an important mechanism for imparting official ideology in age-appropriate ways.[83] Although conditions have changed enormously and youth group membership no longer performs the same functions, one nevertheless finds unmistakable evidence of this effort to reproduce Soviet institutional forms. Moreover, in Russia and Kazakhstan steps have been taken to reinstate Soviet style youth practices, including rallies and construction brigades.[84]

Once again, a brief review of the approaches taken in each country toward relations between state and youth NGOs is helpful in establishing specific differences as well as the overall similarities between them.

Azerbaijan

Predictably, disagreements at the level of state policymaking are relatively invisible in Azerbaijan, where the authoritarian nature of rule has resulted in general compliance with presidential initiatives. Even here, however,

---

[82] On this point see Pilkington, *Russia's Youth and its Culture*, pp. 118–61.

[83] Jeffrey Hahn, "Political Socialization in the USSR: The Komsomol and the Educational System," unpublished PhD thesis, Duke University (1972).

[84] See, respectively, "Osnovnye napravleniia raboty FTsP 'Molodezh Rossii 2006–2010 gg.'," available online at http://kreml.org/interview; and "Kongress molodezhi Kazakhstana podderzhivaet initstiativy Glavy strany," *Kazinform*, March 31, 2004.

different approaches can be detected. For example, a 2002 bill drafted by the Ministry of Youth, Sports, and Tourism, which was intended to provide further assistance to youth organizations, was not passed due to resistance on budgetary and ideological grounds.[85] Yet despite such agreements below the surface, the dominant approach has been to engineer highly structured forms of collaboration between the state and compliant youth groups.

Such state sponsorship has been evident in the Azerbaijani National Youth Forums, at which upwardly mobile children of the elite are exhorted to promote various government initiatives. For example, as Minister of Youth, Sports, and Tourism Abulfaz Garaev informed participants in 2003, "We are sure that all the young people of Azerbaijan will vote for Ilham Aliev." Even in advance of its meeting, the Forum was "expected to pass a resolution, one of the clauses of which is expected to stipulate that all the young people of the Azeri towns and provinces will vote 'for successful furtherance of the democratic elections that were initiated in 1993'."[86] Not surprisingly, the organizers were not disappointed. To date, Azerbaijan has held four national forums, in 1996, 1999, 2001, and 2003, none of which has occasioned significant protest.

Azerbaijan also features an umbrella organization working under the state's aegis. This is the National Assembly of Youth Organizations of Azerbaijan (NAYORA), which was created in 1995 under the Ministry of Youth, Sport, and Tourism, and whose main goal is to coordinate the activities of youth groups.[87] Reflecting the more accommodating approach of the Ministry, NAYORA has not only tried to coopt youth groups, but has also served as a conduit for their demands.[88] By all accounts, however, NAYORA remains a fairly weak actor, both since its institutional support is limited to the Ministry and because it is severely under-funded, which hinders its ability to draw in NGOs.

Recent developments in Azerbaijan include the formation of a pro-presidential youth group as well as overt repression of oppositional youth

---

[85] Interviews, Ministry of Youth, Sports and Tourism, Baku, June 2003. The bill (in original and revised form, 1996 and 1997), translated by Vugar Yagubov, is available online at www.infoyouth.az.

[86] See "The Third Forum of Azeri Youth Has Taken Place in Baku," *Azer-Press News*, October 13, 2003, available via ISI Emerging Markets, online at: www.securities.com.

[87] See the NAYORA website at www.nayora.az. In this semi-official capacity NAYORA replaced the Union of Youth of Azerbaijan, which was established in 1993 as the first descendant of the Komsomol, but which was sidelined after Gaidar Aliev's return to power and the creation of the Ministry of Youth, Sports, and Tourism. Interview with Agadzhan Akhmedov, President, Union of Youth of Azerbaijan, Baku, June 2002.

[88] For example, "Molodezh predstavit pravitelstvu otchet po svoim problemam," Trend News Agency, November 5, 2004, available via ISI Emerging Markets.

organizations. According to one official account, the pro-presidential group, known as Irali, is intended to "unite [the] country's youth around President Ilham Aliyev for solution of all problems, democratization and further development of the country."[89] This unmistakably reflects anxiety about the possibility of an uprising, especially in the aftermath of events in Ukraine, Georgia, and Kyrgyzstan, in which the youth movement played a significant role.[90] By late 2005, along with growing activity on the part of radical youth groups, the regime's attempt to combine coercion with attempted cooptation was increasingly clear. This included a ban on student involvement in political actions (at Baku State University) and the arrests of NGO leaders, as well as an initiative to coordinate the "democratic" actions of establishment groups which participated in the November 2005 parliamentary elections.[91]

Kazakhstan

Much as in Azerbaijan, in Kazakhstan also, the government sought to manage the youth movement by incorporating it within a highly managed national forum. The vehicle chosen for this was the Youth Congress, which had its first meeting in 2001.[92] Over the following year, however, a number of youth groups emerged to challenge the government's plan.[93] As a result of their agitation, contentious politics flared into the open at the second Youth Congress, held in Astana in November 2002.[94] Intended

---

[89] "Republican Youth Movement 'Irali' Established," Sharg News Agency, August 27, 2005, available via ISI Emerging Markets.

[90] "Minister A. Garayev Urges Youth Not to Yield to Instigating Calls of Pro-Opposition Youth Movement 'Yokh'," Trend News Agency, March 24, 2005, available via ISI Emerging Markets.

[91] "Azeri Youth Activist Charged With Coup Attempt," BBC Monitoring, November 14, 2005; "Azeri Movement Condemns 'Political Crackdown' On Students," BBC Monitoring, December 14, 2005; "31 Youth Organizations Joined Statement On Democratic Elections," Trend News Agency, November 25, 2005; all available via ISI Emerging Markets. See also "Azerbaijani opposition youth groups form coalition," Radio Free Europe/Radio Liberty, Newsline, May 4, 2006.

[92] The first Youth Congress was held in Aktau, with Nazarbaev in attendance. "The First Youth Congress of Kazakhstan," Kazakh Information Agency, September 7, 2001.

[93] By far the most important of these youth groups to date has been the Youth Information Service of Kazakhstan (MISK), an NGO whose activities contributed to the rise of grassroots youth movements. Their main complaints have included a lack of proposed funding and institutional support. Interviews, MISK, Almaty, 2003 and 2006.

[94] The importance of this forum for youth policy development was immense, as underscored by the attendance of leading officials including Vice-Premier Baurzhan Mukhamedzhanov, as well as by a three hour meeting between its delegates, Nazarbaev, and the Council of Ministers. "President to Meet Members of the II Congress of the Youth," Kazakh Information Agency, October 30, 2002, available via ISI Emerging Markets.

to orchestrate public support for state policy while smothering what still appeared to be only minor rumblings of dissent, the Congress instead produced exactly the opposite outcome. Initially tensions flared over a range of practical matters, such as insufficient subsidies for student transportation, lack of jobs, and inadequate housing.[95] But increasingly, dissension turned on fundamental procedural matters, especially the directive nature of the conference agenda, which had been conceived before the delegates ever assembled.[96] The meeting was finally concluded without reaching any agreement, but, as already noted above, the disagreements which had been voiced continued to affect the parliament's work. By the end of the Congress, then, the youth movement had established itself as a national political force capable of influencing the development of official policy.

As a result, over the ensuing two years the Nazarbaev regime devoted additional resources to coopting the youth movement, with the goal of harnessing its strength for state and nation building. At least for the meantime, this effort appears to have been successful. A new national student organization, Alliance of Students of Kazakhstan, was established under the auspices of the Ministry of Education, and took over the lobbying activities which had previously galvanized the youth movement.[97] Beginning in 2004 a national "youth parliament" was convened in Almaty, consisting of a small group of about twenty representatives of various political parties and independent but reasonably compliant organizations, partly as a way of preparing the ground for subsequent Youth Congresses.[98] By the time the Fourth Congress was held in Astana in 2005, the government's new program for patriotic education was approved by the

---

[95] The issue of student transportation had already led to a large student protest in Almaty in September 2002, organized by MISK. "Almaty Youth Organizations Demand New Law on State Policy on Youth to Be Adopted," *Kazakh News*, September 5, 2002, available via ISI Emerging Markets.

[96] This revealed a basic incompatibility between the democratic assumptions of many representatives and the authoritarian assumptions of the congress organizers: the charter was only received shortly before congress opening, yet representatives were expected to sign it by the first evening (as indicated on the official congress program). "Konferentsii: V strane sozdana edinaia molodezhnaia organizatsiia – 'Kongress molodezhi Kazakhstana'," *Panorama*, November 15, 2002. See also Evgenia Sidorova, "Kazakstan: Soviet Tactics Making Comeback," Institute of War and Peace Reporting, *Reporting Central Asia*, No. 163, November 22, 2002, www.iwpr.net.

[97] The group's website is http://asker.kz.

[98] "Proba sil," *Kazakhstanskaia pravda*, August 12, 2004; also "V Sentiabre v Kazakhstane nachnet rabotu Molodezhnyi Palrlament," *Kazinform National Company*, July 12, 2005, available via ISI Emerging Markets. Following the Third Congress, formal cooperation agreements took place with the Ministry of Labor on issues related to employment opportunities for young people, and with the Ministry of Culture. "Znakovyi dokument dlia molodezhi," *Kazakhstanskaia pravda*, April 17, 2004; Nursultan Karimbaev, "Molodezh gotova konkurirovat i pobezhdat," *Kazakhstanskaia pravda*, April 2, 2004.

carefully selected delegates, and young people carried a gigantic national flag through the capital's streets.[99]

Several efforts have also been made to recreate the Komsomol, beginning with the formation of the Union of Youth of Kazakhstan (1991), which was intended to provide a seamless transition to post-Soviet organization. This was followed by For the Future of Kazakhstan (1997) and Choice of Youth (2001), which was initially headed by the president's daughter Dariga Nazarbaeva.[100] Because of the failure of each of these state-sponsored groups to rally grassroots support, yet another official youth organization – this time a true umbrella group – was conceived in 2002 and unveiled shortly before the Congress of Youth. Confusingly called the Congress of Youth of Kazakhstan, the new organization was explicitly designated a joint undertaking of the government and independent youth organizations, and was granted plenipotentiary authority for representing youth in policy matters.[101]

This became one of the most controversial issues debated at the second Congress of Youth in Astana. While nominally inclusive and fully representative, the Congress of Youth of Kazakhstan was in fact dominated by the government-backed group Choice of Youth. The plan was apparently to domesticate young people, both by appealing to their democratic instincts (the youth forum was structured as a pseudo-parliamentary meeting) and by offering monetary support for compliant youth NGOs. Instead the group became a lightning rod for criticism of government youth policy, and by extension the entire Nazarbaev regime. Ultimately, the final 2004 law dropped the designation of an official youth organization, and instead called for periodic "forums" to discuss youth policy in which representatives of all independent youth groups might be represented.[102] By 2005, however, along with the taming of the Fourth Youth Congress (as discussed above), a new government-backed group known as Kaisar was formed in a bid to manage the youth movement.[103]

[99] "Proekt vospitaniia chuvstv," *Kazakhstanskaia pravda*, September 20, 2005. Potentially troublesome NGOs were excluded from this gathering.

[100] For the Future of Kazakhstan quite explicitly sought to model itself after the Komsomol, on the grounds that this would provide vital organizational and ideological stability. Interview with Kazybek Shaikh, Deputy Director, For the Future of Kazakhstan, Almaty, 2001.

[101] "O gosudarstvennoi molodezhnoi politike v Respublike Kazakhstan [2002]," article 14, points 4–5.

[102] "O gosudarstvennoi molodezhnoi politike [2004]," article 14, point 4.

[103] "Molodezh Kazakhstana za Nursultana Nazarbaeva – 'Kaisar'," Kazinform National Company, October 7, 2005, available via ISI Emerging Markets. See also "Kazakh security body warns of possible 'conflict' by 'marginal youth'," *Newsline – Transcaucasus & Central Asia*, November 28, 2005, available via ISI Emerging Markets.

Russia

The controversy over state control of youth socialization has been especially evident in Russia, due to the relatively democratic nature of the legislative process. Thus, even while movement toward a unifying national youth policy appeared to be taking place, the underlying formulation of youth policy was becoming increasingly controversial. Unlike in Kazakhstan, however, such controversy appeared initially at the very apex of the policymaking structure. By 2002 two opposing positions were clearly expressed in the form of separate documents, each representing a fundamentally different perspective as well as a different institution. The Ministry of Education's Department of Youth Policy presented its "Initiative of Youth – The Future of Russia," in July.[104] This was countered in September (at President Putin's behest) by the State Council's "Doctrine of Youth of Russia."[105] These documents are worth examining more closely, since they provide an insight into the nature of debates which are still ongoing – and which also exist in more veiled form in Kazakhstan and Azerbaijan – over key issues relevant to globalization, youth culture, and national identity formation.

The document issued by the Department of Youth Policy, a rambling, 228 page affair, spoke at length about the goals and assumptions of state youth policy. As reflected in its very title, the overwhelming thrust of the document was to foster independent youth initiative, and, on this basis, to include young people directly in policymaking.[106] In addition, the Department's statement commented approvingly on the supposed evolution of youth policy in the West, from "natural paternalism" in the 1950s, to a "planetary approach," which called for "cohesion of youth of different regions and countries of the world for solving contemporary problems on an equal footing with adults."[107] The Department's approach was thus to encourage moral education and, at the same time, to empower youth to solve its own problems.[108] This was presented as being clearly preferable to the outmoded, command methods associated with the Soviet period, in which the youth was viewed as an object to be molded according to rigid ideological strictures.

The contrast between the two documents could hardly be more striking. Unlike the Department of Youth Policy's wish to accord youth organizations a significant role in policymaking, the State Council's "Doctrine" declared a need to "change the focus of the government review" of youth

---

[104] "Initsiativa molodykh – budushchee Rossii."   [105] "Doktrina molodezhi Rossii."
[106] "Initsiativa molodykh – budushchee Rossii," e.g., pp. 41–43.   [107] Ibid., p. 201.
[108] Ibid., p. 52.

policy: away from "providing help and guardianship for youth," to "active moral education and drawing youth into social and state structures." In other words, as its authors stated flatly, the objective should be "to take the process of socialization of youth under state control."[109] This was to be achieved through a combination of propaganda and highly centralized institutional oversight. In particular, the State Council called for creating specialized media organs, making schools once more into centers of moral instruction, and even forming a new "federal service for socialization."[110] Among its suggested methods for achieving proper socialization were developing an official "Doctrine of Moral Education," publishing a series of "Family Guide" handbooks to help parents instruct children, and putting out flyers called "You Ought to Know This," which would inform young people of "permissible behavior in problematic situations."[111]

The distance between the opposing positions was articulated by the principals involved, in a remarkable open commentary published in a prominent journal in the spring of 2003.[112] Not only did the representatives of each institution publicly blame the other for deficiencies in youth policy, they also frankly acknowledged the underlying basis for the dispute. The exchange vividly reveals the issues at stake in contention over youth policy.

The head of the State Council's working group, Iurii Neelov (who was also governor of the Yamal-Nenets region) insisted on the need to set standards for youth policy which would be binding throughout the Russian Federation.

Today a common federal approach does not exist. Therefore in the subjects [i.e., regions of Russia] youth policy is realized insofar as there is an understanding of the significance of the problems by the governors. In the doctrine minimal demands are formulated, which must be fulfilled not only at the all-Russian level, but also at the level of the subjects of the RF and local self-government.[113]

For Neelov, in other words, the essence of youth policy was state building, especially the closer integration of the Russian periphery within a system of centralized rule. Building on these points, the working group's deputy head, Sergei Anokhin, went directly to the ideological heart of the matter. "Everyone wants to get away from Soviet experience, to do everything in a modern way somehow," he noted. "But it does not work. They want it to be like in America or West Europe, but our mentality

---

[109] "Doktrina molodezhi Rossii," article 1.   [110] *Ibid.*, articles 3.2.1–3 and 4.2.6.
[111] *Ibid.*, Supplement, 3.2.
[112] The article in question included statements by the head and deputy head of the working group under the State Council as well as the deputy head of the Ministry's Department of Youth Policy. "Molodezh osobogo naznacheniia," *Vremia*, April 23, 2003.
[113] *Ibid.*

and economic base do not allow this." Instead, Anokhin unapologeti-
cally claimed, "The government must control the process of socialization
of youth, its entry into society." While accepting the possibility that youth
organizations could seize the chance to work with the state in formulating
such means and ends, Anokhin flatly rejected the idea that the "initiative
of youth" was worth cultivating per se, or that policymaking should be
predicated on the opinions of youth.

> One also sometimes reads that the doctrine does not consider the interests of
> young people themselves, they do not like it. Excuse me, what are we about? The
> doctrine is not written from the position of youth, but from the position of the
> state. This is a thing of principal importance. The state determines what is neces-
> sary for it in the future, what kind of people it needs. What does it matter what the
> youth wants . . . Maybe [the youth] want only discotheques and nothing more.
> And there is the kind of youth that wants to inject itself and lose consciousness.
> So what, we are going to write about that?![114]

In response, barbed criticism of the State Council's position was
expressed by Tatiana Petrova, Deputy Director of the Department of
Youth Policy. Petrova flatly stated that "without the changes proposed by
the Ministry of Education, the text is not viable. There are many passages
here which even contradict common sense." In particular, she pointed to
the Doctrine's intent to "exert systematic influence on the processes of
socialization of the younger generation," which she equated with illegitimate Soviet and fascist practices. "In my view," Petrova insisted, "control
over socialization – that is what Hitler and Stalin dreamed of. Why is it
now necessary to drag out this moss-covered idea into the light?!"[115]

Such views were entirely consistent with the Department of Youth
Policy's official set of recommendations for working with youth organizations, which stressed the "partnership foundations" of collaborative
work. "Control over these organizations is absolutely inadmissible, [as
is their] administration by state organs of education or heads of educational institutions."[116] In short, these were truly fundamental differences
in terms of the overall orientation toward youth organizations, and thus
relations between state and society as a whole.

Notwithstanding such disagreements, or perhaps because of them, the
preferred approach for managing relations with youth NGOs is through
an orchestrated consultative process. The preferred vehicle for this is
the Youth Chamber, which was established under the state Duma in
2001. Intended as an organ for consultative input on the development

---

[114] *Ibid.*   [115] *Ibid.*
[116] "O detskikh i molodezhnykh obedineniiakh," *Narodnoe obrazovanie*, Nos. 4–5 (April–
May 2000): 340–3.

of youth policy, the Youth Chamber brings together members of parliament, the ministries, local government, and youth NGOs.[117] Still another, free-standing Youth Chamber has recently been created (with numerous regional-level chapters as well as a national body), consisting of representatives of officially registered and acceptable youth NGOs. It thus parallels the Public Chamber, which was formed in 2005 in order to manage civil society by incorporating select representatives into the policy process. According to Speaker of the Duma Boris Gryzlov,

In this country we have hundreds, thousands of youth organizations. They want to make policy themselves – to send their representatives to the Public Chamber . . . in meetings they speak about this directly. Young people do not like it when things are explained to them, as if to little children, how to live, how to love the Fatherland or how to vote.[118]

Here again, the active involvement of young people in social and political life – and the demands this places on state institutions – has a direct bearing on policy. Reflecting a similar approach, the federal program "Youth of Russia" envisions a combination of delegating limited autonomy to youth NGOs, while at the same time maintaining a critical degree of control by the state. Thus, on the one hand, the youth is viewed as "not so much a target group of the Program, but as a subject and primary cadre resource." And yet, in almost the same breath the document adds, "The realization of the complex directions of the Program, which touch on the youth sphere as a whole, foresees the creation of a centralized mechanism for their coordination and dissemination on the regional and municipal levels."[119]

Much as in Azerbaijan and Kazakhstan, in Russia the relevant Komsomol-like group is the Russian Union of Youth, which was formed in 1990 as successor to the faltering Komsomol. A vast umbrella organization which boasts over 200,000 members, the Union collaborates closely with the Department of Youth Policy under the Ministry of

---

[117] "Reglament Obshchestvennoi Molodezhnoi Palaty," available online at: www.duma.gov.ru/family/pagepych.htm. However, pursuant to a change in the membership rules, direct participation in the Youth Chamber is limited to representatives of youth NGOs. See InfoCom – State Duma Press Service, June 29, 2005, available via ISI Emerging Markets. There also exists a Youth Parliamentary Assembly, formed in 2003.

[118] "Legkikh deneg ne byvaet, esli govorit o chestnykh dengakh," *Moskovskii komsomolets*, August 11, 2005.

[119] "Molodezh Rossii na 2006–2010 gody," Article 2. See also "Proekt Strategii gosudarstvennoi molodezhnoi politiki," Article 2.3, where this orientation is defended as most suitable for Russia (in comparison to Belarus, on the one hand, and "countries with developed and self-sufficient institutions of civil society," like the US and Great Britain, on the other).

Education and Science. In keeping with the new policy guidelines, beginning in late 2000 regular meetings began to be conducted between the Department and youth organizations associated with the Union, which were consulted on various topical issues relevant to policymaking. According to former Minister of Education Vladimir Filippov, the purpose of this arrangement was to facilitate coordination between various state agencies seeking to work with local youth organizations in accordance with the goals of the official national program.[120]

In addition, a pro-government (and pro-Putin) group called Walking Together emerged in 2001. For the most part Walking Together made itself known by glorifying the president in terms reminiscent of Soviet times, and by aggressively advocating a new form of ideological rectitude, including several well-publicized attempts to ban the works of prominent authors.[121] The group was superceded in 2005 by another, called Nashi (Ours), which possesses essentially the same attributes.[122] From an official perspective, Nashi offers a useful vehicle for enlisting youth support for various policies, as well as for encouraging service in the army and the state bureaucracy. Reports suggest that the organization has received extensive support from the Kremlin following the Orange Revolution in Ukraine.[123]

Reflections

In sum, already by 2004 something broadly similar was taking place in each of the three countries being examined here. By this time, the youth movement in each country had both gathered strength and splintered. The main national parties (dominated directly or indirectly by the president) had begun to compete for the support of young people, who were seen as potential voters and as key to the future prospects for legitimacy. Each party had its own youth wing, providing an avenue for ambitious young careerists. In all three countries something similar to the

[120] "Minobrazovanie Rossii zakliuchit soglashenie s Natsionalnym Sovetom molodezhnykh i detskikh obedinenii Rossii," July 15, 2003, available online at www.Philippov.ru, Official Website of Vladimir Mikhailovich Filippov, currently a senior government advisor.
[121] "Reincarnation of Soviet Youth League Blessed by Putin, says Russian TV," Russian NTV television broadcast, Moscow, in Russian, October 29, 2001, BBC Monitoring, October 29, 2001, available via ISI Emerging Markets. See also "Putin Youth Movement Finds Another Literary Target," Radio Free Europe/Radio Liberty, Newsline, January 3, 2003, www.rferl.org.
[122] "Putin i 'Nashi' vstretilis' v Sochi," Vesti, May 18, 2006, www.vesti.ru.
[123] See Robert Coalson, "Russian Youth Group 'Nashi' Gathers Momentum," Radio Free Europe/Radio Liberty, Newsline, June 3, 2005, available online at www.rferl.org; also Claire Bigg, "Russia: Here Comes The Sun For Putin's Patriotic Youth," Radio Free Europe/Radio Liberty, Newsline, July 20, 2005, available online at www.rferl.org.

Komsomol had reemerged, while nevertheless remaining a semi-official organization whose legitimacy was suspect, and which faced at least some degree of competition from opposing youth organizations. On the one hand, then, the youth constituted a subject, an emerging political force capable of influencing future youth policy formation. On the other hand, it was the object of organized efforts intended to harness its energy for political reasons. The development of youth policy had thus become thoroughly intertwined with the larger political struggles ongoing in Russia, Kazakhstan, and Azerbaijan. This continues to be true today.

For these reasons, official national youth policy is a highly contested area, encapsulating the disputes which surface in popular discourse concerning the future evolution of society and collective identity. Debate centers on exactly where to set boundaries of voluntary action, or how much leeway to grant the youth movement as a fully autonomous actor. Efforts to manage the process fully from above are evident in Azerbaijan, although the experience in Kazakhstan has increasingly moved in this direction also. In Russia, the picture remains more mixed, as debate continues over the advisability – and practicality – of trying to orchestrate youth activities, as opposed to fostering a genuine dialogue between youth NGOs and the state. Similarly, the extent to which such issues find overt expression at any one moment varies in the three states of interest to us here. Azerbaijan, with its highly authoritarian system and deferential political style, evinces an apparently less disputatious policy development process than is the case in Kazakhstan or (still more so) in Russia. Although disagreements among Azerbaijani policymakers do exist, their expression is generally oblique at best, and the documents framing official policy are few in number, spare in content, and uniform in approach. Disagreements that do surface often take the form of explosive encounters between organized protesters and the police. In contrast, contention in Kazakhstan and Russia is often noisy, and is clearly reflected in public documentation.

Such differences notwithstanding, on the whole the official youth policies of these countries are remarkably similar, both with regard to the hybrid content of prescriptive national youth identity and the general process of engaging young people. This appears to be the result of several factors. One, certainly, is the shared cultural propensities of post-Leninist states. This is evident in the tendency to issue cultural directives, itself a vivid example of institutional holdover from Soviet times.[124] Nevertheless, as a reflection of what we might call post-Leninist culture, it is striking that these impulses to control social and ideological processes is

---

[124] Altstadt, "Azerbaijan's Struggle Toward Democracy."

checked – partly from within the state, though largely from without – by a nascent democratic or "civil society" norm. The result in each country has been an ambivalent effort to maintain a substantial degree of central control over youth organizations, while at the same time conceding to them elements of superficial as well as very real autonomy. Such autonomy is more pronounced and evident in Russia than in Kazakhstan or Azerbaijan, but it is nevertheless palpable in each state.

A second factor explaining the similarity in official youth policy is the existence of shared institutional ties, especially within the intergovernmental framework of the Commonwealth of Independent States (CIS). Despite its manifold weaknesses, the CIS has nevertheless provided a forum within which officials from various branches of government are able to exchange ideas and at times coordinate policymaking. Among other things, this includes periodic meetings between ministers or deputy ministers charged with managing various aspects of youth affairs.[125] While it is often difficult to see such meetings as a "cause" of state policy, official contacts do appear to contribute to shared learning and a degree of legislative uniformity. Indeed, the nature and timing of Ilham Aliev's creation of a pro-presidential youth group in Azerbaijan strongly suggested the direct influence of Russian ideas.[126]

Yet another factor is the new states' comparable positions on the periphery of the world system, and the broadly equivalent socialization pressures to which they are exposed. Officials at all levels are aware of international norms and standards in the area of youth policy, and of the work being conducted in this area by the UN and other leading IGOs.[127] Russia and Azerbaijan are also members of the Council of Europe (since 1996 and 2001, respectively). The Council's Directorate of Youth and Sport provides its own set of guidelines for developing youth policy, and

---

[125] This is the Council for Heads of State Organs on Youth Affairs, which includes Azerbaijan, Armenia, Belarus, Kazakhstan, Kyrgyzstan, Moldova, Russia, Tajikistan, and Ukraine. See "Lushche ploshchadki – molodym," *Kazakhstanskaia pravda*, October 1, 2003. The significance of such meetings within the CIS framework was noted in interviews conducted at the Russian Ministry of Education, Moscow, June 2003. On the CIS framework generally, see John P. Willerton and Geoffrey Cockerham, "Russia, the CIS and Eurasian Interconnections," in James Sperling, Sean Kay, and S. Victor Papacosma, eds., *Limiting Institutions? The Challenge of Eurasian Security Governance* (Manchester and New York: Manchester University Press, 2003), pp. 185–207.

[126] Baku had recently been visited by a delegation from the Russian Ministry of Education and Science, including Sergei Apatenko, the head of the Department of Youth Policy. "Pervyi vitze-spiker Milli Medzhilis prinial delegatsiiu Ministerstva Obrazovaniia i Nauka Rossii," Trend News Agency, February 3, 2005.

[127] For example, see the remarks by Galina Kuprianina, Head of the Department of Youth Policy at the Ministry of Education, stenograph, meeting of the Social Youth Chamber, Russian Duma, April 21, 2003, online at www.duma.gov.ru/family/workpych.htm.

ministerial officials have participated in seminars conducted under its auspices. Members in good standing are expected to observe institutional norms such as "achieving greater transparency, flexibility and rapidity in the implementation of youth policies" and "[encouraging] young people's participation in civil society."[128] Participating in the Council (and formally reproducing its tenets) provides a way of authenticating claims of Europeanness, and thereby enhancing domestic and international legitimacy.[129] It is true that Azerbaijan, and to a lesser extent Russia, have often honored various membership requirements in the breach, especially those regarding local democracy and human rights. And as we have seen, nods in the direction of transparency and civil society are rather perfunctory in these states (again, especially in Azerbaijan). Yet to the extent that such ideas are articulated and exert constraining effects on official conduct, conforming to the requirements of IGOs apparently does play a role.[130] Even for Kazakhstan, which has been denied membership in the Council of Europe, using similar democratic language serves political and diplomatic functions.

The question which remains is how these official policy guidelines are translated into the day-to-day work of identity formation in the sphere of youth socialization. The following chapters examine this process in some detail, in order to elucidate the linkages between discourse and practice, and to explore the role of agency in constructing national youth identity. As we will see, the thrust of local practice is quite different from what is envisioned by most central policymakers. That is, while modified Leninist assumptions continue to shape a largely top-down or state-managed approach on the part of central policy institutions, at the local level a great deal of spontaneous collaboration emerges in everyday practice, tracing a dense social network of entrepreneurship.

---

[128] The Directorate's webpage is www.coe.int/T/E/Cultural_Co-operation/Youth/. See also "On the Youth Policy of the Council of Europe," resolution 6, adopted by the Committee of Ministers, April 16, 1998. Available on-line at http://cm.coe.int/ta/res/1998/98x6.htm.

[129] See Jeffrey Checkel, "Norms, Institutions, and National Identity in Contemporary Europe," *International Studies Quarterly* 43, No. 1 (March 1999): 83–114.

[130] How much is unclear. The importance of the Council of Europe framework is emphasized by Ibrahim Ismailov, an Azerbaijani scholar who focuses on youth policy issues. Private correspondence. However, this was disputed by Namik Chefarov, head of the Department of Youth, Azerbaijan Ministry of Youth, Sports and Tourism, in an interview conducted in Baku, June 2003.

5　Collaborative entrepreneurship

As we saw in chapter 3, the popular discourse in these post-Soviet places is preoccupied with modernization, retraditionalization, and resistance to dissolution (in both literal and figurative terms). And as discussed in chapter 4, much the same holds for national identity policy. The official platforms developed in all three countries make it possible, at least in the abstract, to engage in identity construction at the national and local levels through a combination of strategic innovation and "invented" and resurrected traditions. Ideally, such identity constructs must then be convincingly articulated and enacted, so that young people internalize and reproduce them through their own actions. But what does this imply for the *process* of youth identity construction? In particular, through what modalities do those who implement policy seek to mold the attitudes and conduct of young people? To what extent does this involve interaction among them, in what contexts, and to what particular ends? As the following discussion shows, in each city a complex course of action unfolds whereby the state, acting through its formal auspices, attempts to establish national youth identity while at the same time devolving extensive responsibilities to actors at lower levels of authority. The latter actors, in turn, attempt to foster essentially the same norms and practices both independently and in conjunction with one another as well as the state. The result is not only a striking affinity of values, but also a confluence of organized efforts.

As the previous paragraph suggests, thinking of state actors as social intermediaries also highlights the role of extra-state actors who are also engaged in diffuse policymaking endeavors (including collective identity construction). This, in turn, invokes the role of the entrepreneur, defined by Moe as an "individual who exploits profitable opportunities by providing, or promising to provide, services that are designed to attract support from individuals who might find them of value."[1] Cultural

---

[1] Terry M. Moe, *The Organization of Interests* (Chicago: University of Chicago Press, 1980), p. 36.

entrepreneurship may be considered a particular form of this general category of action. Following Crawford Young, a cultural entrepreneur will be understood here as someone who strategically fashions and activates identity; i.e., who "devotes himself to enlarging the symbolic, solidary resources of the community" by mobilizing dormant or unselfconscious cultural beliefs and practices into overt, ideologized symbols of belonging, thus creating a "catechism of identity."[2] In addition to mobilizing dormant or unselfconscious beliefs, cultural entrepreneurship may also consist of cobbling them together, framing or mediating flows of ideas, and selling them to the public. Thus in Shaw's words (although he uses the term "animateur"), a cultural entrepreneur "is dedicated to the widest cultural diffusion *and* jealous of the standards of the culture he is diffusing."[3] Specifically with regard to national identity formation, then, a cultural entrepreneur is someone able to navigate institutional structure and social process so as to broker specific identity outcomes and assist in their dissemination. This often involves close interaction with state officials, who may respond favorably in hopes of using entrepreneurial initiatives and broad social networks in order to achieve their policy goals.

Cultural entrepreneurship need not be geared to the benefit of society at large; it may instead reflect sectarian or elitist orientations.[4] Nevertheless, with respect to the propagation of national identity entrepreneurial action is generally geared to mass audiences and framed in highly accessible terms. The latter point is important, since art or culture left uninterpreted can serve various purposes or no purpose at all, if its preferred symbolic content is unintelligible to the masses. Therefore cultural entrepreneurs provide the education necessary to "enable people to appropriate the value of a work of art."[5] Such entrepreneurship is all the more crucial under conditions of uncertainty and dense exposure to the outside world. Indeed, by virtue of their negotiating position along the frontier of cultural exchange, entrepreneurs are not only attentive to the national circulation of ideas and aesthetics but are often attuned to receiving and transmitting

---

[2] Crawford Young, *The Politics of Cultural Pluralism* (Madison: University of Wisconsin Press, 1976), pp. 45–46.

[3] Roy Shaw, "The Cultural 'Animateur' in Contemporary Society," *Cahiers d'Histoire Mondiale*, 14 (1972), p. 462.

[4] For example, entrepreneurs may be private actors with strong class roots, whose function is to more narrowly link status with culture. See Paul DiMaggio, "Cultural Entrepreneurship in Nineteenth-Century Boston: The Creation of an Organizational Base for High Culture in America," in Chandra Mukerji and Michael Schudson, eds., *Rethinking Popular Culture: Contemporary Perspectives in Cultural Studies* (Berkeley: University of California Press, 1991), pp. 374–97.

[5] Shaw, "The Cultural 'Animateur'," p. 464.

international ideas.[6] In doing so they move back and forth between formal and informal, public and private, and domestic and international spheres of society, acting to make each intelligible in terms of the other.

In order to explore this process further (and to better evaluate the role of agency in the construction of national youth identity) it is necessary to distinguish three groups of entrepreneurs: state, sub-state, and non-state. For the purposes of this discussion, "state" actors are officials working within the formal governmental and bureaucratic apparatus at the central, regional, and local levels, who make and/or oversee the implementation of youth policy.[7] At the central level this would include individuals working in the relevant ministries as well as members of parliament, especially those directly involved in youth policy matters. In these three cities, however, the state refers to both regional and municipal agencies: the governor's apparatus and regional branches of central ministries, as well as the mayor's apparatus and city government organs. The "state" designation also includes government-organized groups (so-called GONGOs) whose function is to orchestrate NGO activity in this sphere, as discussed in chapter 4. In contrast, "sub-state" actors refers to those in the employ of the state, but who neither exercise authority over policymaking nor hold others accountable for its implementation.[8] As we encounter them here, sub-state actors include teachers, directors of orphanages, librarians, school psychologists, and the staff of state-sponsored youth centers, all of whom are directly involved in the day-to-day work of youth identity construction. Finally, "non-state" actors are those with no formal connection to the process of making, overseeing, or implementing government policy. Such actors are overwhelmingly NGO actors involved in youth affairs, including stereotypical activists as well as independent solo artists and culture afficionados.

---

[6] This provides a potential way of linking the study of cultural globalization with the study of transnational diffusion of norms in the literature on social movements. See Keck and Sikkink, *Activists Beyond Borders*.

[7] In Azerbaijan the Ministry of Youth, Sport, and Tourism is responsible for overseeing youth affairs generally and for supervising participation of other central as well as local agencies for the implementation of youth policy. In Russia, there exists a Department of Youth Policy under the Ministry of Education, which is tasked with interagency planning and with coordinating national with regional and local youth programs. In Kazakhstan analogous functions are served by the Ministry of Culture, Information, and Social Accord in conjunction with the Ministry of Education.

[8] This is analogous to what Foster refers to as "incorporated associations," or associations that are "structurally or operationally connected with the state in some significant way," yet are "formally distinct from . . . the state administration." Kenneth Foster, "Associations in the Embrace of an Authoritarian State: State Domination of Society?" *Studies in Comparative International Development*, 35, No. 4 (Winter 2001), p. 87.

Before examining the interventions they make into youth culture it will first be helpful to situate these categories of actors by looking briefly at central–local relations in the sphere of youth policy, especially the degree of autonomy accorded to each. Once having established these ground rules, it will then be possible to examine the actors themselves, including how they stand in relation to each other as well as to official policy and social discourse, and how they try to shape national identity through direct encounters with youth.

Local governance: vertical and horizontal connections

Realizing the ambitious goals of official youth policy demands careful planning as well as policy coordination among state agencies at the central, regional, and local levels. In addition, it entails directives for state-supported media programming and various other public presentations devoted to appropriate cultural themes. As we have already seen, the youth policies in each country have anticipated the further development of national media outlets aimed at youth audiences. They have also called for creating extensive links between national and local authorities, as part of a systematic effort to implement policy directives and monitor progress toward their achievement. And yet the reality is far more nuanced, as local officials effectively manage everyday policy in highly autonomous and flexible ways.

Kazakhstan provides a good example, where already by 1999 the "Conception" called for establishing close ties with local government departments. Day-to-day oversight was to take place through synchronized efforts on the part of the Ministry of Education and Science, regional branches of the Ministry of Culture, and local officials.[9] And in fact the general approach of orchestrating hierarchical links between state agencies has been consistently maintained, as the 2004 law instructs the Ministry of Culture to "coordinate the activities of central and local executive organs" in carrying out youth policy.[10] In Almaty the regional bureau of the Ministry of Culture works with the city administration's Department of Education, Science, and Culture to ensure that the spirit of national policy is observed. Representing the fruit of these efforts, a citywide program called "Youth and Teenagers" was begun in January 2001, dedicated to building additional youth centers and generally promoting moral and patriotic feelings among the younger

---

[9] "Kontseptsiia gosudarstvennoi molodezhnoi politiki," section V; also "Ved zhizn na meste ne stoit . . . ," *Kazakhstanskaia pravda*, August 5, 2000.
[10] "O gosudarstvennoi molodezhnoi politike," article 4, point 2.2.

generation.[11] In another step which testified to the increasing focus on youth policy, a new Council for Affairs of Youth was created in December 2002 to work alongside the preexisting Department of Youth Affairs under the mayor's office.[12]

Moreover, the bid to re-create the Komsomol at the national level has been paralleled in Almaty (and several other cities) by the formation of a local official youth organization called Talapker (also known as the State Foundation for the Development of Youth Policy). Working under the mayor's apparatus, it provides monetary and other forms of assistance to NGOs, and attempts to coordinate youth group activities.[13] In doing so it also cooperates closely with the ruling party Otan, implementing national policy guidelines and often co-sponsoring events.[14] Talapker's leader at the time, Arman Kudaibergenov, attended the volatile second Congress of Youth, where he pushed for the rapid adoption of federal law on youth policy despite burgeoning protests by independent youth organizations.[15] More routinely, Talapker oversees the opening of new municipal youth centers and organizes numerous events such as "City NEXT," and "Independent Generation," at which local youth are mobilized to show support for city and national policy.[16]

At first glance, the practice of carrying out policy in Kazakhstan suggests a certain degree of deference on the part of local authorities. Thus after the national-level draft law was published in May 2002, the Almaty

[11] I base the observations in this section on interviews conducted at the regional branch of the Ministry of Culture and the city level Department of Education, Science, and Culture. For a discussion of the 2001 program see "Molodym vezde u nas doroga," *Ekspress-K online*, No. 21 (14934), February 2, 2002, available online at www.express-k.kz/. For a brief description of the follow-up version for 2003–05, also entitled "Youth and Teenagers," see "Lushche ploshchadki – molodym," *Kazakhstanskaia pravda*, October 1, 2003.

[12] The Council consists of rectors of local universities, representatives of the city parliament, officials of relevant city government departments, and the heads of select youth organizations. "O Sovete po delam molodezhi pri akime goroda Almaty," Decree 5/813, December 23, 2002.

[13] Decree of Almaty city Akimat, No. 118, March 2, 2001; Interviews with Arman Kudaibergenov, then president of Talapker, Almaty, June 2001 and May 2002.

[14] For example an anti-drug, anti-AIDS rally in Almaty, called "We Choose Life," was co-sponsored by Otan and Talapker. "Skazhi 'net' narkotikam," *Kazakhstanskaia pravda*, June 29, 2004. See also "Otan Party Cares About the Youth," Kazinform, May 14, 2004, available from ISI Emerging Markets, online at www.securities.com.

[15] "Konferentsii: V strane sozdana edinaia molodezhnaia organizatsiia – 'Kongress molodezhi Kazakhstana'," *Panorama*, November 15, 2002. See also Evgenia Sidorova, "Kazakstan: Soviet Tactics Making Comeback," Institute of War and Peace Reporting, *Reporting Central Asia*, No. 163, November 22, 2002, online at: www.iwpr.net.

[16] "Molodym vezde u nas doroga," *Ekspress-K online*, No. 21, February 2, 2002, available online at www.express-k.kz. Following adoption of the Almaty program "Youth and Teenagers" in 2001, monies were allocated for opening new youth centers. Decree 5/812, December 23, 2002, "O dvorovykh klubakh goroda Almaty."

authorities moved to implement it locally – despite the fact that it was not legally binding and that it continued to encounter resistance within parliament and from certain youth organizations.[17] However, although city officials tasked with overseeing youth policy remain cognizant of the themes set out in Nazarbaev's "2030 Plan" and collaborate with their counterparts in the ministerial hierarchy, they also have considerable leeway. The Department of Education, Science, and Culture routinely identifies its own priorities and drafts plans for achieving them without any operational interference from outside.[18] This combination of general subordination and specific autonomy is also characteristic of relations between central and local authorities in Russia and Azerbaijan.

In Azerbaijan local government agencies were also authorized to draft their own programs, which according to national directives "must correspond to the goals, principles and directions of [national] youth policy."[19] And here too, the vision of a hierarchical system of oversight and financial accountability is borne out at the local level in Baku. The key agency overseeing youth affairs is the Main Bureau of Youth, Sport, and Tourism of the Baku City Administration, which in the words of its deputy director, Nasimi Cabbarli, is "one link in the government chain." The Main Bureau contrives its own plan for local youth policy based on national guidelines, often working closely with the Ministry of Youth, Sports, and Tourism to produce festivals or to conduct research and monitoring. Baku is, after all, by far and away the most important city in Azerbaijan, and the Ministry's offices are located nearby. Nevertheless, just as in Almaty, the Main Bureau's plan is drawn up independently, with the Ministry merely providing a formal endorsement. And in this respect the previous command mechanisms of precise specification and rigorous fulfillment has gone by the wayside. For Cabbarli the change is momentous. As he puts it, "In the time of the USSR of course everything was different, now things are set up entirely differently."[20] Regardless of its continued vertical features, then, in the life of a bureaucrat the new system affords far greater flexibility and local control.

Much the same approach prevails in Astrakhan, where local authorities have drafted a framework program requiring "coordination of the work of regional institutions and agencies on questions of implementing state

[17] "O merakh po dalneishei aktivizatsii gosudarstvennoi molodezhnoi politiki v gorode Almaty," Decree 5/734, November 18, 2002.

[18] Interview with Gulia Karsybekova, director of the Department of Education, Science, and Culture, Almaty, June 2002.

[19] "O molodezhnoi politike," article 12, points 1 and 2.

[20] Personal correspondence with Nasimi Cabbarli, deputy head, Main Bureau of Youth, Sport, and Tourism of the Baku City Administration, February 2004.

youth policy in Astrakhan."[21] As a reflection of the top-down aspect of youth policy, all of the goals identified at the national level – patriotism, employment, inter-ethnic tolerance, psychological wellbeing, charitable work, supplementary schooling, and prevention of AIDS and other forms of deviant behavior – are systematically pursued under the framework of the regional program.[22] Ekaterina Lukianova, director of the Astrakhan region Committee on Youth Policy, is formally subordinate to the Ministry of Education and Science and is charged with meeting its policy goals. On the other hand, Astrakhan has had a working youth policy in place since 1997, and from Lukianova's perspective the national Doctrine and other program documents merely provide "recommendations." In formulating plans for regional policy the Committee is guided by contacts with central authorities as well as authorities in other regions of Russia, but – as in Baku – the final plan is the Committee's own doing, and Moscow provides only a rubber stamp.

The situation in Astrakhan is somewhat unusual because Lukianova is a deputy-governor. Not only does this give her special stature at the regional level, thereby allowing her to exert extensive influence on local policy development, but it also strengthens the region's visibility in the eyes of national policymakers. As a result, in 2003 the Astrakhan region Social Service for Youth was designated as one of fifteen nationwide "experimental centers" tasked with training experts, developing new approaches for working with young people, and disseminating lessons learned from this experience.[23] Yet in the most important ways Astrakhan appears to be quite representative of regional practice across Russia. Here as elsewhere, the general approach followed by the Ministry of Education is to grant significant autonomy to regional branches, and to use specific local experiences as a way of informing and cajoling other regional branches to work conscientiously.[24] This may be changing, however, as part of the general drift towards authoritarianism and centralization under Putin. The Doctrine drafted by the State Council envisions a far more

[21] "O gosudarstvennoi molodezhnoi politike v Astrakhanskoi oblasti," Astrakhan region law No. 37, October 6, 1997 (with revisions February 11, 2002), article 10. The region's Committee on Youth Policy also passed a measure aimed at cooperating with federal authorities in carrying out national programs and conducting sociological research on youth and children's organizations. Protocol No. 5, September 27, 2002.

[22] "Realizovyvalas oblastnaia tselevaia Programma gosudarstvennoi molodezhnoi politiki na territorii Astrakhanskoi oblasti na 2001–2003 gody," from *Sotsialno-ekonomicheskoe razvitie Astrakhanskoi oblasti v 2002 godu*, available online at www.astrakhan.net.

[23] Interviews at the Department of Youth Policy; also "Official communication from G.A. Kuprianova," Director of the Department of Youth Policy, Russian Ministry of Education, No. 15-52-325/15-01-21, April 16, 2003.

[24] "Initsiativa molodykh – budushchee Rossii," pp. 149–99; also "Molodezh Rossii."

standardized system, and this vision appears to have been translated into institutional form in mid-2004 by the creation of two new federal organs tasked with monitoring the implementation of federal law in the areas of education and science, including youth policy.[25] Similarly, the creation of a national Youth Chamber led to the establishment of branches in various regions, including Astrakhan.[26] The guidelines of the Ministry of Education's Department of Youth Policy were also faithfully reproduced by the Astrakhan region Committee on Youth Policy, in its own compendium of youth policy guidelines.[27] Nevertheless, local authorities continue to have a great deal of influence over everyday policymaking.

The state sector

The relationship between tiers of local actors in Baku, Astrakhan, and Almaty essentially mirrors the arrangement between central and local state agencies. That is, once again we find an indirect attempt to control through delegation within a loosely hierarchical structure. It is important to recognize, however, that this does not imply any abrogation of responsibility on the part of local officials.[28] Extensive negotiation and reciprocal exchange is often involved in setting up and conducting such events. Thus the goal is not merely to delegate but also to enhance state supervision over youth activities, which otherwise tended to arise "spontaneously," with all the negative implications this carries.[29]

More than anything else, in carrying out national youth identity policy the state depends on the work of extra-state entrepreneurs. Central government officials are fully cognizant of this fact. In Kazakhstan, already by 2000 plans were afoot to enlist mayors for the distribution of funds

[25] Postanovlenie Pravitelstva Rossiiskoi Federatsii ot 17 iunia 2004 g. N 288 g. Moskva O Federalnom agentstva po obrazovaniiu," *Rossiiskaia gazeta*, June 22, 2004; "Postanovlenie Pravitelstva Rossiiskoi Federatsii ot 17 iunia 2004 g. N 300 g. Moskva Ob utverzhdeznii Polozhenie o Federalnoi sluzhbe po nadzoru v sfere obrazovaniia i nauki," *Rossiiskaia gazeta*, June 24, 2004.

[26] "Molodezhnomy palaty: byt," Press Service of the Astrakhan Oblast Duma, April 13, 2004, RIA Avers, available online at www.astrakhan.net.

[27] *Molodezhnaia Politika* (Astrakhan 2000), pp. 2–7. See also "O gosudarstvennoi molodezhnoi politike v Astrakhanskoi oblasti," Article 25.

[28] Schatz makes a similar point, arguing that national identity formation policy implementation in Kazakhstan is "diffuse," as "state officials and quasi-state agents in individual locales . . . endeavored to translate state discourse of Kazakhness into political practice on the ground." However, he suggests that this practice arises due to a lack of funds and/or inadequate planning. At least in the three cities explored here, however, delegation takes place by design and the state continues to play a significant role. Schatz, "The Politics of Multiple Identities," p. 498.

[29] Interviews at the Division of Education, Science and Culture, City Administration, Almaty; interview with Kazybek Shaikh, Deputy Director, For the Future of Kazakhstan, Almaty.

to local artists and other cultural activists, who in turn would undertake various projects aimed at reviving national culture.[30] In addition, Nazarbaev's own conception of identity work called for integrated efforts by governmental and non-governmental organizations, both in order to shape grassroots activities and to produce public spectacles.[31] But crucially, local officials have also actively pursued this approach. Rather than mechanically following the dictates of central policy, in doing so local state actors are expressing a belief about what is required for governance in national identity formation – a belief they share with state actors at the national level.

For example, as a testament to the premium placed on entrepreneurial identity work, a festival was organized in Astrakhan to celebrate "cultural enthusiasts" who dedicated themselves to promoting traditional values and opposing negative influences. In this instance the "enthusiasts" in question were primarily teachers, librarians, and other sub-state actors, but the work of non-state actors was implicitly of equal importance. Notably, the festival was not only subsidized by the regional administration but was presided over by the governor himself.[32] And the reason for this lavish attention and gratitude was not hard to divine. In the opinion of the deputy mayor of Astrakhan city, Vadim Monin, local non-state actors were vital for reproducing the desired national identity among the younger generation. "The culture can defend itself," he argued, "based on the individual efforts of film-makers, journalists, artists, and so on."[33]

Not surprisingly, then, youth organizations are generally well known to state officials, who eagerly seek to work with them by offering modest subsidies and inviting them to participate in state-sponsored events.[34] Precisely the same pattern of intermingling takes place in each city, as state agencies and/or neo-Komsomol organizations invite non-state actors to take part in festivals and to lead workshops on topics related to youth

[30] This was to include subsidies for artists' living and working space. Interview with Beibit Mamraev, staff member, Social-Political Department under the presidential apparatus in Kazakhstan, Almaty, June 2000.

[31] See the published interview with Bolat Baikadamov, deputy head of the Social-Political Department under the presidential apparatus in Kazakhstan, "Ved zhizn na meste ne stoit," *Kazakhstanskaia pravda*, August 5, 2000.

[32] "'Zhivi, glubinka Astrakhanskaia!' Khrani nas ot bespamiatstva i bed!" *Volga*, February 8, 2000.

[33] Interview with Deputy Mayor Vadim Monin, Astrakhan, June 2002.

[34] On this point see Marcia A. Weigle, *Russia's Liberal Project: State-Society Relations in the Transition from Communism* (University Park, PA: Pennsylvania State University Press, 2000), esp. chapter 6. Weigle argues that although the liberal project has failed at the national level, it has flourished at the local level, as many NGOs have emerged to pursue particular goals with substantial autonomy and through networked social and political ties. Weigle also observes that local officials have shifted from ignoring or repressing NGOs, to trying to work with them.

culture, such as interview strategies, standardized test-taking skills, or (except in Baku) sex education. Monin sees his own role as facilitator of this process. The deputy mayor solicits requests for funding from NGOs and selectively aids those representing what he considers wholesome values, in the process effectively commissioning such groups to implement youth policy on behalf of the state.[35] In Baku, the city's Main Bureau of Youth, Sport, and Tourism not only supervises the cultural activities of schools, institutes, and orphanages in every district, but also holds workshops on various youth cultural issues and suggests the inclusion of specific youth organizations. The city administration even recommends specific themes for workshops, seminars, and the like, to be conducted in local schools and other sub-state institutions.[36] And yet the specific content and conduct of such activities is generally outside the purview of local government. According to Cabbarli,

You know, the centers, libraries, and schools prepare and carry out activities independently, we only invite them for discussion. We help them carry out activities, but they are independent from us. But there are simply themes which we suggest to them. For example, activities related to the prevention of drug abuse and AIDS, should be obligatorily conducted in every school.[37]

In this way local state actors are generally on the same wavelength as sub-state actors, and their interactions are almost exclusively cooperative and voluntary. The same holds true for ties between the Baku authorities and local NGOs working in the area of youth culture:

For our part, we cooperate with advice, we take part in their meetings, we give them advice, we are interested in their problems . . . We are like a link connecting them with the [official] organs. For example, [suppose] they want to meet with the law enforcement organs, to conduct some activity. They come to us, and we arrange their meeting.[38]

In Almaty too, state actors (often in conjunction with Talapker, the local state-led organization for youth policy issues) organize various festivals for young people and their institutional chaperones. And as in Baku and Astrakhan, the state provides small amounts of monetary support or, more often, solicits corporate funding for worthwhile organizations.[39]

---

[35] According to Monin, thirty-seven clubs were being funded at a 50 percent level as of summer 2002.

[36] Interview with Parvana Kazymzade, first deputy director, Main Bureau of Youth, Sports, and Tourism, City Administration, Baku.

[37] Personal correspondence with Nasimi Cabbarli, deputy head, Main Bureau of Youth, Sport, and Tourism of the Baku City Administration, February 2004.

[38] *Ibid.*

[39] Interview with Saira Andakhova, staff specialist, City Department of Culture, Almaty, May 2002.

To some extent the pattern of delegation – including the degree of supervision as well as the expectation of immediate value reciprocity – depends on the particular individuals involved. Astrakhan offers a good example. Because the director and deputy director of the regional Committee on Youth Affairs happen to be particularly active and accessible, local youth centers are able to obtain necessary information, legal advice, and some financial support – as long as they meet certain acceptability criteria.[40] Similarly, the regional level official in charge of media issues at the time, Alexei Vasilev, had traveled to the West, and received Open Society Institute funding to conduct "open discussions" for conflict resolution and civil society building. Vasilev funneled money to various youth organizations that wished to establish newspapers or journals, with no restrictions or conditions attached.[41] At least in the Russia of 1998–2005 – and for that matter, in Almaty and Baku during the same period – such flexibility has remained possible.

In addition to such informal contacts, frequent meetings are organized under the state's auspices on various themes, such as conferences on social ills and their possible remedies. These are useful in bringing together state officials as well as numerous non-state actors and practitioners who implement policy on the front lines.[42] Not only do they afford opportunities for state actors to impart official guidelines, but extra-state entrepreneurs also have a chance to voice their own ideas about necessary revisions or possible new government programs. Working with government officials, in Baku and Almaty the local GONGOs (government organized non-governmental organizations), NAYORA and Talapker, are frequently involved in coordinating all such events.[43] Lacking a similar GONGO in Astrakhan, the local authorities tend to operate through the region's Youth Chamber. Just like its national counterpart, the regional

---

[40] Interviews with the following youth organizations in Astrakhan: Social Rehabilitation Center for Girls, Crisis Line "Trust," Center for Youth Creativity, Center for Dance, Center for Biology and Ecology, Center for Tourism (local), Psychological Counseling Center "Behind the Mirror," and American House. See also "Molodezhnaia palata prodolzhaet aktsiiu 'Astrakhan Bez Narkotikov'," *Volga*, June 8, 2001.

[41] Interview with Alexei Vasilev, Oblast Department of Media and Public Relations, Astrakhan. The staff of the magazine *We Are Youth* affirmed that neither Vasilev nor the mayor's office exerted any editorial pressure. Interview with staff of *We Are Youth*, Astrakhan.

[42] A typical example is a conference on drug abuse and AIDS, held at Baku State University and attended by Minister of Education Misir Mardanov. "All-republican conference dedicated to anti-drug addiction and AIDS," *Habarlar-L Digest*, No. 1300, January 12, 2000, from *AzadInform*, December 1, 2000.

[43] For example, "Molodezh predstavit pravitelstvu otchet po svoim problemam," Trend News Agency, November 5, 2004, available ISI Emerging Markets, online at www.securities.com; "Lushche ploshchadki – molodym," *Kazakhstanskaia pravda*, October 1, 2003.

Youth Chamber provides a mechanism for exchanging information as well as legitimating state initiatives through their association with bona fide youth representatives.[44] Regardless of venue and sponsorship, however, in each locale the events themselves and the rationales for holding them are essentially one and the same.

More fundamentally, regardless of the individual officials involved, the general pattern of state relations with extra-state entrepreneurs reflects a willingness to rely on voluntary compliance. Despite their best efforts, state actors cannot oversee the entire project of nation building, and there is a substantial element of devolution involved in their arrangements with actors outside the state. This in itself demonstrates the density of social connections and the strength of ambient discourse. At least within their bailiwick, state actors are conversant with the issues and individuals involved in shaping youth identity. As a consequence they have good reason to believe that there are plenty of "enthusiasts" around, ready to take on the challenges of hybridization.

The sub-state sector

The sub-state level helps illuminate the transition between state and society; that is, it represents the point at which formal oversight and accountability mechanisms are replaced by informal ones. The individuals referred to here as sub-state actors are distinctively positioned within a web of local power relations, and differentiate themselves from state officials in socially well-recognized ways.

By all accounts, those working in schools, orphanages, city youth centers, and libraries generally have rather little to do with state authorities in planning and conducting specific events. While in-house cultural programming is planned months in advance and is formally cleared with the appropriate local government departments, on a day-to-day basis the authorities never interfere with such plans.[45] For example, cultural activities at Russian state-owned institutions, such as schools and orphanages, are nominally subject to dual oversight by the Ministry of Education and the local city administration. Yet in practice such oversight tends to be loose. The Ministry offers guidance about how to observe the various traditional holidays which have become part of the reinvented national heritage. And, as already noted, local officials may suggest topics for presentations and other forums. But ultimately, neither the Minister nor

---

[44] "Molodezhnaia palata prodolzhaet aktsiiu Astrakhan Bez Narkotikov," *Volga*, June 8, 2001.

[45] I base this statement on numerous interviews with sub-state agents as well as authorities responsible for overseeing their activities in each city.

local state actors have been inclined to recreate a Soviet-style degree of control.[46]

Nevertheless, sub-state actors almost always comply with the state's policy guidelines. As already suggested, this is a knowing form of compliance. Sub-state actors are aware of and highly receptive to state priorities in the area of youth culture, and gladly organize their own workshops on appropriate themes. Many even initiate contact, approaching state officials for recommendations of appropriate youth groups or cultural experts to invite to an upcoming event. Not uncommonly, state officials themselves are invited to participate in cultural programs.[47] And yet this is due neither to subordination nor a lack of independent ideas. On the contrary, sub-state actors in each city express confident self-reliance in their strategies for working with young people, including their decisions about organized cultural activities. A typical example is the principal of a middle school in Baku, who sees herself and her teachers as being "completely independent" in their cultural planning, and fully capable of holding any activities they desire, "including gynecology." On the other hand, there are "a lot of holidays" to keep track of and celebrate, and here the ministry and city administration are helpful. Guidance and suggestions are thus as eagerly sought as they are eagerly given.[48]

This high degree of cooperation is perhaps at least partly a generational phenomenon: individuals raised during the Soviet period may well share certain carry-over assumptions about the positive legitimacy of state initiatives. More importantly, however, the commonality of approaches on the part of state and sub-state actors reveals a fundamental affinity with respect to national identity discourse. Teachers, librarians, and the like tend to have many of the same views articulated by state level actors and expressed in official policy statements, including the importance of supervising youth activities and providing moral instruction.

At the same time, sub-state actors are far from insular, and at times serve to bring in influences extending well beyond the state. To cite one example, at an Almaty performance about the dangers of AIDS the actors

---

[46] Interviews with Misir Mardanov, Azerbaijan Minister of Education, Baku; Aida Efendieva, director of School Number 8, Baku; Nariman Bashirov, pro-rector for moral education [vospitanie], Slavianskii Institute, Baku; and Makhbuba (hanim), Orphanage Number 3, Akhmed Li, Baku.

[47] For example, at one high school in Baku the principal and a history teacher organized a ceremony to honor the publication of a treatise on Azerbaijani history, which was attended by professors from Baku State University as well as the deputy head of the district Department for Culture and Human Affairs and the director of the district Department of Education. "Presentation of J. M. Mahmudov's Book 'Fatherland'," *AzadInform*, April 20, 1999, in *Habarlar-L Digest*, No. 779, April 20, 1999.

[48] Interview with Aida Efendieva, principal, School No. 8, Baku, June 2002.

were tenth graders, while various financial and logistical support was provided by the Open Society Institute, the Kazakhstan National AIDS Center, the National Center for the Formation of a Healthy Way of Life, and the Lermontov Theater.[49] In this case we see a mélange of local, national, and transnational actors in play. Furthermore, not being expert on the full range of relevant topics, sub-state actors frequently invite youth group leaders to give presentations. In the process sub-state actors also serve as social conduits for NGOs, providing them with a degree of visibility and potential effectiveness far exceeding what they could otherwise attain through their limited memberships.[50] Repeatedly, extensive networking is evident in such cultural work. In this respect a typical sentiment was attributed to a librarian in Astrakhan, who "sees the success of work only in close contact with schools, clubs, and social organizations."[51]

The non-state sector

Non-governmental youth organizations in these cities cover a dizzying array of themes, including political, professional, cultural, humor, hobbies, and sports. Such groups tend to have small membership and a low social profile despite their best efforts to attract the interest of young people. Thus while many young participants in focus groups held in each city had at least heard of several local NGOs, most were unfamiliar with their specific features and activities. In this respect the condition of youth organizations in Baku, Astrakhan, and Almaty matches the general situation in their respective countries.[52] NGOs suffer from a lack of interest and public trust, and are widely perceived to be no more than vehicles for the personal or political advancement of their leaders.[53] They also tend

---

[49] "'Otorvali mishe lapu . . .'," Transcaspian project, November 28, 2001, available online at www.transcaspian.ru.

[50] I base this statement on numerous interviews with sub-state agents as well as authorities responsible for overseeing their activities in each city.

[51] "Bibliotekar goda – iz sela Obraztsovo," *Volga*, January 11, 2000.

[52] According to Diuk's calculations, only 1 percent of young people in Russia and 15 percent in Azerbaijan participate in either social or political organizations. Moreover, only 1 percent in Russia and 5 percent in Azerbaijan have any involvement in youth organizations. Diuk, "Pervoe svobodnoe pokolenie."

[53] Again according to Diuk, the level of trust in NGOs is 41 percent in Azerbaijan and 21 percent in Russia. *Ibid.* For background on Kazakhstan see Marvin Nowicki, "Kazakhstan's Nonprofit Sector at a Crossroad on the Great Silk Road," *Voluntas*, 11, No. 3 (September 2000): 217–35. Similar conclusions are reached in Sarah E. Mendelson and John K. Glenn, "Democracy Assistance and NGO Strategies in Post-Communist Societies," Carnegie Endowment for International Peace, Working Paper Series, No. 8 (February 2000).

to be only loosely connected with one another, and, at least in objective terms, often compete for money and other resources.[54]

Many are partially subsidized by local government. In addition, many also accept money and other forms of support from foreign donors, including IGOs, transnational NGOs, and private corporations.[55] Such monies are, however, less available in Astrakhan, since IGOs and multi-nationals have a far lower presence there than in Almaty and Baku. Yet the particular source of funding does not appear to play a determining role in shaping the conduct of individual groups, at least those operating in this particular issue-area. Even NGOs that do accept outside funds appear to be reasonably autonomous with regard to the content of their cultural activities.[56]

The autonomy of the non-state sector does not persist simply because state actors have no wish to control it; while largely true, it is also the case that non-state actors tend to have high levels of commitment to pursuing their own agendas. For the same reason, in Baku and Almaty there is well-founded skepticism about the supposed independence of state-backed groups like Talapker and NAYORA. Indeed, a few NGOs flatly refuse to cooperate with the state under current conditions. In the words of the director of one civil liberties organization, "With the pro-government parties and youth organizations we do not cooperate for principled reasons. . . . These artificially created organizations which have been decreed, do not have behind them real live people, are not demanded by the youth and act only within the boundaries delineated by their bureaucrats."[57] Likewise in Astrakhan, the editors of the staunchly liberal/alternative youth newspaper *Youth and Politics* declined to accept funds from the region's Department of Youth Affairs, claiming that it

[54] See James Richter, "Promoting Civil Society?" *Problems of Post-Communism*, 49, No. 1 (January/February 2002): 30–41; also Sarah L. Henderson, *Building Democracy in Contemporary Russia: Western Support for Grassroots Organizations* (Ithaca: Cornell University Press, 2003).

[55] In these three cities some of the most important IGOs and INGOs are: UNICEF, UNDP, Asian Development Bank, USAID, TACIS, Open Society Institute, Eurasia Foundation, Aga Khan Foundation, IREX, ISAR, and Counterpart International. In addition, groups receive corporate funds either as a result of their own efforts or through the good offices of the state. This includes local and national companies as well as major multinationals such as Proctor and Gamble, Coca-Cola, and the leading oil MNCs.

[56] This stands in contrast to the findings of some other researchers who have examined the role of post-Soviet NGOs in different issue-areas. See Mendelson and Glenn, "Democracy Assistance and NGO Strategies in Post-Communist Societies"; also (with relevance to Kazakhstan) Ruth Mandel, "Seeding Civil Society," in Chris M. Hann, ed., *Postsocialism: Ideals, Ideologies and Practices in Eurasia* (New York: Routledge, 2002), pp. 279–96.

[57] Interview with Sagyngaly Yelkeyev, director of Ravnyi Ravnomu, Almaty. Similar views were expressed by Elmari Mamishev, deputy director, Young Lawyers, Baku.

wished to tame the publication and substitute "Soviet propaganda" for their independent positions on issues like AIDS.[58]

However, this does not necessarily translate into mistrust of individual civil servants or official agencies working specifically in the area of youth culture, especially at the local level. On the contrary, even relatively liberal youth NGOs often wish to cooperate with state actors, demurring only when they fear becoming bound up by red tape.[59] Most also find state actors to be reasonably non-obtrusive (as indeed state actors claim). For example, the directors of the Almaty and Baku National Debate Centers, each sponsored by the Open Society Institute, expressed pleasant surprise over the fact that neither had encountered interference from local authorities in conducting their work.[60] Indeed, in many cases the government and fairly politicized NGOs working on specific policy issues have interests in common, which explains why the latter are often keen to take part in events organized by state and sub-state institutions. Thus, although staff members of the Education Center for Youth in Baku work to promote democratic civil society and privately expressed disdain for the state-backed umbrella NAYORA, they also frequently work with it to set up presentations in orphanages, schools, and youth centers. In such instances the objective is to achieve the same ends desired by the state, such as promoting awareness of traditional Azeri culture or teaching computer skills. Similarly, Zan, an Almaty NGO focusing on legal problems of young people, is only too happy to receive support from GONGOs such as Talapker and For the Future of Kazakhstan, who in turn provided such support because of the state's interest in codifying law in this sphere.[61] This is also directly relevant to youth socialization. As Talapker's director argues, a law-governed society is important both normatively and practically, since young people empowered by an understanding of their rights are more likely to become active and productive citizens.[62] Nor is this merely cynical rhetoric, since with the exception of some highly politicized areas the state has a profound interest in cultivating market initiatives and enlisting young people in the reproduction of social order. Thus, working with the state towards shared ends is generally not regarded as threatening a loss of autonomy.[63]

[58] Interview, *Youth and Politics*, Astrakhan, May 2003.
[59] Interview with Alexei Mitin, program coordinator, Akkord, Almaty, June 2002.
[60] Interviews, National Debate Centers, Almaty and Baku.
[61] Interview with Elmira Akhmarova, director of Zan, Almaty. In particular, Kudaibergenov's Foundation provided the start-up costs for Zan's newspaper *Youth and Rights*, which was distributed to schools, universities, orphanages, and juvenile prisons.
[62] "Almaty Youth Organizations Demand New Law on State Policy on Youth to Be Adopted," Radio Free Europe/Radio Liberty, *Kazakh News*, September 5, 2002.
[63] These findings are similar to those reached by Kelly McMann in her excellent study, "The Civic Realm in Kyrgyzstan: Soviet Economic Legacies and Activists'

Of course, NGOs are often stymied in their pursuit of idealistic reform objectives because of the state's resistance. All too often, state agencies are accused of ignoring independent initiatives or repressing those which are too forcefully pushed.[64] In this connection it is important to recognize that – at least in the area of youth culture – most non-state organizations do not fit the stereotypical portrait of NGOs doggedly pursuing democratic or other progressive political goals. Rather, they tend to be informal groups or clubs which are run by middle-aged volunteers, where young people can congregate after school or on weekends. Much as with sub-state actors, then, it is hardly surprising to find a confluence of views on basic questions of identity. This is especially true at the very local level, such as in Astrakhan's Trusovskii district. Here the head of the local Department of Education has close personal and working relationships with youth center leaders, youth groups, and individual specialists of all kinds, and routinely coordinates efforts with them in order to provide young people with a wide range of extra-curricular programs.[65] In the specific area of youth culture, such collaboration is far more the norm than the exception. And, despite significant differences between the political-institutional structures of Russia, Kazakhstan, and Azerbaijan, this pattern of cooperative interaction between state, sub-state, and social organizations is remarkably similar, at least in the sphere of youth socialization.

Having ascertained the key actors and the interconnections between them, the question is how, programmatically, do they seek to achieve desired youth identity outcomes? In fact, as the following chapter shows, their general attitudes and specific strategies speak volumes about the fundamental issues being addressed in this book: processes of national identity formation, assumptions about state–society relations, and how both are affected by globalization.

Expectations," in Pauline Jones Luong, ed., *The Transformation of Central Asia: States and Societies from Soviet Rule to Independence* (Ithaca and London: Cornell University Press, 2004), pp. 213–45. McMann finds that civic groups overwhelmingly desire state assistance and that few are concerned about losing their autonomy in the process.

[64] For an example of such frustrations, see Fuad Aliev (of the Baku-based NGO New Generation of Economists), "Sotsialyi dialog i ego rol v reshenii problem molodezhi Azerbaidzhana: Poisk effektivnykh putei vzaimodeistviia," in Economic Commission for Europe, *Youth of the XXI Century: Realities and Perspectives* (United Nations: New York, 2004), pp. 297–300.

[65] Interviews at Trusovskii district administration, Astrakhan.

6 Shaping national youth identity on the ground

In addition to being highly collaborative, networks of cultural entrepreneurs are characterized by a substantial degree of flexibility in their day-to-day workings. Actors tied to local government institutions are able to mingle with others outside of officialdom, but are also able to draw on the formal accoutrements of the state. Sub-state and non-state actors gain visibility through their association with state-sponsored programs, but may also generate a degree of credibility, or even authority, precisely because they are not representatives of the state. In each case, however, entrepreneurs are able to tap into a variety of organized settings and institutional resources, depending on the situation and their particular needs. This allows them to respond to the attitudes and cultural expectations of young people, and thus to pursue their identity goals in potentially more effective ways. Moreover, in all of these contexts entrepreneurs echo the same themes of rejection, absorption, and assertion discussed previously, but which we now come to understand concretely as applied strategies for shaping youth identity. In exploring their practical interventions in the realm of youth socialization, we uncover separate as well as orchestrated activities and behind-the-scenes communication. We find, in short, a network of actors drawn from various institutional niches, who are not only aware of each other but also – more or less systematically – work together in order to achieve similar goals.

On the whole, as this chapter discusses at length, state and sub-state actors prefer to avoid using overtly authoritarian methods for achieving collective identity goals. Overwhelmingly, state, sub-state, and non-state actors agree that youth attitudes cannot be shaped by fiat, or through a combination of prohibiting and requiring particular conduct. First, entrepreneurs regard coercive measures as being generally inappropriate except when dealing with very young children. There exists a widespread sentiment that attempting to mandate any given behavior smacks of the Soviet approach, which, if nothing else, is considered to be in bad form or archaic. As the head of the Astrakhan Regional Division of Culture commented about such an approach, "Of course we cannot insist on

156

anything, we cannot impose our views . . . This [tossing her hand backwards over her shoulder] . . . no one does this anymore."[1] Not only is coercion widely regarded to be an illegitimate, Soviet-style practice, but it is also viewed as being impracticable. "We fine people for speaking Russian [in order to encourage the use of Kazakh], but it only works for half a day," commented one teacher in Almaty.[2]

This attitude is shaped in part by the views of young people, who sneer at the idea of being forced to comply with normative standards. As one young woman remarked with a smile, "That's how it was done in the time of the [Soviet] Union. They can't do that anymore."[3] Tellingly, a person with a conformist mentality is often derisively referred to by young people as a "Sovok," or Soviet-type person. Activists involved in trying to influence young people are aware of this sea-change in attitudes, and have adjusted accordingly. In the words of a director of a Baku middle school, "Children are much more open now. They insist on having their own opinion. Of course they need to learn manners right from the start, but we cannot *demand* this or that. We cannot punish."[4]

For these reasons, rather than flatly proscribing or mandating specific behaviors, an increasingly pronounced tendency in youth socialization is to resurrect the role of formal ideology and state-led propaganda. To be sure, this is a highly contested aspect of socialization and youth policy. As discussed in chapter 4, even some of those involved in central policy-making consider the very notion of official ideology to be unacceptable. But for many state and sub-state actors, some form of proselytization is indispensable. According to the leader of the semi-official Almaty youth organization, Talapker, "The key problem today is a definite decline in the morals of youth, therefore the law should regulate the ideological composition of youth policy. That is, the developing ideological vacuum should be filled with wide-ranging informational-propaganda activities." Depending on the degree of artfulness used, such "activities" may be rather more subtle than the dogmas propounded by ideologues during the Soviet era. Yet a carefully planned and coordinated approach is clearly favored by many actors close to the state. A typical attitude is expressed by Azerbaijan's Deputy Minister of Youth, Sport, and Tourism, Intiqam Babaev: "It is impossible to forbid, only to manage. We can't use force, but we must explain to young people why [objectionable behavior] is

[1] Interview with Nadezhda Andreevna Liakhova, Astrakhan.
[2] Interview with Balzhan Suzhikova, International Business School, Almaty.
[3] Focus Group, Khazar University, Baku.
[4] Interview with Aida Efendieva, Director, School Number 8, Baku.

bad. They want to get information on what is happening, and we try to counterbalance – it is a counter-propaganda contest."[5]

Still, whether based on official ideology or some less rigid formulation, a key question is exactly how to conduct such identity work in close interaction with youth. For a minority of officials, especially those of the older generation, it is hard to relinquish the Soviet habit of haranguing young people. As former Kazakhstan Minister of Education, Krybek Kusherbaev, argued, "We must promote a healthy way of life not only with the help of videotapes and films on television, but also by going to the discotheques, where, as an eyewitness, narcotics are sold almost openly, by going among the youth, by talking with our children precisely there."[6]

As already noted, these are exactly the kinds of statements which cause young people to roll their eyes in disgust. Not surprisingly, then, almost all entrepreneurs agree that efforts to employ a traditional, heavy-handed moralistic or Soviet approach would be destined to fail. In fact, as warned by the Russian Ministry of the Interior's recommendations, such an approach would be likely to alienate today's youth even further:

In their appearances it is important for workers of interested state organs and social organizations to refrain from extremism – poorly thought-out and exaggerated evaluations, excessive moralization and trying to frighten young people. In the course of interacting with the audience it is also essential to take into account that if narcotics are defined as evil or as something poisonous, anti-social, leading to self-destruction, the end result may be to alienate the auditorium.[7]

This underlines the point that young people are active participants in the socialization process, and that their views and responses are routinely taken into account by most entrepreneurs. Indeed, the anticipated responses of young people often directly influence the form of a planned intervention. For example, many entrepreneurs agree that attempts to proscribe a given behavior typically result in a backlash. As the official responsible for moral education in a Baku University remarked, "Kids are attracted to what is not allowed."[8] For this reason, according to the

---

[5] Interview with Arman Kudaibergenov, Baku, June 2002. Kudaibergenov also expressed similar views in a published interview, "Davaite rasstavim aktsenty," *Novoe Pokolenie*, September 27, 2002, available online at http://www.np.kz/.

[6] "Detiam nuzhny shkoly, kompiutery, goriachaia eda i zdorovye roditeli," *Kazakhstanskaia pravda*, September 18, 1999.

[7] Russian Ministry of Internal Affairs, "Metodicheskie rekomendatsii po realizatsii sotsialnykh profilakticheskikh i reabilitatsionnykh program," Resolution 15–52–521, July 27, 2003 (prepared at the request of the Ministry of Education).

[8] Interview with Nariman Bashirov, Pro-Rector for Vospitanie [moral education], Slavianskii Institute, Baku.

leader of an Almaty youth group, if previously forbidden temptations are no longer illicit, their attraction – and potency – are quickly reduced.

There need to be more options for distraction. You can't say, "The West, or sex and drugs, is *bad*." As soon as you tell someone this is bad, they want to do it. Actually, a greater number of options makes this less attractive. Give people more options and information, and let them choose. Give them experience.[9]

Even aside from questions of legitimacy and potential backlash, the new, more accommodating approach reflects the reality of globalization, especially the nearly unrestricted flow of ideas in the mass media. Indeed, there is a widespread recognition that globalization makes any attempt to impose censorship utterly hopeless. As the deputy director of one Almaty high school remarked, "There is no way to *stop* the West, it would just go underground."[10] And in keeping with prevailing social attitudes, many entrepreneurs regard censorship as counterproductive, since it would inevitably hinder the desirable forms of cultural borrowing needed for economic growth and national development. According to an orphanage director from Almaty, "It is better to know about the real world instead of, as in the Soviet period, burying one's head in the sand."[11] Similarly, in the words of an orphanage director from Baku, "Kids need to see the world and to participate in it, to see who the different people are, to learn their knowledge. They need to understand what independence is and how to handle it with open eyes." In her view this constituted becoming a fully autonomous individual, adept at managing cultural as well as market interactions, while at the same time remaining a thoroughly nationalized citizen of Azerbaijan.[12]

In short, entrepreneurs want young people to *choose* hybridization: i.e., to become actively and voluntarily engaged in the processes of absorption, rejection, and retraditionalization. Not only is this widely regarded to be part of a "democratic" or "free" and post-Soviet society, but it is also considered essential if the benefits of individualism are to be harnessed. As one young activist commented, "We can fight against the harmful aspects of Western influence. But it must come from within, it must be voluntary."[13] The hope, then, is that young people will internalize the appropriate values and essentially police themselves and their peers.

[9] Interview with Zhangir Kainazarov, Association of Young Leaders, Almaty, June 2002.
[10] Interview at Humanities and Linguistics High School, Almaty.
[11] Interview with Anzhela Karasaeva, Director, Orphanage Number 2, Almaty.
[12] Interview with Ms. Makhbuba, Director, Orphaange Number 3, Akhmed Li, Baku.
[13] Interview with Timur Bakiev, member of central staff, Otan [political party], youth wing, Almaty.

Successfully promoting hybridization thus requires artfulness, in addition to commitment and a willingness to connect with young people directly. Above all, as entrepreneurs unanimously agree, young people should not be allowed to go about their business without expert guidance. As one Baku librarian commented wryly, "Even dead people should not be left to their own devices."[14] Instead a concerted effort is made to involve the youth in programs of varying content, whose educational and moral aspects counterbalance and help overcome the alienating effects of Western pop culture. According to the same article praising Astrakhan's cultural enthusiasts, "[t]he villagers prefer their club meetings to the tele-debates and shows which arrive, because here, in the club, what is important is the atmosphere of sincerity and trust, here there are no lies which are strewn about on all the screens and the airwaves, on the pages of the complicit press."[15]

In seeking to impart desirable identity constructs, therefore, many entrepreneurs try to walk the fine line between tiresome moralizing and benign neglect. To some extent this describes a difference between NGO leaders, on the one hand, and state or sub-state actors on the other. The former tend to be less didactic on moral issues, or at least more subtle in suggesting appropriate values. They also tend to be especially willing to negotiate the venues and content of youth socialization, often by delegating much of the responsibility for such matters to young people. For example, in the Almaty-based "Teenager" Center,

We do a monthly newspaper. The kids do it all, except for an editor . . . The choice for a particular article is based on surveys of the kids, which are done in schools. They pick the themes, and then we help them. Suppose they want to write about a rap group. We will listen, and if it is interesting then we do an article . . . We don't give advice, we give information.[16]

To some extent the difference in approach appears to be generational, as younger people are less accepting of propagandistic approaches than people raised under the Soviet system. Yet even younger non-state actors agree that systematic campaigns are essential to inform their peers about pressing social issues, either so as to help them avoid dangers, solve problems, or seize opportunities. According to the leader of one NGO in Almaty,

There is no clear ideological position anymore, compared to the old days with the Komsomol. That is why new non-governmental organization youth groups are

[14] Interview with librarian (name withheld on request), Youth Library, Baku.
[15] "Zhivi, glubinka Astrakhanskaia! Khrani nas ot bespamiatstva i bed!" *Volga*, February 8, 2000.
[16] Interview, "Teenager" Center, Almaty.

needed. The influence of the West is very strong. Kids' behavior is less inhibited; they know their rights; now they experiment a lot, compared to the USSR. This is good: they have their own choice, the choice of making their own living and career. But it can go too far, with the desire for pleasure, for drugs, the quest for easy money.[17]

They also, virtually without exception, advocate cultural hybridization. In the words of a student responsible for organizing events at Astrakhan State University: "A synthesis of culture, a world culture, this is good. But there are also drugs and other forbidden fruit. There is good and bad, and the best thing is to pick."[18] The familiar objective, again, is to draw a sharp distinction between modernization and cultural globalization. Not only are these purposes conveyed in social discourse and propounded in official state policy, they are also consistently reproduced through the actions of intentional agents. Moreover, this is true regardless of age or organizational status, and is equally evident in Astrakhan, Baku, and Almaty.

What follows is an overview of the work of state, sub-state, and non-state actors. Once more, it is convenient to highlight the separate themes of hybridization – absorption, rejection, and assertion – which appear in their interventions, even though in actuality all three are often present at once.

Absorption

Without belaboring the themes already discussed with regard to policy and popular discourse, a prominent feature of cultural entrepreneurship is the affirmation of modernity, and of the central role it assigns to the rational, goal-maximizing individual. This is consciously perceived to be a form of borrowing from the West, and is eagerly embraced as such. More than anything else, "adapting to reality" means encouraging young people to acquire the necessary skills and habits of mind to function in the competitive market.[19] To some extent, such attitudes reflect an increasingly common, neoliberal view that the state should no longer shoulder the burden of providing social entitlements. In the words of an

---

[17] Interview with Elmira Akhmarova, director of Zan, Almaty.

[18] Interview, Astrakhan State University, Inter-University Students' Club, June 2002.

[19] Examples abound from Russian pedagogical journals. See (in translation) E. M. Korzheva, "Adapting Adolescents to Market Relations," *Russian Education and Society*, 38, No. 8 (August 1996): 7–23; L. M. Mitina, "The Personal and Professional Development of the Individual Under the New Socioeconomic Conditions," *Russian Education and Society*, 40, No. 5 (May 1998): 33–51; Zoia Litova, "Preparing School Graduates for Work Under the New Economic Conditions," *Russian Education and Society*, 43, No. 3 (March 2001): 36–44.

official at the Astrakhan Region's Department of Culture, "We need to avoid a mentality according to which youth are given handouts without work."[20]

But again, such attitudes spring as much from below – that is, from society at large – as from state or organized transnational sources. This is perhaps especially true among the younger generation. In each city, youth participants in focus groups unanimously expressed admiration for certain influences which they attributed to the West, including capitalism, foreign investment, computerization, marketization, and high technology. In fact, in promoting such values and institutions entrepreneurs are aware of responding directly to social demands expressed in popular discourse. The leader of state-sponsored Almaty group, Talapker, expressed this succinctly: "Now kids have very strong practical goals related to material values. Therefore there is a need for individuality and individual responsibility."[21] Similarly, according to the head of a youth center in Astrakhan,

We gave out a questionnaire and we looked at the results. We asked them, "What is most important to you?" And they said, "First, money, and second, career." Alright. But it all depends on their level of knowledge, and the choices they make, the education they get. This determines the kind of work they can find.[22]

Interventions designed to foster neoliberal practices, which are often systematically undertaken by entrepreneurs, are thus partly responsive to the immediate demands of young people.

Accordingly, numerous efforts are made to foster rational individualism and prepare the youth for success in the marketplace. For instance, the state holds "Young Business" forums.[23] NGOs provide reading materials on topics such as effective communication, simulated business situations, and client interactions; they also offer seminars with titles like "How to Start Up a Firm," "Theory and Practice of Conversation," and "Personal Growth."[24] Youth groups publish magazines featuring articles such as, "I'd Like to Be a Businessman, Let Me Learn How."

---

[20] Interview, Astrakhan Region Department of Culture, June 2000.

[21] Interview with Arman Kudaibergenov, president (until 2004) of Talapker, Almaty. Kudaibergenov suggested the possibility of "creating a new ideology" of "personal independence, a market economy, the stock exchange, and democratic institutions."

[22] Interview at the Association of Children's and Youth Social Union, main offices, Astrakhan.

[23] "'Almaty Young Business' Fest Coming," *Kazakhstan Today*, February 19, 2004, available ISI Emerging Markets.

[24] Interviews with: staff, Teenage Center, Almaty; and Nabil Seidov, President of Reliable Future, Baku. Reliable Future maintained two libraries stocked with new books on technology, economics, and science.

Children's libraries put up exhibits on "Legal Rights of Youth,"[25] while ordinary libraries present exhibits on "New Possibilities for Economic Entrepreneurship."[26] Young people are encouraged to learn computer skills and familiarize themselves with the Internet. Thus, in keeping with the national campaign "Electronic Russia," the Astrakhan government developed a target plan "Development of Information-Communication Technology for 2003–2004," in which a key goal was "to attract the interest of youth in acquiring practical skills and self-sufficient activity in the area of computer technology."[27] The following year the regional government also established a number of "Centers for Social Access to Information Resources" at various schools, libraries and youth organizations throughout the region.[28] Very similar initiatives have also been launched in Azerbaijan and Kazakhstan, often joining the efforts of state, sub-state, and non-state entrepreneurs.[29] The ability to speak English is also considered essential, providing not only a gateway to knowledge but also a tool for national development. Teaching English and computing are therefore seen as complementary strategies for encouraging modernization.[30] And in each city, individual as well as interactive decision-making skills are encouraged.

This approach has important implications for the practice of identity construction among the youth. For example, the director of Scouts of Azerbaijan invites his young charges to propose specific activities and see them through. Regardless of the exact topic involved (e.g., planning a holiday celebration, a charitable drive, or a demonstration of practical

---

[25] Interviews with Liudmila Soboleva, Chief Librarian, Astrakhan Region Youth Library; and staff, National Children's Library, Almaty.

[26] "V biznesmeny ia b poshel, pust menia nauchat," *Molodezh i Pravo*, 1, No. 2 (February 2001): 24–26, published by the NGO "Zan," Almaty; "Prazdnik predprinimatelstva," *Teenager*, 4, No. 17 (June 2001): 3, published by the NGO "Teenage Center," Almaty.

[27] See Elena Maksimova, "Obiavlen konkurs na lushchii informatsionnyi resurs o rodnom krai," RIA Avers, April 17, 2003, available online at www.astrakhan.net.

[28] "Selchan obuchat kompiuternoi gramotnosti," April 26, 2004, RIA Avers, available online at www.astrakhan.net.

[29] "I Republican scientific-practical conference 'Independent Azeri youth and new information technologies' was held," *AzadInform*, December 14, 1999, in *Habarlar-L Digest*, No. 1252, December 14, 1999; "'Internet Data tsentry' dolzhnyi sposobstvovat vkhozhdeniiu strany v e-ekonomiku," *Panorama* (Almaty), March 9, 2001.

[30] According to one volunteer teacher, "This is helping the positive influence of the West. Learning English you learn the language of the world, and learning computer you learn the information of the world." Interview with Samira Allaverdieva, Youth Volunteer Management Unit, UN Volunteers Program, Baku. Likewise, in addition to providing nativist cultural programs, Reliable Future also holds an English language drama festival. Interview with Nabil Seidov, President, Reliable Future, Baku. See also "Iunym chitateliam: 'latyn XXI veka'!" *Kazakhstanskaia pravda*, February 3, 2000.

skills), each Scout is responsible for initiating and leading an activity with his peers. The obvious and intended goal is fostering individualism:

> Everyone is an individual person, and if I pull rank they will lose initiative. Personal autonomy is crucial to get what you want in life, in family, in business. For that it is necessary to be independent . . . This reflects the reality of the market system . . . Being professional, personable, and able to communicate – all this is essential for success.[31]

In this way, almost regardless of the particular activity in question, by taking charge of such practices in a group setting, members are enrolled in constructing an identity consonant with neoliberal norms. And yet, this is to be an individualism grounded in a larger, shared identity and collaborative framework.

Before concluding this section, it is worth noting that not all interventions are geared to the absorption of prevailing global or Western values. On the contrary, it is possible to locate a range of rather eclectic ideas on offer for young people in each city, including various religious and nationalist movements which represent the West as an alien and undesirable Other. In Baku, for example, there are groups which promote pan-Turkism,[32] while the official "youth portal" at the Ministry of Youth, Sport and Tourism website includes a link on "healthy way of life," where the reader is introduced to Zen Buddhist teachings on living "here and now" in order to overcome feelings of boredom and meaninglessness.[33] Slavic, Orthodox, and Communist groups vie for attention in Astrakhan.[34] Also in each city, fundamentalist Islam is a worrisome undercurrent in the eyes of authorities. And so forth: the West does not cover the entire discursive terrain relevant to youth culture.

On the whole, however, the West is the dominant point of reference for cultural entrepreneurs and young people alike. In popular as well as specialized discourse, one encounters very few references to significant alternative Others in the sphere of youth culture and national youth identity formation – including China, India, Turkey, or (in Baku and Almaty) Russia. The West is also an overwhelmingly attractive reference point in many respects. The rejection of Western values and practices, to which we will turn next, is therefore highly selective. And, like elsewhere in the world, such rejection is geared largely toward facilitating the appropriation of "positive" Western values.

[31] Interview, Scouts of Azerbaijan, Baku, June 2002.
[32] Interview, The Fund of Aid for Youth, Baku, June 2002.
[33] The Ministry's "youth portal" is http://216.92.58.134/ru/youthlife/youthlife5.shtml/.
[34] Interviews with Chelnok (nationalist patriotic organization) and with the regional branch of the Communist Party of Russia, Astrakhan, June 2001.

Rejection

As already discussed, most cultural entrepreneurs are well aware that police actions are ill-suited for achieving their desired outcomes. Indeed, for the most part the key target of rejectionist interventions is not criminal behavior at all, but something far more elusive and subtle. Once more, the overweening fear is disintegration of national identity and the uncritical, wholesale adoption of Western practices. Avoiding this outcome is the apparent goal of various emotional appeals, such warnings about "loss of memory and disaster" and "the frenzied pace of contemporary life."[35] Such overtures reveal the key point: pragmatic concerns cannot be allowed to override traditional-normative ones. Freedom of choice, in other words, is not intrinsically beneficial for its own sake, but only if guided by appropriate values. Organized interventions geared to value rejection thus complement the goals of value absorption; i.e., they reveal a demand for individualism circumscribed by moral boundaries – but boundaries which are internalized instead of imposed. More important than learning to express their individuality, therefore, children need to be taught how to stand up to peer pressure and to resist evil enticements: they must be "taught to fight the dangers of curiosity."[36] And here the entrepreneur steps into the breach. As one Astrakhan official remarked (without a shred of irony!), "We give them a choice: how to say no."[37]

For many of the same reasons, state and sub-state actors – who are especially intent on maintaining the moral *status quo ante* – tend to encourage group events of all kinds. Whereas isolated activities lead down the path of solipsism and anti-social indulgence, organized forms of the same activities are often considered entirely benign. For example, group programs may include group Internet surfing and research, in which young people learn computer skills together. Not only is this linked to an experience of sociality, but under the entrepreneur's watchful eye pernicious influences may be avoided.[38] The overarching objective, again, is to promote individualism, but within acceptable limits.

Other interventions are explicitly geared toward rejection. Thus, under the rubric of promoting a "healthy way of life," various anti-drug,

---

[35] "Zhivi, glubinka Astrakhanskaia! Khrani nas ot bespamiatstva i bed!" *Volga*, February 8, 2000; "Ne zabyvaia narodnye traditsii," *Kazakhstanskaia pravda*, June 28, 2000.

[36] Interview with Gulia Ibrakhanova Karsybekova, Head, Department of Education, Science, and Culture, City Akimat, Almaty.

[37] Interviews at Trusovskii district administration, Astrakhan.

[38] Interview with Akmara Pazilova, Director, Almatynskii raion Youth Center, Almaty, June 2001. See also "'Internet Club' Operates for Popular Enlightenment, but Not for Business Ends," *AzadInform*, November 1, 1999, in *Habarlar-L Digest*, No. 1157, November 1, 1999.

anti-smoking, and anti-drinking activities are planned in each city. These tend to be partly informational, such as explaining the importance of not sharing needles, and partly exhortative, much like the Reagan-era campaign to "say no to drugs."[39] Yet sponsors also try to engage young people in such events by making them enjoyable, either by putting on plays, holding rallies at which music and food will be offered, or by turning them into exciting competitions like poetry or sporting contests. An example is a literature contest in Baku on the theme of drug addiction.[40]

In a less propagandistic vein, Debate Centers in Almaty and Baku hold public discussions as well as smaller forums at individual schools, on such topics as prostitution, the need for a constitutional court, and cultural borrowing from the West – including how much is too much, and how to distinguish the good from the bad.[41] While Astrakhan has no Soros-sponsored Debate Center, here local officials, teachers and NGOs often cooperate to produce much the same setting. Librarians join in such efforts as well, holding reading circles and presenting exhibits, often in conjunction with school activities. For example, at the Regional Children's Library in Astrakhan, the chosen themes over the past several years included: Ecology; Narcotics Abuse; Tuberculosis; The Earth; World War II; Science; Poetry; New Possibilities for Economic Entrepreneurship; AIDS; Day of the Family (including the family's importance in moral upbringing); John Lennon; and Edith Piaf. Strikingly, a new theme was "The Russian Ethnos," which was presented in response to numerous requests from young people, who "want to know their roots." Also in response to requests, the library subscribes to *Rolling Stone* magazine.[42] Very much the same themes are encountered in libraries in Baku and Almaty.[43] In short, while some aspects of socialization are subtle and accommodating, didactic elements surface as well.

Young people appear to have a wide range of reactions to such activities.[44] Big, state-sponsored events engender especially mixed feelings. Many attend begrudgingly, either because they feel beholden to

---

[39] See "Initsiatory molodezhnykh aktsii protiv narkotikov zatrudniaiutsia skazat, naskolko oni effektivny," *Panorama* (Almaty), April 15, 2001; also Marat Yermukanov, "Anti-Drug Efforts of Kazakhstan: Old Methods in New Garbs," *Central Asia – Caucasus Analyst*, February 25, 2004, online at www.cacianalyst.org.

[40] "Best prose dedicated to anti-drug addiction theme to be confirmed on January 14," *AzadInform*, January 10, 2000, in *Habarlar-L Digest*, January 10, 2000.

[41] Interviews at National Debate Centers, Baku and Almaty.

[42] Interview with Liudmila Vasilevna Sobleva, Regional Children's Library, Astrakhan.

[43] I base the above statements on numerous interviews with relevant actors. For a published account (of an Astrakhan librarian's efforts to fight drugs and AIDS) see "Narkotiki: vykhod est!" *Volga*, June 20, 2002.

[44] I base these observations on focus groups as well as numerous – mostly unstructured – interviews with young people.

(sometimes they are bused in directly from school), or because "there is nothing else to do." Some go rarely, on the grounds that the entire spectacle is "just for show." Some appear to feel embarrassed about being associated with a clearly propagandistic message. Others, however, feel no such inhibitions, perhaps because they choose not to read much into the events beyond their superficial aspects. For them, the spectacles afford some entertainment and a place to hang out with friends. And, for many, the underlying message is often not unwelcome, at least as long as it is not excessively belabored. For example, some expressed agreement with the sentiment of anti-smoking or anti-drinking campaigns, even though this was not the main reason why they attended the rally. And yet this is often hard to admit, since it may suggest acquiescence or a "goody-goody" mentality. Thus, when asked about their feelings, young men were often inclined to make ironic (and possibly disingenuous) remarks. For example, one said he was participating in an Anti-Narcotics rally because "it is a good place to buy drugs." One performer, a breakdancer, said he participated partly to curry favor with the authorities and partly to attract potential dance students. And yet, when asked about the general phenomenon of cultural globalization, he responded with the typical litany of complaint and approval: Western influence was positive in encouraging personal freedoms, but it also carried negative messages, including vulgarity and "dissolute behavior."[45]

Nevertheless, especially in less ostentatiously public forums, young people appear to participate freely and even enthusiastically in reproducing the ideas and practices which are propounded by the organizers. This reflects the crucial point – which comes through repeatedly in focus groups and personal interviews – that for the most part they accept, and knowingly reproduce, the essential elements of social discourse concerning the importance of hybridization. As one young man commented (with others in the room nodding agreement), "We don't want to imitate the West, we want to know about it."[46]

This willing embrace of prevailing values was evident, for example, at the Astrakhan Eco-Biological Center, which holds "ecological discos" at which scientific or environmental issues are presented in between dance numbers. According to one of the group's organizers, herself in her early twenties, "It is half party and half about ecological issues."[47] During a break, young attendees enjoyed themselves by decorating eggshells with Russian folk motifs. This was a simple pleasure, but one imbued with a nationalist theme. And in making this artwork in this particular setting,

[45] Interview with Oleg Vladimirovich Kazagashev, dance instructor, Detskii Park, Almaty.
[46] Focus group, Khazar University, Baku.   [47] Interview, Astrakhan, May 2003.

a message was also being fashioned about the ostensibly holistic relationship between environmental concerns, civic volunteerism, and the Russian national spirit. Moreover, for the actors – state, sub-state, and non-state – involved in creating and overseeing the forum, such symbolism is perhaps less important than the act of contributing to "proper" youth socialization, and in doing so not only reaffirming the validity of Russian national identity, but also reconstituting state–society relations and the prevailing normative and institutional order.

Once again, it should be noted that the social discourses in Russia, Azerbaijan, and Kazakhstan are not identical; nor are the organized interventions into youth socialization completely alike. Despite their overwhelming similarities, it is possible to identify differences in nuance or approach across groups of entrepreneurs in different cities. And, just as in the social discourse at large, the most obvious differences have to do with sexuality. Youth organizations tend to reproduce popular views about sex, ranging from the repressive in Baku to the relatively indulgent in Astrakhan. For example, reflecting widespread concerns over the sexual transmission of AIDS, an Astrakhan youth magazine ran a story on a French youth club devoted to abstinence, under the title "The French Do Not Have Sex." On the other hand the journal also provided information about condoms and their appropriate use.[48] In Almaty, too, non-state actors are often non-judgmental about sexual themes. As one youth group organizer explained:

Kids know about the sexual revolution from the Internet. They are concerned about sex and AIDS. That is normal, it is natural. At one of the schools some teachers started a "club of virgins," but the boys just laugh. It is silly. We talk about all of these things. And we also give them information about condoms.[49]

In contrast, in Baku the Youth Enlighteners instruct young mothers to avoid breast-feeding in public; it goes without saying that sex before marriage is sinful. Thus, according to the group's leader, a woman in her early twenties, one of the main "negative" aspects of Western influence is overt sexuality, including its reflection in provocative dress.[50] And, of course, even in Astrakhan religiosity is correlated with attitudes about sexuality and how best to instruct the youth on such matters. This was strikingly evident at a meeting targeting young people in a local youth center, where a group called "For You" discussed its methods for presenting information about safe sex, including demonstrations of how to

---

[48] Interview at My Molodye youth group, Astrakhan.
[49] Interview, "Teenager" Center, Almaty.
[50] Interview with Rugiia Iusifova, executive director of the Youth Enlightened Organization of Azerbaijan, Baku, June 2003.

use condoms. A deputy head of the region's Department of Youth Affairs was present and fully supportive (the city has its own AIDS Center, which often cooperates with "For You"). But also in attendance was a furiously blushing priest (after all, another kind of cultural entrepreneur), who swiftly denounced the notion of "giving choices" to young people about morally circumscribed issues, and launched into a diatribe about moral lassitude and Orthodox Christian values.[51] While the priest spoke the room was silent, and young people as well as NGO members lowered their eyes. When he departed, however, there were wry smiles and slight headshakes, and the discussion carried on as before.

Also not surprisingly, age matters: even in Astrakhan, older entrepreneurs tend to hold more traditional views on a variety of moral issues. For example, Liudmila, the leader of a modeling club in Astrakhan, is acutely aware of Western influences and strives to keep her charges from falling prey to its vulgar excesses. Although she considers sex before marriage to be acceptable if the relationship is based on love, smoking is decidedly unacceptable, and anyone caught swearing is immediately expelled. In Liudmila's view, much of her work is directed toward stemming the tide of moral degeneracy by reinforcing traditional values and gender roles. "In reality this is a club for young women to learn how to be ladylike," she explains. "I teach them how to walk, how to dress attractively with regard to styles and colors, how to put on make-up, to talk to people, [to use] proper manners. The main goal is to give them self-confidence." And, by shoring up the traditional notions of femininity in these ways, a supposedly essential element of Russian culture is also preserved.[52] Interestingly, Liudmila's young models appear to embrace her views wholeheartedly. In follow-up interviews, several of them enthusiastically echoed the same attitudes about love, sex, "decency," and the virtues of being "ladylike."

In mediating youth culture across all of these contexts, "administrative methods" are the exception rather than the rule. In certain situations, however – especially those having to do with criminal enterprises, the perceived "culture of violence," and physical spaces devoted to aberrant behavior – the authorities quickly resort to coercive solutions. Such repressive measures reflect a tendency to conflate drug abuse, crime, and generalized immorality. For example, President Aliev closed all casinos

[51] Forum at Youth Center "Ulitka," Astrakhan.
[52] Interview at Liudmila's [unnamed] modeling club, Astrakhan, May 2003. Interviews with members suggested that such ideals pervaded the club. Similar mores were embodied in the "Pearl of Kapchagay" beauty contest, which was organized by the Youth Union of Kazakhstan and held in Almaty in October 2002. Interview, Youth Union of Kazakhstan, Almaty, June 2003.

in Azerbaijan in 1998, citing a pervasive presence of organized crime and prostitution. Although gambling is welcomed in Astrakhan and Almaty, here too, as in Baku, police conduct frequent raids on night clubs, which are regarded (with some basis in fact) as proverbial dens of iniquity. The underlying attitude was expressed in a report by the Russian Federal Anti-Drug Service on the social and physical environment in discos, which it portrayed as almost inevitably breeding drug abuse. According to the report, "The volume of the music, the lights and the general atmosphere in the hall are very difficult to handle without drugs. More than 30 to 40 minutes without 'doping,' not necessarily Ecstasy, is impossible to tolerate."[53] In such ways, the rising incidence of drug addiction and generally "deviant" conduct has gone hand-in-hand with rising social anxiety and efforts to stamp out the most virulent threats.[54] Beyond the problematic behavior in question, a key factor tying together all repressive acts is widespread unease over the emergence of alien cultural environments and their troubling identity implications.

In addition to wanton immorality, violence is also considered a special problem for which extreme measures are often required. To a significant extent such attitudes are tied to fears of terrorism. In Russia the spiraling crisis in Chechnya had already raised vivid concerns, but in Azerbaijan and Kazakhstan terrorism was also a growing source of anxiety well before September 2001. These anxieties colored perceptions of the globalization of youth culture, leading state and sub-state actors to take steps to bar aggressive behavior, even when it appeared only in virtual form. In Astrakhan, the Committee on Youth Affairs launched a crackdown on computer clubs starting in 2001, supposedly due to widespread violations of local health and safety codes. According to the official statement released by Director of the Committee on Youth Policy Ekaterina Lukianova, the goal was "to develop computer clubs, to make them more civilized."[55] In a private interview, however, she acknowledged the real issue: the video games being played were "extremely aggressive," and "people are sick of such violence."[56]

In Russia and Kazakhstan, worries about rampant violence have raised suspicions over the recent practice of observing Halloween. In 2003 the holiday was banned in schools by the Moscow Department of Education.

---

[53] Quoted in Carl Schreck, "Anti-Drug Agents Targeting City Clubs," *Moscow Times*, April 28, 2004.

[54] As of late 2005, there were tentative plans in Russia to begin drug testing of students. "Studenty sdadut testi na narkotiki," *Kommersant*, September 20, 2005.

[55] "Deiatelnost kompiuternykh klubov vziali pod control organy gosudarstvennoi vlasti," April 28, 2004, RIA-Avers, online at www.Astrakhan.net/.

[56] Interview, Astrakhan, May 2003.

According to the decree, practices associated with Halloween included a "cult of death or mockery of death, identification with spirits of evil, etc.," which not only violated the secular character of public education but was also "detrimental to the psychological and spiritual-moral health" of participants.[57] Echoes of this sentiment can be detected in Astrakhan and Almaty. Although local authorities have not imposed any blanket prohibitions, at least one school in Almaty did decide to ban Halloween on the grounds that it was "too fierce."[58] Still, such measures are generally reserved for particularly dangerous or extreme forms of misconduct. As stratagems for socialization, far more common approaches are persuasion, negotiation, and setting a proper example. In the words of a staff member from a youth rehabilitation center in Astrakhan, "We try to avoid saying 'don't.' Instead we promote other activities: sports, reading, travel. We model a healthy way of life. Being friends with your parents; participating in cultural activities; realizing your internal possibilities."[59]

Assertion

As we have already seen, an essential component of the "healthy way of life" is perceived to be a thorough grounding in traditional culture. This was reflected in an article from an Astrakhan newspaper extolling the region's "librarian of the year." The description of the winner's accomplishments offers a veritable "How To" guide for fostering Russian national identity:

The priority directions in the work of the library have become the moral and economic education [related to] the rebirth of national traditions, family life and regional enlightenment . . . By opening up the national, cultural wealth of the village the library transforms itself here into an exhibit hall, there into a museum, there into a playground and a place for interesting meetings. The ethnographic corner "Russian Chamber" attracts particular attention; here are articles of peasant life, so near and so far, native to all . . . [In addition] activities for organizing family time were introduced into practical work some time ago. "Family, wife, children" month takes place annually on International Family Day and Mother's Day. The exhibits "We and Our Family," "Kaleidoscope of Family Time," "For You, Parents" signify and tell about the wonderful life of the family . . . Meetings of parents and teenage sons at "round tables" dedicated

---

[57] Instead of Halloween, the decree called for establishing a new holiday "in conformity with the basic values of Russian culture" which could be celebrated together with teachers and parents. "Khellouin opasen dlia vashego zdorovia," *Izvestiia*, October 25, 2003.

[58] Interview with administrator [name withheld by request], High School No. 111, Almaty, June 2002.

[59] Interview with Rosa, "Zazerkale" Center, Astrakhan.

to questions of defense of the Fatherland help teens define their views for the future.[60]

In Astrakhan, Almaty, and Baku similar efforts are continuously undertaken by cultural entrepreneurs. In each city the common antidote for runaway globalization is traditional culture, which is seen as providing a powerful source of social glue. In part, traditional culture is seen as a corrective to harmful global influences – and for that matter, also native ones, like saturation with vodka. A typical, wishful attitude was expressed by the deputy mayor of Astrakhan: "If they sing folksongs they won't start using drugs."[61] But traditional culture is also considered a powerful prop of national identity. According to Azerbaijan's Minister of Education Misir Mardanov, notwithstanding the priority placed on attaining world standards in curriculum and other educational matters, the importance of inculcating national identity remained unsurpassed.

School children should learn a national foundation, and a world foundation. This applies not only to subjects such as geography, history, and literature, but also to morality. The key is to adjust the balance between knowledge and personal conviction. And here, the majority – [wagging his finger for emphasis] the *majority* – must be national.[62]

Such views epitomize the emphasis placed on historical narratives by entrepreneurs. Similarly, "arts and crafts" activities often intentionally include traditional folk themes, so young people will "know their national identity."[63] A favored approach is to introduce the youth to practitioners of indigenous art forms. An example in one Almaty high school is the program "My Kazakhstan," featuring yurts, ancient folk customs, national costumes, native literature and poetry recitals, and traditional dances.[64] Here again non-state actors are in accord with state and sub-state actors with regard to the importance of learning national culture. Thus, student organizers at an inter-university club in Astrakhan include a significant number of traditional Russian performances, which are well attended by students. And here, too, such ideas resonate with the wishes of young people. Not only do many students enjoy such entertainment, but they also consider it to be an appropriate expression of shared values.

---

[60] "Bibliotekar goda – iz sela Obraztsogo," *Volga*, January 11, 2000.
[61] Interview with Vadim Monin, deputy mayor, Astrakhan. Likewise, according to the head of a local youth group, "Folklore, costumes, literature, traditions – we present all kinds of styles, at special celebrations. This helps to ward off bad influences." Interview, NGO "Sources," Astrakhan.
[62] Interview, June 2002.   [63] Interview, "Zhasulan" Youth Center, Almaty.
[64] Interview at Humanities and Linguistics High School, Almaty.

As one said, "We like our own national themes, something which is really Russian. We want to be ourselves, not just like Americans."[65]

Another strategy for reconstructing youth identities involves reviving the habit of going to the library, although here the emphasis is not so much on nativist themes as on "good literature," especially the literary classics. Naturally, librarians are in the forefront of this effort, but they are joined by teachers and many other state and extra-state activists from the older generation. Moreover, as one librarian in Baku pointed out, libraries provide another opportunity for entrepreneurial intervention: "We cannot do much, but we can give guidance. . . . If a kid comes in with a question, she can give suggestions and ideas, and then we can give *encouragement* for good ideas . . . For example, patriotism."[66]

A related idea was voiced by an instructor at a Pedagogical Institute, who insisted that exposure to high culture was the key to making good choices in all areas. "It is necessary to enlighten, not just educate," she explained. "They should learn about beauty, flowers, cultural matters. What is love, art, ballet, opera. . . . They must have knowledge of the world, knowledge of life's potential, in order to be able to choose the best from the West."[67]

Dramatic and musical theater also provides a marvelous vehicle for promoting intangible virtues. Such programs allow the entrepreneur to weave specific social lessons into a broader cultural pastiche, perhaps linked to state institutions and platforms. This frequently involves conscious manipulation of social identities which are ostensibly primordial but dormant. For example, Russian national identity is claimed to be generous and charitable; in Astrakhan these qualities are enacted in youth cultural performances and outreach programs, such as helping invalids or providing charity to the poor.[68] Similarly, the goal of the state-funded Center for Children's and Youth's Creativity in Astrakhan is "to inculcate feelings of goodness, attentiveness, empathy for others, benevolence, sincerity in experiences."[69] In Almaty, the regional governor's office promotes programs which reflect the allegedly intrinsic Kazakh preference for friendship, consideration for guests, non-aggressiveness, and consensus.[70] In sum, because the corrosive effects of post-industrial modernization are

---

[65] Interviews, Astrakhan State University, Inter-University Students' Club, June 2002 and May 2003.

[66] Interview, Children's Library, Baku.

[67] Interview with Lida, State Pedagogical College, Almaty.

[68] Interview with Valentina Liakhova, head, Oblast Division of Culture, Astrakhan.

[69] "Chem sovershennee vospitanie, tem shastlivee narody," *Volga* (Astrakhan), January 12, 2000.

[70] Interviews at the Division of Culture, Information and Social Accord, Department of Youth Affairs, City Akimat, Almaty.

too powerful to be entirely contained, cultural programs provide a compensatory strategy, including an emphasis on socially integrated values and identities. This serves to channel youthful ambitions in a direction conducive to the maintenance of established institutional ties.

In addition to simply asserting traditional values, entrepreneurs also interweave elements of Western and supposedly indigenous culture, so as to support nation- and state-building goals. In part, this means encouraging "healthy" forms of integration, much as with other interventions aimed at selective absorption. In addition, melding traditional cultural themes with racy Western ones is intended to promote decontamination, not merely by watering down the concentration of cultural toxins but also by subsuming them within a broader narrative of legitimate symbols, thereby defusing their novel or provocative aspects. And by incorporating foreign elements which are in high demand, entrepreneurs are able to accommodate young people's desires, and thereby perhaps gain a reciprocal measure of legitimacy.

Activists therefore try to promote hybridization by providing mixed programs in which modern, international culture is sandwiched between more traditional offerings. For example, at the annual youth cultural festival in Almaty the list of music groups is drawn partly from requests by young people themselves, and includes Western bands (like Nazareth) as well as Russian and local bands. Such music festivals are a "present for kids from the mayor," in the words of the director of the city's Department of Culture. Nevertheless, she includes some healthful "presents" likely to be more appreciated by audience members in their later years: "Unfortunately they might not like classical and folk music, but we include it anyway so they know it and so they might learn it."[71] The same stratagem was evident in the inclusion of rock music alongside traditional folk and classical music in an Astrakhan festival. In the words of the official responsible for this arrangement, "We need to give kids what they want, and at the same time provide a varied exposure. Globalization should mean mutual benefit and accumulation of cultural outlooks, not erosion. Children should get native and foreign culture."[72] And the very same arguments were made by Azerbaijan's Deputy Minister of Culture, Sevda Mamedalieva. "It is important for young people to be exposed to the world's culture," she argues, "but the key is that their own must be preserved." She therefore accepts the need to offer a wide range of performances, including "folklore, traditional instruments, classical,

[71] Alma Beisebaeva, Director of the City Administration Department of Culture, Almaty.
[72] Interview with Leonid Volkov, Head of Division of Youth, Tourism, and International Ties, Oblast Administration, Astrakhan, July 2001.

popular-modern festivals, jazz, and [twisting her mouth in disgust] even rap and breakdance!"[73] Almost without exception, then, cultural activists recognize that ultimately, the only chance for traditional culture to survive is if it is freely chosen by young people themselves. Many appear to have faith this will, indeed, be the case. According to Natasha, a music teacher in Almaty,

We give them everything: the West, the East, traditional, Russian. A mixture. Classics are good for the soul, for learning. They like it once they get into it. But we also use jazz, spirituals, Gershwin, and occasionally rock songs or folk songs . . . Rock – the kids say it's vivid. They don't want to think. It's loud. Rap, rock – they are repetitive, like a narcotic. Of course, even rock can be interesting. There are good groups with interesting melodies. But the best are old songs, like the ones sung by grandparents, which are rich and full of cultural worth. And the kids like them better; they are prettier.[74]

A related stratagem for promoting hybridization involves coopting the veneer of modernity and technological sophistication, as a way of consolidating traditional practice. For example, in Baku the Council of Youth encourages a synthesis of classical jazz with traditional *mugam* instrumentation and style (a related form, which uses harder rock sounds, is known as "industrial mugham").[75] In other conscious efforts to mimic the "modern" Western style, the Baku NGO Reliable Future sponsored a combination performance of rock music together with orchestra and chorus, while in its annual youth cultural festival in Almaty the state-backed Talapker included a new version of dombra, the ancient instrument of the steppes, but now set in a contemporary arrangement with "big sound."[76] Again, the gambit being played here involves using Western form to cultivate traditional content, without the former insidiously undermining the latter's effect.

Once more, it is worth stressing the point that even young people, including cultural activists or members of youth groups, often endorse these ideas. A striking example comes from an inter-university club in Astrakhan, whose organizers – working together with the region's Committee on Youth Affairs – include deviant artists such as punk-rockers in their programming in hopes that the broader exposure they gain may transform them. To take a case in point, the club invited a group of "extreme breakdancers." The result was exactly as hoped. "In the

---

[73] Interview with Sevda Mamedalieva, Azerbaijan Deputy Minister of Culture, Baku, June 2002.
[74] Interview with Natasha, private Arts Academy, Almaty.
[75] Interview with Agadzhan Akhmedov, Council of Youth of Azerbaijan, Baku.
[76] Interviews with Nabil Seidov, president of Reliable Future, Baku; and Alma Beisebaeva, Director of the City Administration Department of Culture, Almaty.

festival they saw actors, dancers. They changed their style, they stopped smoking and drinking, and they started training. Actually they ended up doing ballet."[77]

In addition to making these sorts of manipulative calculations, older entrepreneurs also have simpler goals: holding mixed cultural events at least serves the purpose of maintaining a degree of adult supervision. For this reason the deputy director of one Almaty school organizes evenings at local night clubs and includes programming content she personally finds in bad taste, such as breakdance and Britney Spears. After all, in her view, hosting such events is "better than letting them take place on the street."[78]

Finally, and in another resounding echo of popular discourse, a major emphasis is placed on sports and physical fitness. Such activities are not only healthy and popular, but are considered to be positively related to feelings of nationalism, including willingness to serve in the armed forces. Not surprisingly, in view of the Nagorno-Karabakh conflict, this is particularly true in Azerbaijan, where organized sports are officially viewed as a means of instilling patriotism.[79] However, it is also increasingly true in Russia, as part of the Federal Program to promote "Patriotic Education." In addition to sports, visceral nationalism is cultivated by excursions to military bases as well as by singing and discussing patriotic hymns. But everywhere it is the *organization* of sport, not merely the sport itself, which is important. Sports centers typically promote good hygiene, a spirit of camaraderie, and national identity (often by touting the exploits of one or another national team). For these reasons, in the words of one rhapsodic newspaper article, in Astrakhan's sports centers "children not only develop physically, but also acquire vitally important habits."[80]

The foregoing analysis has emphasized the importance of planned interventions, undertaken largely (though not entirely) by adult society, which are intended to shape the identities of young people. Nevertheless, as we have also seen, the process of youth socialization incorporates the interests and demands of youth to a substantial extent, and canny agents

---

[77] Interview, inter-university club, Astrakhan State University, May 2003.

[78] Interview at Humanities and Linguistics High School, Almaty.

[79] For example, karate competitions are held to mark World Azerbaijanians' Solidarity Day. "Competition Between Karate Federations' Clubs Was Held," *AzadInform*, January 3, 2000, in *Habarlar-L Digest*, No. 1284, January 3, 2000. Promoting sports is also an act of constituency building. See "Military Tourism and Sport Games Promote Martial Patriotic Spirits of Youth," *AzadInform*, December 10, 1999, in *Habarlar-L Digest*, No. 1111, October 12, 1999.

[80] "Chem sovershennee vospitanie, tem shastlivee narody," *Volga* (Astrakhan), January 12, 2000.

operate on both sides of the exchange, seeking to influence the content of shared values. State, sub-state, and non-state actors involved in this project are not only affected by social discourse, but must respond to it – and specifically, to the sensibilities of young people – in order to effectively pursue their agendas. In examining the approaches they use, one is struck by the degree of similarity between popular discourse and specialized entrepreneurial discourse. This consists of the thematic embrace of key neoliberal values, coupled with rejection of "excessive" individualism and the assertion of national particularism. Yet while similarities abound, it is also possible to detect differences. In contrast to the popular discourse, which is often uncertain or ambivalent about identity boundary issues, cultural entrepreneurs – whether pursuing an official standard of nationalism or merely working to promote social solidarity – invariably come down hard on the side of strictly delimited borrowing. And as we have seen, they also engage in systematic interventionist strategies for achieving their cultural ends. This is equally true for each of the three cities we have examined in Russia, Kazakhstan, and Azerbaijan.

Finally, although cultural entrepreneurs are variously located within the social fabric, collaboration between them goes a long way toward bridging the gap between formal state agencies and spontaneous grassroots action. This happens in ways we may not expect. As the above analysis shows, in many respects nationalists and state-builders are the same people: that is, they speak overwhelmingly the same language of identity, one bound up with place and tradition, and yet one also increasingly inflected by globalization and the quest for modernity. Furthermore, the manner in which they cooperate reveals the workings of a true social movement arising in response to globalization – yet one which is hardly oppositional. On the contrary, the social process implicated in mediating globalization in the sphere of youth identity serves to reaffirm and, at the same time, reconstitute the state as both the instrument and embodiment of social order.

7   Conclusions

In exploring national youth identity construction under globalization, I have highlighted the role of strategic actors and organized social settings. Doing so, I hope, offers a particular set of insights into the process of social identity construction, more for what this reveals about society and its encounter with globalization than for its ability to capture and explain the identities held by young people.[1] For this purpose, as I have argued, it is essential to explore the microprocesses through which ideal or prescriptive identities are constructed. This in turn allows us to understand and explain identity formation in terms of the meanings of various constructs, as well as the reasons for which they are strategically employed. As we have seen, understanding *how* national identity is formulated and publicly articulated sheds considerable light on *why* this takes place, at least with regard to the reasons and meanings that inform the process. Moreover, the preceding chapters have shown that – at least under conditions of globalization – national identity formation rests not simply on passive diffusion but on decisions and interventions undertaken at the national and local levels, in the pursuit of social and political goals. While I have focused mainly on strategic actors, including their interrelations and planned interventions, we have also seen that such entrepreneurs are sensitive to the anticipated wishes and demands of young people, whose socialization they seek to influence. These observations imply something worth reflecting on at some length: mediating globalization is a thoroughly social endeavor, and the manner in which it is pursued helps shape state–society relations.

[1] This points up some of the limitations of this study: youth identity outcomes are shaped by a number of factors, many of which are not directly or entirely subject to strategic calculation. Thus, in addition to formal state policymaking, culture, international context, and discursive processes are also in play at the domestic and international levels. While attempting to remain sensitive to such factors, therefore, the present analysis makes no claim to being truly comprehensive. Nor has it attempted systematically to measure youth attitudes and identities themselves. There is, to be sure, some reason to believe that the findings presented here have descriptive validity. Still, strictly speaking such questions go beyond the scope of this book.

National identity and globalization

We have seen that the construction of national youth identity in Russia, Kazakhstan, and Azerbaijan is hardly an insular matter. On the contrary, perhaps especially in the area of national identity formation, the relationship between state and society is powerfully influenced by globalization. Governments and mass publics are constantly exposed to voluminous flows and, at the same time, are made excruciatingly aware of the opportunities and threats posed by them. This is as true in cultural terms with respect to national identity, as it is in economic terms with respect to trade, investment, employment, and welfare legislation. The results are familiar. Much like social discourse at large, elite discourse is also highly critical of Western popular culture, which is viewed as threatening to rupture social stability by replacing collective identification with self-indulgent or solipsistic pursuits. To offset these tendencies, the emerging strategic narrative champions native-traditional values and patriotic attachments. At the same time it embraces modernization, while seeking to harness the latter to nation- as well as state-building goals. Along the way many of the fundamental assumptions of neoliberalism are reproduced, including the importance of individual volition and rational action. Arguably this smuggles in the entire package of westernized identity constructs which entrepreneurs wish to avoid. Yet although many are aware of this irony, they tend to regard it as a gambit – the outcome of which they can control.

In addition to understanding the superficial content of this narrative, exploring the process of identity construction in a fine-grained fashion allows us to grasp more fully the underlying ambivalence associated with it. What we find is that this ambivalence stems from the inherently paradoxical nature of each of the main strands of hybridization – absorption, rejection, and assertion – as well as from the tensions between them.

One example of this is the multiple, partially contradictory meanings associated with absorption. First, there is obviously an element of instrumentality to such narratives, especially their presumed usefulness in promoting marketization and efficiency. However, the endorsement of modernization and individualist values should not be read simply as part of a calculated or Machiavellian undertaking engineered by elites.[2] On the contrary, individualism in particular appears to be embraced for purely normative reasons, embodied in notions of "freedom" and "progress," as well as for pragmatic development reasons. At the same time, there is a way in which absorption is collectively fantasized as the reclamation of

---

[2] Ernst B. Haas, "Nationalism: An Instrumental Social Construction," *Millennium*, 22, No. 3 (Summer 1993): 505–45.

something lost, and therefore as part of the necessary process of becoming unique and whole again as a nation. In fact, despite the patterned similarities of capital markets, production processes, and rational individualist outlooks, something unique does often take place: through its intermingling with local patterns of culture and social organization, absorption produces a particular inflection of global discourse and practice. It is in part by weaving such nuances into a larger tapestry of difference that the state seeks to justify its existence as guardian of the nation. And yet this is never entirely successful. Inevitably, ambivalence results from seeking to recapture the nation by incorporating within it something quintessentially foreign.

In much the same way, claims of hoary customs and timeless beliefs are partly designed to facilitate and legitimate their exact opposite. That is, globalization – widely regarded as an inevitability – is responded to by the mobilization of tradition, yet this is often intended to make liberalization possible, either by compensating for, or denying, the reality of cultural change. To be sure, local governments often seek to capitalize on nostalgia as a way of attracting foreign capital.[3] Yet this is far more than mere instrumentalism. Instead, national identity assertion is part and parcel of a larger social discourse in which narratives of traditionalism and modern developmentalism are sought for their own, internally legitimate and legitimating qualities.[4] Assertion thus represents another intrinsically problematic strand of hybrid identity construction, inasmuch as it functions both to resist and promote particular aspects of homogenization. The same basic insight also applies to rejection. Like assertion, it also enables sameness, in this case by narrowly delineating what is *not* absorbed, and then constructing out of these elements a veritable fetish of difference which serves to mask the extent of absorption. What we find, then, in uncovering the deeper layers of meaning associated with national identity formation, is a dynamic interrelatedness among the constituent strands of hybridity, including both contradiction and complementarity. In the former Soviet spaces we have visited, entrepreneurs are busy juggling these identity constructs while wrestling with their paradoxical meanings.

Why is it worth trying to understand how globalization is mediated on the periphery of the world? Quite aside from its anthropological interest, I would suggest that this is worth doing, in part, because it reveals something fundamental about the nature, and perhaps also the

---

[3] As argued by Beth Mitchneck, "The Heritage Industry Russian Style: The Case of Yaroslavl'," *Urban Affairs Review*, 34, No. 1 (September 1998): 28–51.

[4] As Jusdanis observes, nation building is thus a synthetic process in which culture and politics are fully intertwined. Jusdanis, *Necessary Nation*, pp. 91–5.

durability, of the identities that arise through this process. First, it exposes the strategic character and belabored artificiality of many of the constructs in play, including the effort required to synthesize and legitimate an overarching narrative of nationalism. Moreover, coming to terms with the dynamic properties of the identity constructs themselves implies an important corollary: by virtue of their dynamism they are also potentially unstable. Both elements – modern and traditional – threaten to collapse into each other, raising the constant specter of either homogenization or backlash. Nevertheless, as discussed in chapter 1, extreme instability is highly atypical. Instead, as our former Soviet case studies exemplify, in general one finds rather robust forms of hybridization; indeed, this appears to be heavily over-determined. The more interesting question, then, is *how* such hybrid identity outcomes emerge. What has this study revealed about state–society relations and the nature of agency, in the context of national identity formation and youth socialization?

Social process and social effects

Coming to grips with agency, I would argue, requires understanding the social process of identity construction, including the formal and informal channels through which it takes place. One component of this process consists of government policy, and is initiated at the top of the political hierarchy. To a large extent, however, identity construction proceeds through decentralized forms of agency, including dispersed social actors as well as local institutions nominally under the purview of the state. Rather than resulting from organized pressure campaigns, this decentralized organization of identity construction reflects consensus and cooperation among autonomous actors. It is strongly influenced by domestic institutional legacies, while also remaining responsive to pressures and opportunities arising from the international context. More specifically, in our three post-Soviet settings we notice several important conditions: a high degree of intersubjective agreement on collective identity questions, lingering (yet contested) statist assumptions, and a nearly unrivaled discourse of neoliberalism. All these have combined to produce a particular process of national youth identity construction. Before turning to some reflections about state–society relations and social process more broadly, it is worth briefly reviewing and synthesizing these points.

The cohesion of identity discourse

One of the key findings of this study is the existence, in these globalizing locales, of a remarkably harmonious discourse on matters of national youth identity. Certainly the single most pervasive and urgently articulated idea within this discourse concerns the "need to be national," which in turn consists, at least prescriptively, of basic self–Other differentiations as well as a set of legitimating values and norms. As our case studies demonstrate, the nationalist idea is so powerful and ubiquitous because it works on several levels at once. That is, it fulfills a deep social psychological need for solidarity, offers potential empowerment through identification with national tradition and glory, and stands as a dominant legitimating principle for social organization.[5] One has to wonder to what extent this discursive uniformity reflects a basic cultural commonality, perhaps arising from shared Soviet experience, which then becomes expressed in broadly similar responses to globalization.

Nevertheless, to say that national youth identity discourse is remarkably cohesive is not to suggest that it is completely homogeneous. Particularist discourses are also articulated, pertaining to local, tribal, ethnic, and Islamist identity constructs, none of which show signs of disappearing.[6] Certainly it is possible to find constituencies which favor starkly opposing worldviews, including cosmopolitanism versus national-traditionalism.[7] And as discussed in chapter 4, at the level of central government – i.e., in the framing of official legislation – one *does* find a good deal of contention, as well as diktat. Below this level, however, where identity is reproduced and negotiated in everyday places, the process takes on a quite different cast. In sum, although alternative discourses exist, the dominant narrative is one of strategic hybridization.

Of course, the existence of a dominant narrative does not mean that it will always remain so, or that the outcomes associated with it are entirely predictable. The formation of a relatively homogeneous national identity is best understood as a tendency, or better yet as a project, inasmuch as it is intentionally shepherded by politically canny elites. As such, the future prospects of a unifying national identity are uncertain at best; neither globalization nor particularistic identities arising in response to it are inevitabilities, but are themselves contingent developments subject to change. Still, in the places we have examined – marked as they are by rapid integration into international social and economic life – there is a

---

[5] Hall, *National Collective Identity*, pp. 34–44. See also Castells, *The Power of Identity*.

[6] As emphasized in Pinar Akçali, "Nation-State Building in Central Asia: A Lost Case?" *Perspectives on Global Development and Technology*, 2, Nos. 3/4, (2003): 409–29. In fact, as Shatz observes, delegating the implementation of identity policy to local actors appears to be having unintended effects in some areas, including the renewal of tribal identifications. Schatz, "The Politics of Multiple Identities."

[7] Surucu, "Modernity, Nationalism, Resistance." As Rosenau argues, these may be further categorized with reference to their global or local orientation as well as their specific strategies for dealing with globalization. James N. Rosenau, *Distant Proximities: Dynamics beyond Globalization* (Princeton and Oxford: Princeton University Press, 2003).

high degree of social accord on basic matters of national identity, which may well have lasting consequences.

Lingering Leninism

The ubiquity of statist attitudes suggests that a Soviet institutional legacy is in play.[8] We glimpse such institutional holdover in a number of ways, including the impulses of state actors to propound official youth policy doctrine, and to engineer or coopt the national youth movement. The very idea that it is possible to successfully design and oversee youth identity from above smacks of the Soviet planning mentality. Furthermore, the notion that the entire process might effectively be coordinated by the centralized political apparatus testifies to a highly bureaucratized, command-based organizational culture, again much like that which developed during the USSR. Besides the impulse to craft such policies, the fact that they are still widely considered acceptable speaks volumes about the social expectations of state-led political change. As Roy argues, in these tendencies to regard the state as dominant yet benign we glimpse a continuation of the "Soviet habitus."[9] Observers have noted that this attitude extends even to many NGOs, which might be assumed to insist on maintaining some distance from government agencies.[10] And of course, democratic safeguards have been only weakly institutionalized in post-Soviet political structure.[11] Not surprisingly, then, current developments in each of these countries reflect resurgent authoritarianism.

[8] Stephen Hanson, "The Leninist Legacy and Institutional Change," *Comparative Political Studies*, 28, No. 2 (July 1995): 306–14. Kubik distinguishes between "explicit" and "implicit" legacies, where the former is intentionally and the latter habitually transmitted. However, in the present study both forms of transmission are apparent. Kubik also refers to ideologically tinged "scenarios" for the future, as opposed to parameters of institutional development. Jan Kubik, "Cultural Legacies of State Socialism: History-Making and Cultural-Political Entrepreneurship in Postcommunist Poland and Russia," in Grzegorz Ekiert and Stephen E. Hanson, eds., *Capitalism and Democracy in Central and Eastern Europe: Assessing the Legacy of Communist Rule* (Cambridge: Cambridge University Press, 2003), pp. 317–51.

[9] Roy, *The New Central Asia*, p. 165.

[10] Squier makes this point in analyzing the 2001 Civic Forum, in which the Russian government attempted to forge ties with the NGO community: "[T]he main difference of opinion among NGOs that the Civic Forum revealed was the relative comfort that charities and service-provision organizations felt regarding the government. Many of the human rights leaders . . . noted with dismay that the majority of the organizations seemed perfectly willing to subordinate themselves to a centralized government body, so long as the government began spending money to address the problems on which they worked." John Squier, "Civil Society and the Challenge of Russian Gosudarstvennost," *Demokratizatsiya*, 10, No. 2 (Spring 2002), pp. 177–78.

[11] Karen Dawisha and Bruce Parrott, *Russia and the New States of Eurasia: The Politics of Upheaval* (New York: Cambridge University Press, 1994), pp. 147–57.

Delegitimation of totalitarian methods

And yet, while the Leninist impulse persists, it is also powerfully counteracted by other forces. The most important of these is the delegitimation of full totalitarianism, as part of the collapse of the USSR. Trying to impose any monolithic perspective is therefore widely considered unacceptable or embarrassing, as revealing a crude and outdated Soviet worldview. Furthermore, the global norm of democracy is clearly a presence in each society's political culture. While full substantive democracy is far from being realized, and while political opponents are still persecuted in Kazakhstan, Azerbaijan, and even in Russia, the permissible bounds of public engagement have widened immeasurably – a fact well understood by state elites and non-state activists alike. Democratic ideas have also found broad discursive resonance, as evidenced by the widespread idea that it is "normal" or "civilized" for people to express different views, to tolerate others' opinions, and to seek compromise solutions when disagreements arise. For these reasons, even if they have not personally internalized such norms, state actors in these post-Soviet spaces are operating under real – and strikingly similar – normative constraints.[12] Failure to follow through on the Leninist impulse thus represents an acknowledgment that the state cannot mandate one point of view without risking its legitimacy, both in the eyes of the younger generation and the international community.

Naturally, such developments are not entirely consistent, and it is sometimes difficult to determine whether state actors who profess democratic ideals actually apply them in practice. An example is the Astrakhan official in charge of youth cultural matters, Ekaterina Lukianova. While allowing young people and actors outside the state considerable leeway in pursuing their own ends, Lukianova also cracks down on unsavory, independent video gamers, and denies funding to excessively non-conformist youth groups. How do we understand such behavior? Does it reveal a fundamental lack of democracy or an insistence on maintaining minimal standards of decency? Such questions often require minute examination of particular contexts and individuals, which goes beyond the scope of this study. For the most part, however, there is no question that state actors are far more tolerant of non-conformist behavior, and more willing to cede everyday authority, than their Soviet predecessors were. At the same time, while some officials are perhaps sincerely democratic, it should also be noted that adopting this posture has strategic benefits as

---

[12] For a somewhat related argument regarding the overriding similarities among post-communist countries at the level of mass society, see Marc Morje Howard, *The Weakness of Civil Society in Post-Communist Europe* (New York: Cambridge University Press, 2003).

well. That is, the new openness helps to legitimate state authority by distinguishing it from the illegitimate Soviet model. Allowing alien culture to flourish, therefore, not only accommodates the popular demand for Western symbols and individualist values, but also helps consolidate new institutions and empowers actors operating within these new boundaries.

The corollary of this shift in prevailing norms is that asserting one's own initiative has become not only possible, but also personally, professionally, and socially validating. This is noticeable among sub-state as well as non-state actors. One finds NGOs undertaking youth socialization with only limited state partnership, and sometimes without any at all. Teachers, librarians, and the like also frequently make their own decisions on strategic matters of national identity formation, invoking the illegitimacy of Soviet diktat as their justification for doing so. Even when the state's support is enlisted, this is often done in calculated ways, designed to widen a given actor's access to resources or target audiences while still retaining autonomy. For all these reasons, despite their reflexive tendencies to exert control, state officials recognize that social conduct cannot be fully shaped from above. Instead, to be successful in current conditions identity formation must be narrative, everyday, and diffuse.[13]

Nowhere is this more true than in the realm of youth culture, with its endemic alienation and resistance to authority. Rather than simply imparting ideas from above, negotiation and careful manipulation are often required. Once more, this finding underscores the point that young people are active participants in identity construction. This fact is fully recognized by activists at all levels, who constantly anticipate and accommodate young people's views, and often try to involve them in dialogue about issues relevant to youth socialization. In sum, the Soviet-style statist reflex is offset, perhaps increasingly, by an inclination to assert independence – and this is equally true of young people as well as state, sub-state, and non-state actors of all ages. By doing so, such actors constitute themselves as modern, sophisticated, and socially empowered individuals imbued with legitimacy.

For similar reasons, the state is also constrained to allow non-state actors to claim a high degree of autonomy over the process of socialization. To be sure, insofar as this is officially endorsed by the state, such activities take place under the state's aegis or in accordance with general state policy guidelines. And despite an absence of overt coercion, there is

---

[13] Similarly, as Semenenko observes, there continues to be only a "weak correlation between the dynamic of institutional development and changes in individual consciousness, between hierarchical institutions and network forms of interaction of social subjects." Irina S. Semenenko, "Globalizatsiia i sotsiokulturnaia dinamika: lichnost', obshchestvo, kultura," *Polis*, No. 1 (January 2003): 5–23.

also a considerable amount of subtle pressure and cooptation involved, reflecting an effort to influence non-state interventions. Nevertheless, it is precisely because the state appears not to be associated with national youth identity formation much of the time, that the process works as well as it does. Indeed, non-state entrepreneurs are generally able to operate in this realm as they see fit, interacting with local state, sub-state, and other non-state actors, as well as with young people, on the basis of their shared convictions about the need for strategic hybridization.

The functional linkage between neoliberal content and process

Attaining "modernity," understood as cutting-edge technology and vibrant market institutions, is as much about the symbolic aspects of legitimacy and modernity as it is about reaping practical and material benefits. As such, the enormous international pressures to conform are matched locally by the desire to catch up. Yet becoming modern in practice necessitates entrepreneurial initiative and decentralization, which in turn requires the average individual to be reconstructed. Therefore, instead of Homo Sovieticus – whether in its original collectivist form or its Brezhnevite incarnation as risk-averse rule follower – it has been necessary to fashion a thoroughly post-Soviet person: rational, risk-acceptant, profit oriented, and empowered to act independently in pursuit of personal and national goals.[14] We thus find state and extra-state actors bent on educating young people to take their place in the new society, both by instilling in them specific market-based skills, and by constructing them as autonomous agents.

But changes in identity constructs and personal motivations are related to globalization in a larger institutional sense as well. That is, as globalization creates new associations and scales of production which transcend borders and threaten to elude control, states seek to adapt organizationally. As part of this process, the effort to reshape individual mentalities is increasingly paralleled by a tendency to delegate decision-making from public to private actors, especially in the economic sphere. Far from taking place spontaneously, this devolution of monitoring and decision-making authority is actively fostered by many states as a way of retaining ultimate control over outcomes, with territoriality now operating at several scales both above and below nation-state boundaries.[15] As a result of such

[14] See John Meyer and Ronald Jepperson, "The 'Actors' of Modern Society: The Cultural Construction of Social Agency," *Sociological Theory*, 18, No. 1 (March 2000): 100–20.

[15] See the contributions to Rodney Bruce Hall and Thomas J. Biersteker, eds., *The Emergence of Private Authority in Global Governance* (New York: Cambridge University Press,

disaggregation and structured devolution the state is potentially able to expand its regulatory and managerial capacity.[16] I suggest that something fundamentally similar is occurring in the process of constructing young people as well-socialized citizens.[17] Of course, not all such delegation is highly formalized or planned far in advance; at times it is implicit, *ad hoc*, or *de facto*. Nevertheless, instead of a state dominated approach, we find one in which private and semi-private actors assert – and are granted – extensive ability to mediate cultural flows and construct youth identity guidelines, often in association with state organized efforts.

A few qualifications need to be made here. First and most obviously, decentralization is not some irresistible requirement imposed by external forces, but instead represents a deliberate choice. When this occurs as part of a strategy of promoting trade and investment, it reflects certain ideological assumptions – which not all state actors share. Second, the degree of decentralization which takes place varies according to issue-area; economic delegation hardly implies political decentralization, especially with regard to matters of key national importance. Third, economic decentralization may occur for other reasons besides seeking international integration, and may reveal state weakness rather than an adaptive bid to enhance state capacity. Ironically, Kazakhstan furnishes an excellent example of the latter two points. Not only has the Nazarbaev regime steadfastly resisted democratization and true political decentralization, it has also allowed much economic decentralization to take place by default. Rather than a strategy of responding to global pressures, we often find mere capitulation to the demands of entrenched local strongmen.[18]

Nevertheless, the above observations about purposive devolution in response to globalization remain relevant to our discussion, because while the applicability of this concept is questionable in the spheres of

---

2003); also Jamie Peck, "Neoliberalizing States: Thin Policies/Hard Outcomes," *Progress in Human Geography* 25, 3 (2001): 445–55; Karen Litfin, "Sovereignty in World Ecopolitics," *Mershon International Studies Review*, 41, No. 2 (November 1997): 167–204.

[16] James Fulcher, "Globalisation, the Nation-state and Global Society," *Sociological Review*, 48, No. 4 (November 2000): 522–43; Linda Weiss, *The Myth of the Powerless State* (Ithaca: Cornell University Press, 1998).

[17] One is again reminded of Ong's insight, that one important component of the Chinese diaspora includes the acquisition of "flexible citizenship," in which individuals are constructed as mobile and culturally protean as an adaptation to neoliberal globalization. Ong, *Flexible Citizenship*.

[18] See Pauline Jones Luong, *Institutional Change and Political Continuity in Post-Soviet Central Asia: Power, Perceptions, and Pacts* (Cambridge and New York: Cambridge University Press, 2002); also Pauline Jones Luong, "Economic Decentralization in Kazakhstan: Causes and Consequences," in Luong, ed., *The Transformation of Central Asia: States and Societies from Soviet Rule to Independence* (Ithaca: Cornell University Press, 2003), pp. 182–210.

economics and high politics (especially in Kazakhstan and Azerbaijan), it is altogether applicable in the national identity sphere. The places we have examined provide a telling example of adaptation to cultural globalization, including the loss of control it entails with respect to the flow of ideas. We see this vividly in the state's approach to managing national youth identity formation: the state not only works with extra-state actors in developing youth policy, but also essentially sub-contracts policy implementation in ways that allow these actors a great deal of authority. Insofar as this arrangement contributes to stable governance and control over ultimate identity outcomes, it represents an adaptive form of state-building which involves a partial reconfiguration of sovereignty. In short, cultural globalization creates conditions that favor state delegation, much like other forms of delegation to private actors under conditions of globalization. And this in turn has important consequences for national identity. In particular, one finds a close linkage between the *institutional process* of engaging globalization through integration, on the one hand, and the *configuration of individualism*, on the other. Heightened individual autonomy and decentralization thus appear to be interrelated: they are each cultural artifacts and functional components of neoliberalism. In this sense it seems accurate to say that the collaborative, top-down and bottom-up process of youth socialization is, in itself, another example of globalization's hybrid effects.

To be clear, however, while there are important institutional reasons for delegation, this is not a sufficient explanation. Delegation is also made possible by two other factors already discussed: the delegitimation of Soviet methods and the emergence of a new consensus articulated in social discourse. Without the delegitimation of Soviet methods, the still palpable statist reflex might easily reassert itself, thereby preventing any real decentralization. Similarly, without the pervasive reproduction of a new discourse, it is questionable whether state actors would so confidently recognize like-minded sub-state and non-state actors, and so readily entrust important functions to them. And vice versa: in the absence of such a shared discourse, it seems unlikely that extra-state actors would so willingly turn to the state. It thus seems plausible that the pattern of state–society collaboration we have uncovered is most likely to emerge under conditions of globalization, high discursive consensus, and acceptable avenues for non-state social organization.

Collaboration and state–society relations

The last condition, the existence of acceptable avenues for non-state social organization, begs an important question in post-Soviet settings: to

Conclusions

what extent is social organization really acceptable outside the bounds of the state? Furthermore, how is the state situated in the sphere of national identity formation, and what insights does the present study yield for state–society relations more broadly? By way of an answer, I suggest that what these post-Soviet places reveal is how profoundly shared under-standings of social order influence relations between state and society. Indeed, the social demand for order is, in itself, one key dimension of stateness.[19] Challenges to sovereignty, territoriality, and identity pro-duced by globalization evoke responses at the national and local levels, on the part of actors who both demarcate and transcend the bound-aries between state and non-state. In doing so, they draw on the cultural repertoires at hand – quotidian local, imagined indigenous, and ideal-ized foreign – all of which become deeply hybridized in the bargain. It is within this liminal terrain (what Featherstone calls "dialogical space") that national identity is negotiated, and through which the nation and state are mutually constituted in everyday practice.[20]

What we find, paradoxically, is that by challenging self–Other distinc-tions and threatening to disrupt social structure, globalization actually ends up *reinforcing* the state. First, the Other is always present under glob-alization, creating a constant and ever-present need for differentiation and defense. In addition, constructing national identities also requires pro-pounding sameness in the form of shared values and the existence of close social bonds.[21] The latter task gains urgency inasmuch as absorp-tion of the new capitalist ethos tends to transgress established normative boundaries, which in turn requires a reimposition of order.[22] In these ways – by insinuating itself in the production of sameness and difference, and by standing as the guarantor of the nation's territorial integrity – the state manages to continually reproduce itself and to underscore its own salience.

We have seen how this process unfolds: quite aside from official procla-mations and programs, government actors at all levels are always lurking

[19] As Doty argues, the state represents a fundamental collective desire for stability and order (or "fully coded unity"), which becomes manifested in concrete social practices and institutions. Roxanne Lynn Doty, "Racism, Desire, and the Politics of Immigration," *Millennium*, 28, No. 3 (1999), p. 593. See also Yael Navaro-Yashin, *Faces of the State: Secularism and Public Life in Turkey* (Princeton: Princeton University Press, 2002), esp. pp. 132–36.

[20] Featherstone, *Undoing Culture*, pp. 111 and 117; see also Ronald Axtmann, "The State of the State: The Model of the Modern State and its Contemporary Transformation," *International Political Science Review*, 25, No. 3 (July 2004): 259–79.

[21] On this point see Rogers Brubaker and Frederick Cooper, "Beyond 'Identity'," *Theory and Society*, 29, No. 1 (February 2000): 1–47.

[22] I refer again to Roxanne Lynn Doty's discussion of this duality. Doty, "Racism, Desire, and the Politics of Immigration."

helpfully in the background, dispensing small favors, distributing funds, offering places to meet, and connecting entrepreneurs.[23] Yet this represents, by and large, not so much a manipulative strategy as a collective social endeavor. Consequently, a full account of state agency certainly includes the bureaucracy, but one far removed from the soulless labyrinth depicted by Kafka. Instead we find an engaged and sensitive ensemble of everyday actors, endowed with at least some degree of privileged resource control, but who are at the same time conversant with and responsive to popular discourse. Castells makes the point well: "[L]ocal and regional governments are, at the same time, the manifestation of decentralized state power, the closest point of contact between the state and civil society, and the expression of [parochial] cultural identities."[24]

In addition to state actors, what we have called "sub-state" actors play a crucial role in mediating globalization. Their expertise helps create attractive spectacles,[25] while their separation from the state proper allows them to mediate identity problems in socially acceptable ways. "Non-state" actors are also vital for the success of youth socialization, because their independence and ability to relate to young people (often as peers) makes them especially convincing purveyors of ideas. Insofar as their attitudes and goals concerning youth identity formation coincide with those of the state, such actors are politically invaluable – both for constructing national (youth) identity, and for legitimating extant institutions. We thus find cultural entrepreneurs engaged in the process of contesting and constructing social order, in which they are at once local members of the general public, and at the same time are deeply complicit in building the state.[26]

---

[23] In Appadurai's terms, in mediating globalization the state plays the role of "arbitrageur": screening flows from outside and then artfully combining their elements, with selective value added, in order to establish itself as benevolent champion of the nation. Appadurai, *Modernity at Large*, p. 42.

[24] Castells, *The Power of Identity*, p. 271. The state is thus, as Steinmetz argues, "shot through with circuits of meaning that cut across the state–society frontier." George Steinmetz, "Introduction: Culture and the State," in George Steinmetz, ed., *State/Culture: State-Formation After the Cultural Turn* (Ithaca and London: Cornell University Press, 1999), p. 12.

[25] As Adams observes in analyzing the production of cultural performances in Uzbekistan, the state depends on cultural elites to create attractive displays, thereby mobilizing the masses to support state-sanctioned programs. Laura Adams, "Cultural Elites in Uzbekistan: Spectacle, Seduction and the State," in Jones Luong, ed., *Transformation of Central Asia*, pp. 93–119.

[26] In Bourdieu's terms, through this process entrepreneurs act to generate and deposit cultural capital into the state's coffers. See Pierre Bourdieu, "The Forms of Capital," in J. G. Richardson, ed., *Handbook of Theory and Research for the Sociology of Education* (New York: Greenwood Press, 1986), pp. 241–58.

Consequently I would argue that – at least in these places and with respect to these particular issues – what we see in local responses to globalization is an important degree of social embeddedness on the part of the state, as well as what Peter Evans has called "complementarity" in the division of labor and goals.[27] The result is potentially consistent with the development of civil society, understood as the expansion of social groups and organizations outside the formal jurisdiction of the state, especially on the basis of social networks which cut across heterogeneous groups.[28] Admittedly, the pattern being followed in Kazakhstan, Russia, and Azerbaijan does not mirror the experience of the West. Yet here one must distinguish between liberal and statist trajectories of state–society development. As Henry Hale argues,

Whereas the liberal notion conceives of social organizations existing and operating independently of the state, the statist version sees the state and society as integrally related, part of the same organic whole. . . . The state's role is to protect non-state society, ensuring its continued existence, as well as to protect the interests of the state itself, which is seen as the embodiment of the nation.[29]

Hale suggests that in such cases nonstate society may be seen as "completing the state rather than diminishing it."[30] And, I would add, through its engagement with cultural entrepreneurs the state augments social organization. What we see in each of these post-Soviet sites, then, is the emergence of civil society and collaborative action – or the expansion of the public sphere – in the area of national identity formation, as an outgrowth of broadly shared understandings expressed in social discourse.

Many readers will doubtless find this conclusion rather perplexing, since it seems so clearly at odds with the generally top–down pattern of governance in these post-Soviet states. I would argue, however, that governance – and the degree of social involvement in political

[27] See Peter Evans, "Government Action, Social Capital, and Development: Reviewing the Evidence on Synergy," in Peter Evans, ed., *State–Society Synergy: Government and Social Capital in Development* (Berkeley: International and Area Studies, University of California at Berkeley, 1997), pp. 178–209.

[28] On social networks as precursors of civil society in Russia, see James L. Gibson, "Social Networks, Civil Society, and the Prospects for Consolidating Russia's Democratic Transition," *American Journal of Political Science*, 45, No. 1 (Jan. 2001): 51–68. On civil society development in response to globalization, see Ergun Ozbudun and E. Fuat Keyman, "Cultural Globalization in Turkey: Actors, Discourses, Strategies," in Berger and Huntington, eds., *Many Globalizations*, pp. 296–319.

[29] Henry Hale, "Civil Society from Above? Statist and Liberal Models of State-Building in Russia," *Demokratizatsiya*, 10, No. 3 (Summer 2002), p. 309.

[30] *Ibid.* On this point see also B. Michael Frolic, "State-Led Civil Society," in Timothy Brook and B. Michael Frolic, eds., *Civil Society in China* (Armonk, NY, and London: Sharpe, 2000), pp. 46–67; and Foster, "Associations in the Embrace of an Authoritarian State."

projects – varies greatly according to the issue at stake. In certain arenas, including high politics as well as issue-areas like the environment or
property rights, social discourse tends to be sharply contested but also
narrowly articulated, with few people actively engaging the key questions
at stake. Within these arenas the public sphere contracts, and formal
state institutions play a dominant role. Thus, despite the rumblings of
dissent associated with the "colored revolutions" in Georgia, Ukraine,
and Kyrgyzstan, at least for the foreseeable future the regimes in Russia,
Azerbaijan, and Kazakhstan have consolidated their power, and appear
able to rule in highly authoritarian style. While seeming to be imposed
from above, however, another way of understanding this outcome is that
it reflects prevailing social understandings of order within the formal
political arena. Conversely, *in the arena of national identity formation –
including the perceived collision between youth identity and globalization – the prevailing social discourse is both broadly articulated and
highly consensual. State–society relations are powerfully influenced as
a result: the public sphere greatly expands, and governance comes to
be shared by state and extra-state actors, who look to each other for
help.[31] As we have seen, this emerges through dialogue between formally designated and self-appointed entrepreneurs, as well as between
the youth and those seeking to shape youth socialization. The take-away
lesson from the foregoing discussion, then, is that state–society relations –
like the boundaries between public and private – vary across issue-area
depending on intersubjective understandings of order, which are themselves constituted through discourse. Seen from this perspective, too, the
state's preoccupation with national identity formation becomes under-
standable not merely as functionally necessary or cynically self-interested
behavior, but as an expression of the abiding social character of the
state.

Nor does this outcome appear to be limited to post-communist settings.[32] Much the same dynamic is described by Rogers Smith, who
argues that a deep "sense of peoplehood" arises from diffuse interactions

---

[31] An expression of this is Kirill Razlogov, El'na Orlova, and Evgenii Kuz'min, "Rossiiskaia
kul'turnaia politika v kontekste globalizatsii," *Otechestvennye zapiski*, No. 4 (2005), available online at http://www.strana-oz.ru.

[32] In addition to the former USSR, a fascinating glimpse into just such a blurring of state
and social boundaries is provided by Jing Wang in her observations on the official Chinese discourse of popular culture. According to Wang, since the late Deng period the
central state has extensively reorganized the hierarchy of governing institutions, and now
collaborates with a range of increasingly local (including non-state) social organizations
extending down to the street committee level. In this way, the state is simultaneously
weakened (formally) yet also strengthened (practically) in its ability to police illicit cultural and economic activities. See Wang, "The State Question."

between leaders and constituents.[33] Such collaboration may in fact be fairly typical and routine elsewhere, constituting a subtle and often unnoticed feature of relatively consensual polities. If so, it would be important to know how such collaboration is generated and sustained, and how various individuals and groups come to play active parts. Answering these questions in future studies will require exploring "state–society relations," not only through an appreciation of power as expressed in formal and informal rules, but, perhaps more importantly, through an examination of social networks and meanings.[34]

Is this agency, and why does it matter?

Before ending, we return to a key analytical problem: how to evaluate the significance of the micro-decisions and interventions involved in constructing identity. The individuals we have examined here stand astride massive global flows of ideas, and it is not always clear to what extent their actions are truly autonomous, as opposed to being predetermined by disparities in power and knowledge, or prefigured by dominant discourses of legitimate action. Are these individuals – both inside and outside of the state bureaucracy – best understood as creative conjurers of new social identities, or as mere reproducers of ideas and practices established elsewhere? After all, as chapter 1 discusses at length, strategic hybridization is basically the same phenomenon everywhere in the world. Specific local distinctions in terms of the emphases placed on absorption versus assertion or rejection amount to only minor variations on a global theme. Observing that social actors are needed to mediate particular outcomes represents a weak claim for agency, since it essentially concedes that larger structures are implicated in producing the general pattern. From this standpoint "agency" simply describes the performance of exogenously determined political action, much in the way the propagation of institutions is understood by world polity theorists: to the extent that individual actors figure in such accounts, they are best viewed as "enactors of scripts rather more than . . . self-directed actors."[35]

---

[33] Rogers M. Smith, *Stories of Peoplehood: The Politics and Morals of Political Membership* (New York: Cambridge University Press, 2003), p. 32.

[34] An important discussion along these lines is E. Fuat Keyman, *Globalization, State, Identity/Difference: Toward a Critical Social Theory of International Relations* (Atlantic Highlands, NJ: Humanities Press, 1997). See also Gilbert M. Joseph and Daniel Nugent, "Popular Culture and State Formation in Revolutionary Mexico," in Gilbert M. Joseph and Daniel Nugent, eds., *Everyday Forms of State Formation: Revolution and the Negotiation of Rule in Modern Mexico* (Durham and London: Duke University Press, 1994), pp. 3–23.

[35] Meyer *et al.*, "World Society and the Nation-State," p. 150.

Instead, I would argue that something more significant is taking place in these post-Soviet locales. In making this argument, to repeat a point discussed earlier, I conceptualize agency rather modestly as the innovative use of discursive and/or symbolic power in order to produce change in established patterns of social outcomes. Accordingly, the key to evaluating the significance of actors' interventions is not whether the results are "extraordinary" in the sense that they are categorically different from outcomes produced elsewhere under similar conditions. Instead, the question is implicitly a counterfactual one: whether the outcomes we see with regard to the content and process of identity construction would have occurred regardless of the specific interventions launched by state and extra-state entrepreneurs. In other words, in mediating the cultural and institutional space between global flows and local conditions, did the actors involved produce something substantially new? And here, I would submit, the answer is decidedly *yes*, both with respect to social networks and discourse.

Certainly the state, sub-state, and non-state actors we have examined do not invent identity constructs out of whole cloth. On the contrary, ambient social discourse echoes many of the ideas purveyed by policy-makers and entrepreneurs, and some of this emanates from beyond the state's borders. Still, these actors – especially in local settings and in direct contact with the youth – provide crucial value-added by accentuating certain features and dampening others, refashioning the constructs and meanings in play, managing the ambivalence generated in the course of hybridization, and translating the resulting pastiche into a narrative suitable for consumption by young audiences. Where novel practices do not already resonate with preexisting culture, the transmission of ideas – such as individualism, efficiency-seeking, and other liberal concepts – are facilitated by the construction of appropriate narratives, which often draw on indigenous symbols (including actual or putative traditional culture).

In part, the practice of constructing national identity under globalization thus parallels the transfer of norms, in which "cultural match" is required for successful uptake of foreign ideas.[36] And as Acharya points out, where cultural match does not already exist it has to be fashioned through "localization," in order to make international norms resonate with prior beliefs and identities.[37] It should be emphasized, then, that pre-existing cultural configurations should not be seen as insurmountable

---

[36] On cultural match see Checkel, "Norms, Institutions and National Identity"; also Cortell and Davis, "Understanding the Domestic Impact of Norms," pp. 73–6.
[37] Amitav Acharya, "How Ideas Spread: Whose Norms Matter? Norm Localization and Institutional Change in Asian Regionalism," *International Organization*, 58, No. 2 (April 2004): 239–75.

barriers, but rather as constraints which can potentially be overcome by agency. Indeed, it may be suggested that one measure of agency is the ability to reconcile truly innovative ideas with a traditionalist discourse. In this respect, to refer back to our earlier discussion of this problem, entrepreneurs in these former Soviet cities display a measure of true "virtuosity" by expanding the discursive repertoire and the range of culturally viable practice.

Additionally, agency as we encounter it here consists of creating networks and, through them, formulating discursive strategies and carrying them out. Along the way, entrepreneurs have fashioned among themselves surprisingly inclusive and mutually responsive interconnections. This in itself constitutes an insufficiently appreciated social mechanism, one which helps explain how state–society relations and national identity formation are linked in the context of globalization. Moreover, to emphasize a point made above, such action is highly consequential – not only in shaping idealized national identity constructs (and potentially influencing youth identity outcomes in the bargain), but in reconstituting the state through the institutionalization of prevailing practices and beliefs. In sum, far from being scripted performers, these actors resemble "principled activists" within transnational networks, as described by Keck and Sikkink: "[n]o mere automatic 'enactors,' these are people who seek to amplify the generative power of norms, broaden the scope of practices these norms engender, and sometimes even renegotiate or transform the norms themselves."[38] Cultural entrepreneurs perform precisely such functions, and do so, moreover, in evolving political contexts which they help shape by their actions.

It is appropriate at this point to briefly revisit one of the questions posed at the outset, about the viability of distinct national identity constructs in an era of globalization. While it is far too early to say what effects globalization will ultimately have, it seems rather arbitrary to assume that the inroads made by Western culture will ineluctably widen, or that hybrid cultural frameworks cannot remain stable. In Russia, Kazakhstan, and Azerbaijan it remains an open question whether youth audiences will embrace the identities which are so assiduously being constructed for

---

[38] Viewing their agency from this standpoint offers a way of linking the study of cultural globalization, and its active mediation, with the study of transnational diffusion of norms and the literature on social movements. See Keck and Sikkink, *Activists Beyond Borders*, p. 35. The foregoing discussion also has clear parallels to McAdam, Tarrow, and Tilly's influential work on social category formation within social movements. Thus, we find abundant evidence of brokerage, certification, attribution of threats and opportunities, and social appropriation of identities. Douglas McAdam, Sidney Tarrow, and Charles Tilly, *Dynamics of Contention* (New York: Cambridge University Press, 2001).

them. This may depend in large part on whether cultural entrepreneurs can create a compelling narrative, one that combines the promise of modernization with the emotional allure of belonging. In addition, it may well be that *how* identity is constructed has a bearing on its likely success. To what extent is this process inclusive and spontaneous, as opposed to being peremptorily imposed by the state? Where a high degree of consensus and social cooperation combine, there are perhaps better prospects for mediating cultural flows and maintaining a unique identity in the face of globalization.

In closing, this brings us back again to the role of individual agents and the interconnections between them. In the area of national youth identity formation we find the entrepreneur partly in the role of chaperone and partly in the role of guardian of tradition and culture. In their public interventions – just as in official and semi-official discourse – a number of contrasting normative claims are advanced, each with significant implications for state–society relations and the future prospects of legitimacy. As these claims are presented by the various actors explored in this study, they tend to invoke a juxtaposition of two sets of values: the foreign, modern, and material *versus* the native, traditional, and ideal. The cultural entrepreneur seeks to reconcile the tensions between them, manipulating symbols of the latter set in order to bound, sanitize, and partially displace those in the former. At the same time the entrepreneur also tries to salvage some of the foreign, modern, and material – especially the modernizing power of individualism. This involves crafting a new national identity as well as separating global flows into discrete components, some of which are shored up while others are discounted or even discarded. Such artistry requires a subtle touch and sleight of hand, to divert the youth from temptation while at the same time offering at least some material benefits – and this, despite the state's empty cupboard. It is the entrepreneur's job to choreograph this intricate step. As Ulf Hannerz envisions it:

Local cultural entrepreneurs have gradually mastered the alien cultural forms which reach them through the transnational commodity flow and in other ways, taking them apart, tampering and tinkering with them in such a way that the resulting new forms are more responsive to, and at the same time in part outgrowths of, local everyday life.[39]

Hannerz is probably too optimistic, at least for the places explored in this book. But the image of using culture to craft political tools does

[39] Ulf Hannerz, "Scenarios for Peripheral Cultures," in Anthony D. King, ed., *Culture, Globalization, and the World System: Contemporary Conditions for the Representation of Identity* (Minneapolis: University of Minnesota Press, 1997), p. 124.

identify the quest of the state and its social interlocutors to remain insin-
uated in the process of change. And it does capture the interplay of the
native and foreign, the new and old, and the common and extraordinary aspects of identity hybridization. I would only add that the *way in
which this is attempted* reveals a great deal about the evolving relationship
between state and society. That is, not only does it illuminate the texture
of identities fashioned thereby – interwoven as they are from notions of
sameness and difference – but it also helps us to see that national identity formation constitutes a medium through which society is reproduced
and renegotiated, and through which the state itself congeals, as an outgrowth of social discourse and action. This is perhaps the most important
insight to be gained from exploring the process of identity construction
in post-Soviet space and elsewhere, in the context of globalization.

References to scholarly works

Abaza, Mona, "Shopping Malls, Consumer Culture and the Reshaping of Public Space in Egypt," *Theory, Culture and Society*, 18, No. 5 (October 2001): 97–122

Abbasov, Il'gam, "Uchebniki istorii epokhi nezavisimosti," *Azerbaidzhan v Mire*, 1, No. 3 (2006), available online at www.realazer.com/mag.

Abu-Lughod, Lila, "The Romance of Resistance: Tracing Transformations of Power through Bedouin Women," *American Ethnologist*, 17, No. 1 (February 1990): 41–55

Acharya, Amitav, "How Ideas Spread: Whose Norms Matter? Norm Localization and Institutional Change in Asian Regionalism," *International Organization*, 58, No. 2 (April 2004): 239–75

Adams, Laura, "Cultural Elites in Uzbekistan: Spectacle, Seduction and the State," in Pauline Jones Luong, ed., *The Transformation of Central Asia: States and Societies from Soviet Rule to Independence* (Ithaca: Cornell University Press, 2003), pp. 93–119

Akçali, Pinar, "Nation-State Building in Central Asia: A Lost Case?" *Perspectives on Global Development and Technology*, 2, Nos. 3/4 (2003): 409–29

Albrow, Martin, *The Global Age: State and Society Beyond Modernity* (Stanford: Stanford University Press, 1997)

Alessandrini, Anthony C., "'My Heart's Indian for All That': Bollywood Film between Home and Diaspora," *Diaspora: A Journal of Transnational Studies*, 10, No. 3 (Winter 2001): 315–40

Alexander, Jeffrey C., *The Meanings of Social Life* (New York: Oxford University Press, 2003)

Alexander, Jeffrey C., and Philip Smith, "The Discourse of American Civil Society: A New Proposal for Cultural Studies," *Theory and Society*, 22, No. 2 (April 1993): 151–207

Alger, Chadwick, "Local Response to Global Intrusions," in Zdravko Mlinar, ed., *Globalization and Territorial Identities* (Brookfield, VT: Ashgate, 1992), pp. 77–104

Aliev, Fuad, "Sotsialyi dialog i ego rol v reshenii problem molodezhi Azerbaidzhana: Poisk effektivnykh putei vzaimodeistviia," in Economic Commission for Europe, *Youth of the XXI Century: Realities and Perspectives* (United Nations: New York, 2004), pp. 297–300

Allworth, Edward, "History and Group Identity in Central Asia," in Graham Smith, Edward Allworth, and Vivien Law, eds., *Nation-Building in the*

Post-Soviet Borderlands: The Politics of National Identities (Cambridge: Cambridge University Press, 1998), pp. 67–90

Alonso, William, "Citizenship, Nationality and Other Identities," *Journal of International Affairs*, 48, No. 2 (Winter 1995): 585–99

Altstadt, Audrey, "Azerbaijan's Struggle Toward Democracy," in Karen Dawisha and Bruce Parrott, eds., *Conflict, Cleavage, and Change in Central Asia and the Caucasus* (Cambridge: Cambridge University Press, 1997), pp. 110–55

Amin, Hussein, and Hanzada Fikry, "Media, Sex, Violence, and Drugs: Egypt's Experience," in Yahya Kamalipour and Kuldip Rampal, eds., *Media, Sex, Violence, and Drugs in the Global Village* (New York: Rowman and Littlefield, 2001), pp. 219–33

Anderson, Benedict, *Language and Power: Exploring Political Cultures in Indonesia* (Ithaca: Cornell University Press, 1990)

Imagined Communities: Reflections on the Origin and Spread of Nationalism (Verso: London and New York, 1991)

Ang, Ien, "Desperately Guarding Borders: Media Globalization, 'Cultural Imperialism', and the Rise of 'Asia'," in Yao Souchou, ed., *House of Glass: Culture, Modernity, and the State in Southeast Asia* (Singapore: Institute of Southeast Asian Studies, 2001), pp. 27–45

Appadurai, Arjun, *Modernity at Large: Cultural Dimensions of Globalization* (Minneapolis and London: University of Minnesota Press, 1996)

Arnett, Jeffrey, "The Psychology of Globalization," *American Psychologist*, 57, No.10 (October 2002): 774–63

Axtmann, Ronald, "The State of the State: The Model of the Modern State and its Contemporary Transformation," *International Political Science Review*, 25, No. 3 (July 2004): 259–79

Badie, Bertrand, *The Imported State: The Westernization of the Political Order*, translated by Claudia Royal (Stanford: Stanford University Press, 2000)

Bahrampour, Firouz, *Turkey: Social and Political Transformation* (Brooklyn: Theo. Gaus' Sons, 1967)

Ball, Alan M., *Imagining America: Influence and Images in Twentieth-Century Russia* (New York: Rowman and Littlefield, 2003)

Banks, Jack, "MTV and the Globalization of Popular Culture," *Gazette*, 59, No. 1 (1997): 43–60

Barber, Benjamin, *Jihad vs. McWorld: How Globalism and Tribalism are Reshaping the World* (New York: Ballantine Books, 1995)

Barnett, Michael, "Culture, Strategy and Foreign Policy Change: Israel's Road to Oslo," *European Journal of International Relations*, 5, No. 1 (1999): 5–36

Barth, Fredrik, "Introduction," in Fredrik Barth, ed., *Ethnic Groups and Boundaries: The Social Organization of Cultural Difference* (Boston: Little, Brown, and Co., 1969), pp. 9–38

Bauman, Zygmunt, "Modernity and Ambivalence," in Mike Featherstone, ed., *Global Culture: Nationalism, Globalization and Modernity* (London: Sage Publications, 1990), pp. 143–69

Befu, Harumi, "Globalization Theory from the Bottom Up: Japan's Contribution," *Japanese Studies*, 23, No. 1 (May 2003): 3–22

Beissinger, Mark, *Nationalist Mobilization and the Collapse of the Soviet State* (Cambridge: Cambridge University Press, 2002)

Bentley, Jerry H., "Cross-Cultural Interaction and Periodization in World History," *American Historical Review*, 101, No. 3 (June 1996): 749–70

Berking, Helmuth B., "Ethnicity is Everywhere: On Globalization and the Transformation of Cultural Identity," *Current Sociology*, 51, No. 3–4 (May 2003): 248–64

Biersteker, Thomas J., "The 'Triumph' of Neoclassical Economics in the Developing World: Policy Convergence and Bases of Governance in the International Economic Order," in James N. Rosenau and Erenst O. Czempiel, eds., *Governance without Government: Order and Change in World Politics* (Cambridge: Cambridge University Press, 1992), pp. 102–31

Bigg, Claire, "Russia: Here Comes The Sun For Putin's Patriotic Youth," Radio Free Europe/Radio Liberty, *Newsline*, July 20, 2005, available online at www.rferl.org

Billington, James H., *Russia in Search of Itself* (Baltimore and London: Johns Hopkins University Press, 2003)

Biswas, Shampa, "W(h)ither the Nation-State? National and State Identity in the Face of Fragmentation and Globalisation," *Global Society: Journal of Interdisciplinary International Relations*, 16, No. 2 (April 2002): 175–98

Boli, John, and George M. Thomas, eds., *Constructing World Culture: International Nongovernmental Organizations since 1875* (Stanford: Stanford University Press, 1999)

Bonnett, Alastair, *The Idea of the West: Culture, Politics and History* (New York: Palgrave, 2004), pp. 107–22

Bossen, Claus, "Festival Mania, Tourism and Nation-Building in Fiji: The Case of the Hibiscus Festival, 1956–1970," *The Contemporary Pacific*, 12, No. 1 (Spring 2000): 123–54

Boulanger, Clare L., "Inventing Tradition, Inventing Modernity: Dayak Identity in Urban Sarawak," *Asian Ethnicity*, 3, No. 2 (September 2002): 221–21

Bourdieu, Pierre, "The Forms of Capital," in J. G. Richardson, ed., *Handbook of Theory and Research for the Sociology of Education* (New York: Greenwood Press, 1986), pp. 241–58

  The Logic of Practice, translated by Richard Nice (Stanford: Stanford University Press, 1990)

  "Scattered Remarks," *European Journal of Social Theory*, 2, No. 3 (August 1999): 334–40

Braga e Vaz da Costa, Maria Helena, "Representation and National Identity in Rio de Janeiro: Walter Salles, Jr.'s, *A Grande Arte*," *Studies in Latin American Popular Culture*, 20 (2001): 165–85

Brass, Paul R., *The Politics of India Since Independence*, second edn. (Cambridge and New York: Cambridge University Press, 1994)

Breuilly, John, *Nationalism and the State*, 2nd edition (Chicago: University of Chicago Press, 1994)

Brison, Karen J., "Constructing Identity through Ceremonial Language in Rural Fiji," *Ethnology*, 40, No. 4 (Fall 2001): 309–27

Brooks, Stephen G., "The Globalization of Production and the Changing Benefits of Conquest," *The Journal of Conflict Resolution*, 43, No. 5 (October 1999): 646–70

Brown, Hilary, "American Media Impact on Jamaican Youth: A Cultural Dependency Thesis," in Hopeton S. Dunn, ed., *Globalization, Communications and Caribbean Identity* (New York: St. Martin's Press, 1995), pp. 56–82

Brubaker, Rogers, *Nationalism Reframed: Nationhood and the National Question in the New Europe* (Cambridge: Cambridge University Press, 1996)

Brubaker, Rogers, and Frederick Cooper, "Beyond 'Identity'," *Theory and Society*, 29, No. 1 (February 2000): 1–47

Bruner, M. Lane, "Rhetorics of the State: The Public Negotiation of Political Character in Germany, Russia, and Quebec," *National Identities*, 2, No. 2 (July 2000): 159–75

Bucholtz, Mary, "Youth and Cultural Practice," *Annual Review of Anthropology*, 31 (2002): 525–52

Buell, Frederick, *National Culture and the New Global System* (Baltimore: Johns Hopkins University Press, 1994)

Buttel, Frederick, "Some Observations on the Anti-Globalization Movement," *Australian Journal of Social Issues*, 38, No. 1 (February 2003): 95–116

Buzgalin, Aleksander, "Russia's Generation XXI: Caught Between Pragmatism, Radicalism And . . . Antiglobalism?" Jamestown Foundation, *Russia and Eurasia Review*, 1, No. 9 (October 8, 2002)

Calhoun, Craig, "Social Theory and the Politics of Identity," in Craig Calhoun, ed., *Social Theory and the Politics of Identity* (Oxford: Blackwell, 1994), pp. 10–36

Callahan, William A., "Beyond Cosmopolitanism and Nationalism: Diasporic Chinese and Neo-Nationalism in China and Thailand," *International Organization*, 57, No. 3 (Summer 2003): 481–517

"Remembering the Future: Utopia, Empire, and Harmony in 21st-Century International Theory," *European Journal of International Relations*, 10, No. 4 (December 2004): 569–601

Camilleri, Joseph, "State, Civil Society, and Economy," in Joseph Camilleri, Anthony Jarvis, and Albert Paolini, eds., *The State in Transition: Reimagining Political Space* (Boulder, CO: Lynne Rienner, 1995), pp. 209–28

Canclini, García Néstor, *Hybrid Cultures: Strategies for Entering and Leaving Modernity* (Minneapolis: University of Minnesota Press, 1995)

Cardoza, Kavitha, "Parental Control Over Children's Television Viewing in India," *Contemporary South Asia*, 11, No. 2 (July 2002): 135–61

Carnoy, Martin, and Diana Rhoten, "What Does Globalization Mean for Educational Change? A Comparative Approach," *Comparative Education Review*, 46, No. 1 (February 2002): 1–9

Carruthers, Ashley, "National Identity, Diasporic Anxiety, and Music Video Culture in Vietnam," in Yao Souchou, ed., *House of Glass: Culture, Modernity, and the State in Southeast Asia* (Singapore: Institute of Southeast Asian Studies, 2001), pp. 119–49

Castells, Manuel, *The Power of Identity* (Malden, MA: Blackwell, 1997)

Cesari, Jocelyne, "Global Multiculturalism: The Challenge of Heterogeneity," *Alternatives: Global, Local, Political*, Supplement, 27, No. 1 (February 2002): 5–19

Cha, Seong Hwan, "Modern Chinese Confucianism: The Contemporary Neo-Confucian Movement and its Cultural Significance," *Social Compass*, 50, No. 4 (December 2003): 481–91

Chadwick, Andrew, "Studying Political Ideas: A Public Political Discourse Approach," *Political Studies*, 48, No. 2 (Special Issue, 2000): 283–301

Chaney, David, *Cultural Change and Everyday Life* (New York: Palgrave, 2002)

Chapman, David W., John Weidman, Marc Cohen, and Malcolm Mercer, "The Search for Quality: A Five Country Study of National Strategies to Improve Educational Quality in Central Asia," *International Journal of Educational Development*, 25, No. 5 (September 2005): 514–30

Chatterjee, Partha, *The Nation and its Fragments: Colonial and Postcolonial Histories* (Princeton: Princeton University Press, 1993)

Checkel, Jeffrey, "Norms, Institutions, and National Identity in Contemporary Europe," *International Studies Quarterly* 43, No. 1 (March 1999): 83–114

Chen, Feng, "Rebuilding the Party's Normative Authority," *Problems of Post-Communism*, 45, No. 6 (November/December 1998): 33–41

Cherednichenko, Tatiana, *Rossiia 90-kh: Aktualnyi leksikon istorii kultury* (Moscow: Novoe Literaturnoe Obozrenie, 1999)

Cheshkov, Marat, "Globalizatsiia: sushchnost, nyneshniaia faza, perspektivy," *Pro et Contra*, 4, No. 4 (Fall 1999), available online at http://pubs.carnegie.ru/

Chua, Beng-Huat, "Between Economy and Race: The Asianization of Singapore," in Ayse Oncu and Petra Weyland, eds., *Space, Culture and Power: New Identities in Globalising Cities* (London: Zed Books, 1997), pp. 23–41
  "World Cities, Globalisation and the Spread of Consumerism: A View of Singapore," *Urban Studies*, 35, Nos. 5/6 (May 1998): 981–1000
  "'Asian-Values' Discourse and the Resurrection of the Social," *positions*, 7, No. 2 (Fall 1999): 573–92

Clifford, James, *Routes: Travel and Translation in the Late-Twentieth Century* (Cambridge: Harvard University Press, 1997)

Coalson, Robert, "Russian Youth Group 'Nashi' Gathers Momentum," Radio Free Europe/Radio Liberty, *Newsline*, June 3, 2005, available online at www.rferl.org

Cohn, Bernard S., "Representing Authority in Victorian India," in Eric Hobsbawm and Terence Ranger, eds., *The Invention of Tradition* (Cambridge and New York: Cambridge University Press, 1983), pp. 165–210

Comaroff, Jean, and John Comaroff, "Millennial Capitalism: First Thoughts on a Second Coming," *Public Culture* 12, No. 2 (Spring 2000): 291–343

Compton, Jr., Robert W., *East Asian Democratization: Impact of Globalization, Culture, and Economy* (Westport and London: Praeger, 2000)

Condee, Nancy, "Body Graphics: Tabooing the Fall of Communism," in Adele Marie Barker, ed., *Consuming Russia: Popular Culture, Sex, and Society Since Gorbachev* (Durham: Duke University Press, 1999), pp. 339–61

Condry, Ian, "The Social Production of Difference: Imitation and Authenticity in Japanese Rap Music," in Heide Fehrenbach and Uta G. Poiger, eds.,

Transactions, Transgressions, and Transformations: American Culture in Western Europe and Japan (New York: Berghahn Books, 2000), pp. 166–84

Connor, Walker, *Ethnonationalism: The Quest for Understanding* (Princeton: Princeton University Press, 1994)

Cooke, Steven, and Fiona McLean, "Picturing the Nation: The Celtic Periphery as Discursive Other in the Archaeological Displays of the Museum of Scotland," *Scottish Geographical Journal*, 118, No. 4 (2002): 283–98

Cornell, Svante, *Small Nations and Great Powers: A Study of Ethnopolitical Conflict in the Caucasus* (Richmond: Curzon Press, 2001)

Coronil, Fernando, *The Magical State: Nature, Money, and Modernity in Venezuela* (Chicago: Chicago University Press, 1997)

Cortell, Andrew, and James Davis, "Understanding the Domestic Impact of Norms: A Research Agenda," *International Studies Review*, 2, No. 1 (Spring 2000): 65–87

Cowen, Tyler, *Creative Destruction: How Globalization is Changing the World's Cultures* (Princeton and Oxford: Princeton University Press, 2002)

Croucher, Sheila, *Globalization and Belonging: The Politics of Identity in a Changing World* (Lanham, MD: Rowman and Littlefield, 2004)

Cruz, Consuelo, "Identity and Persuasion: How Nations Remember Their Pasts and Make Their Futures," *World Politics*, 52, No. 3 (April 2000): 275–312

Daughtry, J. Martin, "Russia's New Anthem and the Negotiation of National Identity," *Ethnomusicology*, 47, No. 1 (Winter 2003): 42–67

Davis, Eric, "The Museum and the Politics of Social Control in Modern Iraq," in John Gillis, ed., *Commemorations: The Politics of National Identity* (Princeton: Princeton University Press, 1994), pp. 90–104

Dawisha, Karen, and Bruce Parrott, *Russia and the New States of Eurasia: The Politics of Upheaval* (New York: Cambridge University Press, 1994)

De Grandis, Rita, "The Voice of Alejandro 'Negro' Dolina: Towards a Repositioning of Populist Discourse," *Studies in Latin American Popular Culture*, 16 (1997): 127–45

Delanty, Gerard, "Consumption, Modernity and Japanese Cultural Identity: The Limits of Americanization?" in Ulrich Beck, Nathan Sznaider and Rainer Winter, eds., *Global America? The Cultural Consequences of Globalization* (Liverpool: Liverpool University Press, 2003), pp. 114–33

Delgado, Fernando P., "Chicano Ideology Revisited: Rap Music and the (Re)articulation of Chicanismo," *Western Journal of Communication*, 62, No. 2 (Spring 1998): 95–113

Derné, Steve, "The (Limited) Effect of Cultural Globalization in India: Implications for Culture Theory," *Poetics*, 33, No. 1 (February 2005): 33–47

Diawara, Manthia, "Toward a Regional Imaginary in Africa," in Frederic Jameson and Masao Miyoshi, eds., *The Cultures of Globalization* (Durham and London: Duke University Press, 1998), pp. 103–24

DiMaggio, Paul, "Cultural Entrepreneurship in Nineteenth-Century Boston: The Creation of an Organizational Base for High Culture in America," in Chandra Mukerji and Michael Schudson, eds., *Rethinking Popular Culture: Contemporary Perspectives in Cultural Studies* (Berkeley: University of California Press, 1991), pp. 374–97

Diouf, Mamadou, "Engaging Postcolonial Cultures: African Youth and Public Space," *African Studies Review*, 46, No. 2 (September 2003): 1–12

Dirlik, Arif, "Markets, Culture, Power: The Making of a 'Second Cultural Revolution' in China," *Asian Studies Review*, 25, No. 1 (March 2001): 1–33

Diuk, Nadia, "Pervoe svobodnoe pokolenie: Molodezh, politika i identichnosti v Rossii, Ukraine i Azerbaidzhane," *Polit.ru*, December 27, 2003, www.Polit.ru "The Next Generation," *Journal of Democracy*, 15, No. 3 (July 2004): 59–66

Dosybiev, Anton, "Kazakhstan: School Gang Violence On the Rise," Institute of War and Peace Reporting, *Reporting Central Asia*, No. 253 (December 16, 2003), available online at www.iwpr.net

Doty, Roxanne Lynn, "Racism, Desire, and the Politics of Immigration," *Millennium*, 28, No. 3 (1999): 585–606

Dubin, Boris, "'Protivoves': symvolika Zapada v Rossiia poslednykh let," *Pro et Contra*, 8, No. 3 (April 2004): 23–35

Duff, Ernest A., "Attack and Counterattack: Dynamics of Transculturation in the Caribbean," *Studies in Latin American Popular Culture*, 12 (1993): 195–202

Dujunco, Mercedes, "Hybridity and Disjuncture in Mainland Chinese Popular Music," in Richard King and Timothy Craig, *Global Goes Local: Popular Culture in Asia* (Vancouver: University of British Columbia Press, 2002), pp. 25–39

Dutt, Sagarika, "Identities and the Indian State," *Third World Quarterly*, 19, No. 3 (September 1998): 411–35

Eitzen, Hilda, "Nawriz in Kazakhstan: Scenarios for Managing Diversity," in Ingvar Svanberg, ed., *Contemporary Kazakhs: Cultural and Social Perspectives* (New York: St. Martin's, 1999), pp. 73–101

Esenova, Saulesh, "Soviet Nationality, Identity, and Ethnicity in Central Asia: Historic Narratives and Kazakh Ethnic Identity," *Journal of Muslim Minority Affairs*, 22, No. 1 (April 2002): 11–38

Evans, Peter, "Government Action, Social Capital, and Development: Reviewing the Evidence on Synergy," in Peter Evans, ed., *State–Society Synergy: Government and Social Capital in Development* (Berkeley: International and Area Studies, University of California at Berkeley, 1997), pp. 178–209

Featherstone, Mike, *Undoing Culture: Globalization, Postmodernism and Identity* (London: Sage Publications, 1995)

Fenster, Mark, "Understanding and Incorporating Rap: The Articulation of Alternative Popular Musical Practices within Cultural Practices and Institutions," *Howard Journal of Communications*, 5, No. 3 (Spring 1995): 223–44

Ferguson, James G., "Of Mimicry and Membership: Africans and the New World Society," *Cultural Anthropology*, 17, No. 4 (November 2002): 551–71

Fernando, Chitra, "Asian Xenophobia against the West," *Annals of the American Academy of Political and Social Science*, 318 (July 1958): 83–88

Fierke, Karin M., "Links Across the Abyss: Language and Logic in International Relations," *International Studies Quarterly*, 46, No. 3 (September 2002): 331–54

Finckenauer, James, *Russian Youth: Law, Deviance and the Pursuit of Freedom* (New Brunswick: Transaction Publishers, 1995)

Finnemore, Martha, *National Interests in International Society* (Ithaca: Cornell University Press, 1996)

Fischer, Edward F., "Cultural Logic and Maya Identity," *Current Anthropology*, 40, No. 4 (August–October 1999): 473–99

Fitzgerald, T. K., *Metaphors of Identity* (Albany: State University of New York Press, 1993)

Foster, Kenneth, "Associations in the Embrace of an Authoritarian State: State Domination of Society?" *Studies in Comparative International Development*, 35, No. 4 (Winter 2001): 84–109

Foster, Robert J., "Making National Cultures in the Global Ecumene," *Annual Review of Anthropology*, 20 (1991): 235–60

French, Howard W., "Despite an Act of Leniency, China has its Eye on the Web," *New York Times*, June 27, 2004, Section 1, p. 6

Frolic, B. Michael, "State-Led Civil Society," in Timothy Brook and B. Michael Frolic, eds., *Civil Society in China* (Armonk, NY, and London: Sharpe, 2000), pp. 46–67

Fulcher, James, "Globalisation, the Nation-state and Global Society," *Sociological Review*, 48, No. 4 (November 2000): 522–43

Gable, Eric, "The Culture Development Club: Youth, Neo-Tradition, and the Construction of Society in Guinea-Bissau," *Anthropological Quarterly*, 73, No. 4 (October 2000): 195–203

Garon, Sheldon, *Molding Japanese Minds: The State in Everyday Life* (Princeton: Princeton University Press, 1997)

Geertz, Clifford, *The Interpretation of Cultures* (New York: Basic Books, 1973)

Gellner, Ernest, *Nations and Nationalism* (Oxford: Basil Blackwell, 1983)

   Culture, Identity, and Politics (Cambridge: Cambridge University Press, 1987)

Gibson, James L., "Social Networks, Civil Society, and the Prospects for Consolidating Russia's Democratic Transition," *American Journal of Political Science*, 45, No. 1 (Jan. 2001): 51–68

Giddens, Anthony, *Modernity and Self-identity: Self and Society in the Late Modern Age* (Stanford: Stanford University Press, 1991)

Glenn, John, *The Soviet Legacy in Central Asia* (New York: St. Martin's, 1999)

Goff, Patricia M., "Invisible Borders: Economic Liberalization and National Identity," *International Studies Quarterly*, 44, No. 4 (December 2000): 533–62

Gokhale, Balkrishna Govind, "Nehru and History," *History and Theory*, 17, No. 3 (October 1978): 311–22

Gong, Gerrit W., *The Standard of "Civilization" in International Society* (New York: Oxford University Press, 1984)

Guano, Emanuela, "Spectacles of Modernity: Transnational Imagination and Local Hegemonies in Neoliberal Buenos Aires," *Cultural Anthropology*, 17, No. 2 (May 2002): 181–210

Guha, Ramachandra, "Cricket and Politics in Colonial India," *Past and Present*, No. 161 (November 1998): 155–190

Guo, Yingjie, and Baogang He, "Reimagining the Chinese Nation," *Modern China*, 25, No. 2 (April 1999): 142–70

Gusfield, Joseph R., "Tradition and Modernity: Misplaced Polarities in the Study of Social Change," *The American Journal of Sociology*, 72, No. 4 (January 1974): 351–62

Gvosdev, Nikolas, "The New Party Card? Orthodoxy and the Search for Post-Soviet Russian Identity," *Problems of Post-Communism*, 47, No. 6 (November-December 2000): 29–38

Haas, Ernst B., "Nationalism: An Instrumental Social Construction," *Millennium*, 22, No. 3 (Summer 1993): 505–45

Hachigian, Nina, "The Internet and Power in One-Party East Asian States," *Washington Quarterly*, 25, No. 3 (Summer 2002): 41–58

Hahn, Jeffrey, "Political Socialization in the USSR: The Komsomol and the Educational System," unpublished PhD thesis, Duke University (1972)

Hale, Henry, "Civil Society from Above? Statist and Liberal Models of State-Building in Russia," *Demokratizatsiya*, 10, No. 3 (Summer 2002): 306–21

Hall, Rodney Bruce, *National Collective Identity: Social Constructs and International Systems* (New York: Columbia University Press, 1999)
    "The Discursive Demolition of the Asian Development Model," *International Studies Quarterly*, 47, No. 1 (March 2003): 71–99

Hall, Rodney Bruce, and Thomas J. Biersteker, eds., *The Emergence of Private Authority in Global Governance* (New York: Cambridge University Press, 2003)

Hall, Stuart, "The Local and the Global: Globalization and Ethnicity," in Anthony King, ed., *Culture, Globalization, and the World System: Contemporary Conditions for the Representation of Identity* (Minneapolis: University of Minnesota, 1997), pp. 19–39

Hannerz, Ulf, *Cultural Complexity: Studies in the Social Organization of Meaning* (New York: Columbia University Press, 1992)
    "Scenarios for Peripheral Cultures," in Anthony D. King, ed., *Culture, Globalization, and the World System: Contemporary Conditions for the Representation of Identity* (Minneapolis: University of Minnesota Press, 1997), pp. 107–28
    "Thinking about Culture in a Global Ecumene," in James Lull, ed., *Culture in the Communication Age* (London and New York: Routledge, 2001), pp. 54–71

Hansen, G. Eric, *The Culture of Strangers: Globalization, Localization and the Phenomenon of Exchange* (Lanham, MD: University Press of America, 2002)

Hanson, Stephen, "The Leninist Legacy and Institutional Change," *Comparative Political Studies*, 28, No. 2 (July 1995): 306–14.

Hay, Colin, "What Place for Ideas in the Structure–Agency Debate? Globalisation as a 'Process Without A Subject'," *First Press: Writing in the Critical Social Sciences* (2001), available online at www.theglobalsite.ac.uk/press/

Hedetoft, Ulf, "The Nation-State Meets the World: National Identities in the Context of Transnationality and Cultural Globalization," *European Journal of Social Theory*, 2, No. 1 (February 1999): 71–94
    The Global Turn: National Encounters with the World (Aalborg, Denmark: Aalborg University Press, 2003)

Held, David, Anthony McGrew, David Goldblatt and Jonathan Perraton, *Global Transformations: Politics, Economics and Culture* (Stanford: Stanford University Press, 1999)

Henderson, Sarah L., *Building Democracy in Contemporary Russia: Western Support for Grassroots Organizations* (Ithaca: Cornell University Press, 2003)

Herzfeld, Michael, *Ours Once More: Folklore, Ideology and the Making of Modern Greece* (Austin: University of Texas Press, 1982)

Hintze, Otto, "The Formation of States and Constitutional Development: A Study in History and Politics," in Felix Gilbert, ed., *The Historical Essays of Otto Hintze* (New York: Oxford University Press, 1975), pp. 159–77

Hobsbawm, Eric, "Introduction: Inventing Traditions," in Eric Hobsbawm and Terence Ranger, eds., *The Invention of Tradition* (Cambridge and New York: Cambridge University Press, 1983), pp. 1–14

Hobsbawm, Eric, and Terence Ranger, eds., *The Invention of Tradition* (Cambridge and New York: Cambridge University Press)

Holden, T. M., and Azrina Husin, "Moral Advertising in Malaysian TV Commercials," in Richard King and Timothy Craig, *Global Goes Local: Popular Culture in Asia* (Vancouver: University of British Columbia Press, 2002), pp. 138–59.

Holm-Hansen, Jorn, "Political Integration in Kazakhstan," in Pal Kolsto, ed., *Nation-Building and Ethnic Integration in Post-Soviet Societies: An Investigation of Latvia and Kazakstan* (Boulder, CO: Westview, 1999), pp. 153–226

Hopf, Ted, *Social Construction of International Politics: Identities and Foreign Policies, Moscow, 1955 and 1999* (Ithaca and London: Cornell University Press, 2002)

Horsman, Mathew, and Andrew Marshall, *After the Nation-State: Citizens, Tribalism and the New World Disorder* (London: Harper-Collins, 1994)

Howard, Keith, "Exploding Ballads: The Transformation of Korean Pop Music," in Richard King and Timothy Craig, eds., *Global Goes Local: Popular Culture in Asia* (Vancouver: University of British Columbia Press, 2002), pp. 80–95

Howard, Marc Morje, *The Weakness of Civil Society in Post-Communist Europe* (New York: Cambridge University Press, 2003)

Howes, David, ed., *Cross-Cultural Consumption: Global Markets, Local Realities* (London: Routledge, 1996)

Hozic, Aida, "The Political Economy of Global Culture – A Case Study of the Film Industry," in Reneo Lukic and Michael Brint, eds., *Culture, Politics, and Nationalism in the Age of Globalization* (Burlington, vt: Ashgate, 2001), pp. 55–78

Hroch, Miroslav, *Social Preconditions of National Revival in Europe* (Cambridge: Cambridge University Press, 1985)

Hruby, Laura, "A Rapper in Baku: Coolio Gives Concert at Heidar Aliyev Palace," *EurasiaNet*, April 9, 2004, available online at www.eurasianet.org

Huntington, Samuel P., *The Clash of Civilizations and the Remaking of World Order* (New York: Simon and Schuster, 1996)

Indzhigolian, Anzhela, "O sotsializiruiushchem vozdeistvii Internet (na primere rossiiskikh i kazakhstanskikh studentov)," unpublished paper prepared for the Second Russian Congress of Sociologists, Moscow, 2003

Inkeles, Alex, "Convergence in Societal Systems," in Eliezer Ben-Rafael and Yitzhak Sternberg, eds., *Identity, Culture and Globalization* (Leiden, Boston and Cologne: Brill, 2001), pp. 161–75

International Crisis Group, *Youth in Central Asia: Losing the New Generation*, Asia Report No. 66 (October 31, 2003), www.crisisweb.org

Issawi, Charles, *Cross-Cultural Encounters and Conflicts* (New York and Oxford: Oxford University Press, 1998)

Itoh, Mayumi, *The Globalization of Japan* (New York: St. Martin's Press, 2000)

Iwabuchi, Koichi, *Recentering Globalization: Popular Culture and Japanese Transnationalism* (Durham: Duke University Press, 2002)

Jackson, Patrick Thaddeus, "Hegel's House, Or 'People Are States Too'," *Review of International Studies*, 30, No. 2 (April 2004): 281–87

Jackson, Peter, "Local Consumption Cultures in a Globalizing World," *Transactions of the Institute of British Geographers*, 29, No. 2 (June 2004): 165–78

Jackson, Robert H., "The Weight of Ideas in Decolonization," in Judith Goldstein and Robert O. Keohane, eds., *Ideas & Foreign Policy: Beliefs, Institutions and Political Change Society* (Ithaca: Cornell University Press, 1993), pp. 111–38

Jameson, Frederic, "Globalization as a Philosophical Issue," in Frederic Jameson and Masao Miyoshi, eds., *The Cultures of Globalization* (Durham and London: Duke University Press, 1998), pp. 54–77

Jayasuriya, Kanishka, "Globalization and the Changing Architecture of the State: The Politics of the Regulatory State and the Politics of Negative Coordination," *Journal of European Public Policy*, 8, No. 1 (February 2001): 101–23

Jenkins, Henry, "Pop Cosmopolitanism: Mapping Cultural Flows in an Age of Media Convergence," in Marcelo Suarez-Orozco and Desirée Qin-Hilliard, eds., *Globalization: Culture and Education in the New Millennium* (Berkeley: University of California Press, 2004), pp. 114–40

Johansson, Perry, "Consuming the Other: the Fetish of the Western Woman in Chinese Advertising and Popular Culture," *Postcolonial Studies*, 2, No. 3 (November 1999): 377–88

Jowitt, Ken, *The Leninist Response to National Dependency* (Berkeley: Institute of International Studies, University of California, 1978)

Jumagulov, Erbol, "Kazaks Despair at Childrens' Gambling," Institute of War & Peace Reporting, *Reporting Central Asia*, No. 210 (June 11, 2003), www.iwpr.net

Jumagulov, Erbol, and Eduard Poletaev, "Kazak Cops Hammer Counter-Culture," "Kazak Cops Hammer Counter-Culture," Institute of War & Peace Reporting, *Reporting Central Asia*, No. 62 (July 27, 2001), www.iwpr.net

Jusdanis, Gregory, *The Necessary Nation* (Princeton: Princeton University Press, 2001)

Kalathil, Shanthi, and Taylor C. Boas, *Open Networks, Closed Regimes: The Impact of the Internet on Authoritarian Rule* (Washington, DC: Carnegie Endowment for International Peace, 2003)

Kamrava, Mehran, "State-Building in Azerbaijan: The Search for Consolidation," *Middle East Journal*, 55, No. 2 (Spring 2001): 216–37

Kang, Jong, "Lethal Combination: Sex and Violence in the World of Korean Television," in Yahya Kamalipour and Kuldip Rampal, eds., *Media, Sex,*

Violence, and Drugs in the Global Village (New York: Rowman and Littlefield, 2001), pp. 153–65

Karin, Erlan, and Andrei Chebotarov, "The Policy of Kazakhization in State and Government Institutions in Kazakhstan," in Natsuko Oka, ed., *The Nationalities Question in Post-Soviet Kazakhstan* (Chiba, Japan: Institute of Developing Economies, Japan External Trade Organization, 2002), pp. 69–108

Keck, Margaret, and Kathryn Sikkink, *Activists Beyond Borders: Advocacy Networks in International Politics* (Ithaca: Cornell University Press, 1998)

Keesing, Roger, "Creating the Past: Custom and Identity in the Contemporary Pacific," *The Contemporary Pacific*, 1, No. 1 (1989): 19–42

Keyder, Caglar, "Whither the Project of Modernity? Turkey in the 1990s," in Sibel Bozdogan and Resat Kasaba, eds., *Rethinking Modernity and National Identity in Turkey* (Seattle: University of Washington Press, 1997), pp. 37–51

"The Housing Market from Informal to Global," in Caglar Keyder, *Istanbul: Between the Global and the Local* (Lanham, MD: Rowman and Littlefield, 1999), pp. 143–71

Keyman, E. Fuat, *Globalization, State, Identity/Difference: Toward a Critical Social Theory of International Relations* (Atlantic Highlands, NJ: Humanities Press, 1997)

Khanbu, Pirouz, "The Metamorphosis of Architecture and Urban Development in Azerbaijan," *Azerbaijani International* 6, No. 4 (Winter 1998) available online at www.azer.com

Khasanova, Gulnara, "Nation-Building and Values in Russian Textbooks," in Pal Kolsto and Helge Blakkisrud, eds., *Nation-Building and Common Values in Russia* (Lanham, MD: Rowman and Littlefield, 2004), pp. 269–99

Kim, Samuel S., and Lowell Dittmer, "Whither China's Quest for National Identity?" in Lowell Dittmer and Samuel S. Kim, eds., *China's Quest for National Identity* (Ithaca: Cornell University Press, 1993), pp. 237–90

King, Anthony, "Thinking with Bourdieu Against Bourdieu: A 'Practical' Critique of the Habitus," *Sociological Theory*, 18, No. 3 (November 2000): 417–33

Kissane, Carolyn, "History Education in Transit: Where To for Kazakhstan?" *Comparative Education*, 41, No. 1 (February 2005): 45–69

Kitley, Philip, "Subject to What?: A Comparative Analysis of Recent Approaches to Regulating Television and Broadcasting in Indonesia and Malaysia," *Inter-Asia Cultural Studies*, 2, No. 3 (December 2001): 503–14

Kloos, Peter, "The Dialectics of Globalization and Localization," in Don Kalb et al., eds., *The Ends of Globalization: Bringing Society Back In* (Lanham, MD: Rowman and Littlefield, 2000), pp. 281–297

Kolesova, L. S., "Adolescents as a Group that is Vulnerable to Narcotics Addiction and HIV Infection," *Russian Education and Society*, 45, No. 4 (April 2003): 39–53, translated from the original in *Pedagogika*, No. 1 (January 2002): 34–41.

Kolsto, Pal, "Bipolar Societies?" in Pal Kolsto, ed., *Nation-Building and Ethnic Integration in Post-Soviet Societies: An Investigation of Latvia and Kazakstan* (Boulder: Westview, 1999), pp. 15–43

"Epilogue," in Pal Kolsto and Helge Blakkisrud, eds., *Nation-Building and Common Values in Russia* (Lanham, MD: Rowman and Littlefield, 2004), pp. 327–39

Korff, Rüdiger, "Globalisation and Communal Identities in the Plural Society of Malaysia," *Singapore Journal of Tropical Geography*, 22, No. 3 (November 2001): 270–83

Korzheva, E. M., "Adopting Adolescents to Market Relations," *Russian Education and Society*, 38, No. 5 (August 1996): 7–23

Kowert, Paul A., "National Identity: Inside and Out," *Security Studies*, 8, No. 2/3, (Winter 1998/99–Spring 1999): 1–34

Kraidy, Marwan, "Hybridity in Cultural Globalization," *Communication Theory*, 12, No. 3 (August 2002): 316–39

Kratochwil, Friedrich, and John Ruggie, "International Organization: A State of the Art or an Art of the State?" *International Organization*, 40, No. 4 (Autumn 1986): 753–75

Kubik, Jan, "Cultural Legacies of State Socialism: History-Making and Cultural-Political Entrepreneurship in Postcommunist Poland and Russia," in Grzegorz Ekiert and Stephen E. Hanson, eds., *Capitalism and Democracy in Central and Eastern Europe: Assessing the Legacy of Communist Rule* (Cambridge: Cambridge University Press, 2003), pp. 317–51

Kuehnast, Kathleen, "From Pioneers to Entrepreneurs: Young Women, Consumerism, and the 'World Picture' in Kyrgyzstan," *Central Asian Survey*, 17, No. 4 (December 1998): 639–54

Kuru, Ahmet, "Between the State and Cultural Zones: Nation Building in Turkmenistan," *Central Asian Survey*, 21, No. 1 (March 2002): 71–90

Kuzio, Taras, "Kazakhstan Grapples with Cultural Revival Dilemmas," *EurasiaNet*, January 17, 2002, available online at www.eurasianet.org/

Laffey, Mark, "Adding an Asian Strand: Neoliberalism and the Politics of Culture in New Zealand," in Jutta Weldes *et al.*, eds., *Cultures of Insecurity: States, Communities, and the Production of Danger* (Minneapolis and London: University of Minnesota Press, 1999), pp. 233–60

Laing, Dave, "The Music Industry and the 'Cultural Imperialism' Thesis," *Media, Culture and Society*, 8 (1986): 331–41

Laitin, David, *Hegemony and Culture: Politics and Religious Change among the Yoruba* (Chicago and London: University of Chicago Press, 1986)

Landau, Jacob M., and Barbara Kellner-Heinkele, *Politics of Language in the Ex-Soviet Muslim States* (Ann Arbor: University of Michigan Press, 2001)

Lapid, Yosef, "Culture's Ship: Returns and Departures in International Relations Theory," in Yosef Lapid and Friedrich Krachtowil, eds., *The Return of Culture and Identity in International Relations* (London: Lynne Reinner, 1996), pp. 3–20

Larkin, Brian, "Indian Films and Nigerian Lovers: Media and the Creation of Parallel Modernities," in Jonathan Xavier Inda and Renato Rosaldo, eds., *The Anthropology of Globalization: A Reader* (Malden, MA: Blackwell, 2002), pp. 350–78

Lashley, Lynette, "Television and the Americanization of the Trinbagonian Youth: A Study of Six Secondary Schools," in Hopeton S. Dunn, ed.,

Globalization, Communications and Caribbean Identity (New York: St. Martin's Press, 1995), pp. 83–97

Latouche, Serge, *Westernization of the World: The Significance, Scope and Limits of the Drive towards Global Uniformity*, translated by Rosemary Morris (Cambridge, MA: Polity Press, 1996)

Lee, Molly, "The Impacts of Globalization on Education in Malaysia," in Nelly Stromquist and Karen Monkman, eds., *Globalization and Education: Integration and Contestation Across Cultures* (Blue Ridge Summit, PA: Rowman and Littlefield, 2000), pp. 315–32

Legrain, Philippe, "Cultural Globalization is Not Americanization," *Chronicle of Higher Education*, 49, No. 35 (May 9, 2003), B7

Levchenko, Maksim, "Nash shans," *Vreneia* (Almaty), January 9, 2003.

Levitt, Peggy, "Social Remittances: Migration Driven Local-Level Forms of Cultural Diffusion," *The International Migration Review*, 32, No. 4 (Winter 1998): 926–48

Liechty, Mark, "Media, Markets and Modernization: Youth Identities and the Experience of Modernity in Kathmandu, Nepal," in Vered Amit-Talai and Helena Wulff, eds., *Youth Cultures: A Cross-Cultural Perspective* (London and New York: Routledge, 1995), pp. 166–201

Lincoln, Bruce, *Discourse and the Construction of Society: Comparative Studies of Myth, Ritual, and Classification* (New York: Oxford University Press, 1989)

Lipsitz, George, *Dangerous Crossroads: Popular Music, Postmodernism, and the Poetics of Place* (London and New York: Verso, 1994)

LiPuma, Edward, "History, Identity and Encompassment: Nation-Making in the Solomon Islands," *Identities* 4, No. 2 (December 1997): 213–44

Litfin, Karen, "Sovereignty in World Ecopolitics," *Mershon International Studies Review*, 41, No. 2 (November 1997): 167–204

Litova, Zoia, "Preparing School Graduates for Work Under the New Economic Conditions," *Russian Education and Society*, 43, No. 3 (March 2001): 36–44.

Litzinger, Ralph, "Reimagining the State in Post-Mao China," in Jutta Weldes et al., eds., *Cultures of Insecurity: States, Communities, and the Production of Danger* (Minneapolis and London: University of Minnesota Press, 1999), 293–318

Lukes, Steven, *Essays in Social Theory* (New York: Columbia University Press, 1977)

Luong, Pauline Jones, *Institutional Change and Political Continuity in Post-Soviet Central Asia: Power, Perceptions, and Pacts* (Cambridge and New York: Cambridge University Press, 2002)

"Economic Decentralization in Kazakhstan: Causes and Consequences," in Pauline Jones Luong, ed., *The Transformation of Central Asia: States and Societies from Soviet Rule to Independence* (Ithaca: Cornell University Press, 2004), pp. 182–210

Lynch, Daniel C., *After the Propaganda State: Media, Politics, and "Thought Work" in Reformed China* (Stanford, CA: Stanford University Press, 1999)

"International 'Decentering' and Democratization: The Case of Thailand," *International Studies Quarterly*, 48, No. 2 (June 2004): 339–62

Macdonald, Sharon, and Gordon Fyfe, eds., *Theorizing Museums: Representing Identity and Diversity in a Changing World* (Cambridge, MA: Blackwell, 1996)

Madhok, Balraj, *Indianization* (New Delhi: S. Chand and Co., 1970)

Mandel, Ruth, "Seeding Civil Society," in Chris M. Hann, ed., *Postsocialism: Ideals, Ideologies and Practices in Eurasia* (New York: Routledge, 2002), pp. 279–96

Markowitz, Fran, *Coming of Age in Post-Soviet Russia* (Urbana and Chicago: University of Illinois Press, 2000)

Martin-Barbero, Jesus, "Transformations in the Map: Identities and Culture Industries," *Latin American Perspectives*, 27, No. 4 (July 2000): 27–48

Mazrui, Ali, and Michael Tidy, *Nationalism and New States in Africa from about 1935 to the Present* (London: Heineman, 1984)

McAdam, Douglas, Sidney Tarrow, and Charles Tilly, *Dynamics of Contention* (New York: Cambridge University Press, 2001)

McAnulla, Stuart, "Structure and Agency," in David Marsh and Gerry Stoker, eds., *Theory and Methods in Political Science* (London: Palgrave, 2002), pp. 271–91

McCarthy, Susan, "Gods of Wealth, Temples of Prosperity: Party-State Participation in the Minority Cultural Revival," *China: An International Journal*, 2, No. 1 (March 2004): 28–52

McCormack, Gavan, "New Tunes for an Old Song: Nationalism and Identity in Post-Cold War Japan," in Roy Starrs, ed., *Nations Under Siege: Globalization and Nationalism in Asia* (New York: Palgrave, 2002), pp. 137–67

McDaniel, Tim, *The Agony of the Russian Idea* (Princeton: Princeton University Press, 1996)

McGray, Douglas, "Japan's Gross National Cool," *Foreign Policy*, No. 130 (May/Jun 2002): 44–54

McMann, Kelly, "The Civic Realm in Kyrgyzstan: Soviet Economic Legacies and Activists' Expectations," in Pauline Jones Luong, ed., *The Transformation of Central Asia: States and Societies from Soviet Rule to Independence* (Ithaca and London: Cornell University Press, 2004), pp. 213–45

McNeely, Connie, *Constructing the Nation-State: International Organization and Prescriptive Action* (Westport, CT: Greenwood Press, 1995)

Melucci, Alberto, *Challenging Codes: Collective Action in the Information Age* (Cambridge: Cambridge University Press, 1996)

Mendelson, Sarah E., and John K. Glenn, "Democracy Assistance and NGO Strategies in Post-Communist Societies," Carnegie Endowment for International Peace, Working Paper Series, No. 8 (February 2000)

Metzger, Robert A., "King of the Nilesat," *Wired*, 6, No. 10 (October 1998), available online at www.wired.com/wired/

Meyer, Birgit, and Peter Geschiere, "Introduction," in Birgit Meyer and Peter Geschiere, eds., *Globalization and Identity: Dialectics of Flow and Closure* (Oxford: Blackwell, 1999), pp. 1–15

Meyer, John W., John Boli, George M. Thomas, and Francisco Ramirez, "World Society and the Nation-State," *American Journal of Sociology*, 103, No. 1 (July 1997): 144–81

Meyer, John, and Ronald Jepperson, "The 'Actors' of Modern Society: The Cultural Construction of Social Agency," *Sociological Theory*, 18, No. 1 (March 2000): 100–20

Migdal, Joel, "The State in Society: An Approach to Struggles for Domination," in Joel Migdal, Atul Kohli, and Vivienne Shue, eds., *State Power and Social Forces: Domination and Transformation in the Third World* (Cambridge: Cambridge University Press, 1994), pp. 7–34.

    State in Society: Studying How States and Societies Transform and Constitute One Another (Cambridge and New York: Cambridge University Press, 2001)

Milliken, Jennifer, "Discourse Study: Bringing Rigor to Critical Theory," in Karin Fierke and Knud Jorgensen, eds., *Constructing International Relations: The Next Generation* (Armonk, NY, and London: M. E. Sharpe, 2001), pp. 136–59

Mitchneck, Beth, "The Heritage Industry Russian Style: The Case of Yaroslavl'," *Urban Affairs Review*, 34, No. 1 (September 1998): 28–51

Mitina, L. M., "The Personal and Professional Development of the Individual Under the New Socioeconomic Conditions," *Russian Education and Society*, 40 No. 5 (May 1998): 33–51.

Moe, Terry M., *The Organization of Interests* (Chicago: University of Chicago Press, 1980)

Mookerji, Radha, *Nationalism in Hindu Culture* (Delhi: S. Chand and Co., 1957)

Morris, Stephen D., "Between Neo-liberalism and Neo-indigenismo: Reconstructing National Identity in Mexico," *National Identities*, 3, No. 3 (November 2001): 239–55

Mosse, George, *Nationalism and Sexuality: Respectability and Abnormal Sexuality in Modern Europe* (New York: Howard Fertig, 1985)

Murphy, Craig N., *International Organization and Industrial Change: Global Governance Since 1850* (New York: Oxford University Press, 1994)

Nandy, Ashis, *The Intimate Enemy: Loss and Recovery of Self under Colonialism* (Delhi: Oxford University Press, 1983)

Narumi, Hiroshi, "Fashion Orientalism and the Limits of Counter Culture," *Postcolonial Studies*, 3, No. 3 (November 2000): 293–309

Navaro-Yashin, Yael, *Faces of the State: Secularism and Public Life in Turkey* (Princeton: Princeton University Press, 2002)

Neklessa, Aleksandr, "Konets tsivilizatsii, ili Zigzag istorii," *Znamia*, No. 1 (1998): 165–79

Neumann, Iver B., *The Uses of the Other: "The East" in European Identity Formation* (Minneapolis: University of Minnesota Press, 1999)

    "Returning Practice to the Linguistic Turn: The Case of Diplomacy," *Millennium: Journal of International Studies*, 31, No. 3 (2002): 627–51

Nilan, Pam, "Young People and Globalizing Trends in Vietnam," *Journal of Youth Studies*, 2, No. 3 (October 1999): 353–70

Norberg-Hodge, Helena, "The March of the Monoculture," *Ecologist*, 29, No. 3 (May/June 1999): 194–7

Norris, Pippa, and Ronald Inglehart, "Islamic Culture and Democracy: Testing the 'Clash of Civilizations' Thesis," *Comparative Sociology*, 1, Nos. 3/4 (August 2002): 235–63

Nowicki, Marvin, "Kazakhstan's Nonprofit Sector at a Crossroad on the Great Silk Road," *Voluntas*, 11, No. 3 (September 2000): 217–35

OAS, "Cultural Industries in the Latin American Economy: Current Status And Outlook In The Context Of Globalization," available online at www.oas.org/culture/pub.html

Ohmae, Kenichi, *The End of the Nation State: The Rise of Regional Economies* (New York: The Free Press, 1995)

Olcott, Martha Brill, *Kazakhstan: Unfulfilled Promise* (Washington, DC: Carnegie Endowment for International Peace, 2002)

Olson, Laura J., *Performing Russia: Folk Revival and Russian Identity* (New York: Routledge-Curzon, 2004)

Omelchenko, Elena, and Uliana Bliudina, "On the Outside Looking In? The Place of Youth in Russia's New Media and Information Space," in Hilary Pilkington, ed., *Looking West: Cultural Globalization and Russian Youth Culture* (State College, PA: Penn State University Press, 2002), pp. 21–49

Omelchenko, Elena, and Moya Flynn, "Through Their Own Eyes: Young People's Images of 'the West'," in Hilary Pilkington, ed., *Looking West: Cultural Globalization and Russian Youth Culture* (State College, PA: Penn State University Press, 2002), pp. 77–100

Oncu, Ayse, "The Myth of the 'Ideal Home' Travels Across Cultural Borders to Istanbul," in Ayse Oncu and Petra Weyland, eds., *Space, Culture and Power: New Identities in Globalising Cities* (London: Zed Books, 1997), pp. 56–72

    "Istanbulites and Others: The Cultural Cosmology of Being Middle Class in the Era of Globalism," in Caglar Keyder, ed., *Istanbul: Between the Global and the Local* (Lanham, MD: Rowman and Littlefield, 1999), pp. 95–119

Ong, Aihwa, *Flexible Citizenship: The Cultural Logics of Transnationality* (Durham and London: Duke University Press, 1999)

Oppenheim, Lois Hecht, "Latin America and the Cultural Consequences and Contradictions of Globalization," *Perspectives on Global Development and Technology*, 2, No. 1 (2003): 54–76

Ozbeck, Meral, "Arabesk Culture: A Case of Modernization and Popular Identity," in Sibel Bozdogan and Resat Kasaba, eds., *Rethinking Modernity and National Identity in Turkey* (Seattle: University of Washington Press, 1997), pp. 211–32

Ozbudun, Ergun, and E. Fuat Keyman, "Cultural Globalization in Turkey: Actors, Discourses, Strategies," in Peter Berger and Samuel Huntington, eds., *Many Globalizations: Cultural Diversity in the Contemporary World* (New York: Oxford University Press, 2002), pp. 296–319

Paasi, Anssi, "The Political Geography of Boundaries at the End of the Millennium: Challenges of the De-territorializing World," in Heikki Eskelinen, Ilkka Liikanen, and Jukka Oksa, eds., *Curtains of Iron and Gold: Reconstructing Borders and Scales of Interaction* (Aldershot: Ashgate, 1999), pp. 9–24

Pal, Bipin Chandra, "Hinduism and Indian Nationalism," in Elie Kedourie, ed., *Nationalism in Asia and Africa* (New York and Cleveland: The World Publishing, 1970), pp. 338–52

Paolini, Albert, *Navigating Modernity: Postcolonialism, Identity, and International Relations* (Boulder: Lynne Rienner, 1999)

Paranjape, Makarand, "Reworlding Homes: Colonialism, 'National Culture', and Post-National India," in Geeti Sen, ed., *India: A National Culture?* (Thousand Oaks, CA: Sage Publications, 2003), pp. 114–26

Parmenter, Lynn, "Internationalization in Japanese Education: Current Issues and Future Prospects," in Nelly Stromquist and Karen Monkman, eds., *Globalization and Education: Integration and Contestation Across Cultures* (Blue Ridge Summit, PA: Rowman and Littlefield, 2000), pp. 237–54

Peck, Jamie, "Neoliberalizing States: Thin Policies/Hard Outcomes," *Progress in Human Geography* 25, 3 (2001): 445–55

Petro, Nicolai N., *Crafting Democracy: How Novgorod Has Coped With Rapid Social Change* (Ithaca: Cornell University Press, 2004)

Phillips, Andrew, and Paul James, "National Identity between Tradition and Reflexive Modernization: The Contradictions of Central Asia," *National Identities*, 3, No. 1 (March 2001): 23–35

Pieterse, Jan Nederveen, "Globalization as Hybridization," in Mike Featherstone, Scott Lash, and Roland Robertson, eds., *Global Modernities* (London: Sage, 1995), pp. 45–68

Piirainen, Timo, "The Fall of an Empire, the Birth of a Nation: Perceptions of the New Russian National Identity," in Chris Chulos and Timo Piirainen, eds., *The Fall of an Empire, the Birth of a Nation: National Identities in Russia* (Burlington, VT: Ashgate, 2000), pp. 161–96

Pilkington, Hilary, *Russia's Youth and its Culture: A Nation's Constructors and Constructed* (London and New York: Routledge, 1994)

"Reconfiguring 'the West': Style and Music in Russian Youth Cultural Practice," in Hilary Pilkington, ed., *Looking West: Cultural Globalization and Russian Youth Culture* (State College, PA: Penn State University Press, 2002), pp. 165–200

"Youth and Popular Culture: The Common Denominator?" in Russel Bova, ed., *Russia and Western Civilization: Cultural and Historical Encounters* (New York: M. E. Sharpe, 2003), pp. 319–50

Pilkington, Hilary, with Elena Starkova, "'Progressives' and 'Normals': Strategies for Glocal Living," in Hilary Pilkington, ed., *Looking West: Cultural Globalization and Russian Youth Culture* (State College, PA: Penn State University Press, 2002), pp. 101–32

Polkinghorne, Donald E., *Narrative Knowing and the Human Sciences* (Albany: State University of New York Press, 1988)

Pollner, Melvin, *Mundane Reason: Reality in Everyday and Sociological Discourse* (Cambridge: Cambridge University Press, 1987)

Polozhenie molodezhi i realizatsiia gosudarstvennoi molodezhnoi politiki v Rossiiskoi Federatsii: 2002 god, report prepared by the Department of Youth Affairs of the Ministry of Education and Science (December 17, 2003), http://www.ed.gov.ru/junior/news/

Polozhenie molodezhi v Rossii: Analiticheskii doklad (Moscow: Mashmir, 2005), http://stat.edu.ru

Poluekhtova, Irina, "Amerikanskie filmy kak factor sotsializatsii molodezhi v Rossii 90-kh godov," in Vladimir S. Magun, ed., *Sotsialnye izmeneniia v Rossii i molodezh* (Moscow: Moscow Social Science Foundation, 1997), pp. 57–81

Price, Monroe, *Media and Sovereignty: The Global Information Revolution and Its Challenge to State Power* (Cambridge, MA: The MIT Press, 2002)

Rae, Heather, *State Identities and the Homogenisation of Peoples* (Cambridge: Cambridge University Press, 2002)

Rajadhyaksha, Ashish, "The 'Bollywoodization' of the Indian Cinema: Cultural Nationalism in a Global Arena," *Inter-Asia Cultural Studies*, 4, No. 1 (April 2003): 25–39

Rampal, Kuldip, "Cultural Bane or Sociological Boon? Impact of Satellite Television on Urban Youth in India," in Yahya Kamalipour and Kuldip Rampal, eds., *Media, Sex, Violence, and Drugs in the Global Village* (New York: Rowman and Littlefield, 2001), pp. 115–30

Ratner, Carl, "Agency and Culture," *Journal for the Theory of Social Behaviour*, 30, No. 4 (September 2000): 413–34

Rausin, Sigrid, "Signs of the New Nation: Gift Exchange, Consumption and Aid on a Former Collective farm in North-West Estonia," in Daniel Miller, ed., *Material Cultures: Why Some Things Matter* (Chicago: Chicago University Press, 1998), pp. 189–213

Rawkins, Phillip M., "An Approach to the Political Sociology of the Welsh Nationalist Movement," *Political Studies*, 27, No. 3 (September 1979): 440–57

Raz, Aviad E., "Domesticating Disney: Onstage Strategies of Adaptation in Tokyo Disneyland," *Journal of Popular Culture*, 33, No. 4 (Spring 2000): 77–99

Razlogov, Kirill, El'na Orlova, and Evgenii Kuz'min, "Rossiiskaia kul'turnaia politika v kontekste globalizatsii," *Otechestvennye zapiski*, No. 4 (2005), http://www.strana-oz.ru

Regev, Motti, "'Rockization': Diversity within Similarity in World Popular Music," in Ulrich Beck, Nathan Sznaider and Rainer Winter, eds., *Global America? The Cultural Consequences of Globalization* (Liverpool: Liverpool University Press, 2003), pp. 219–21

Renwick, Neil, "Japan.com," *National Identities*, 3, No. 2 (July 2001): 169–85

Rhoten, Diana, "Education Decentralization in Argentina: A 'Global-Local Conditions of Possibility' Approach to State, Market, and Society Change," *Journal of Education Policy*, 15, No. 6 (November-December 2000): 593–619

Richter, James, "Promoting Civil Society?" *Problems of Post-Communism*, 49, No. 1 (January/February 2002): 30–41

Rigi, Jakob, "Conditions of Post-Soviet Youth and Work in Almaty, Kazakhstan," *Critique of Anthropology*, 23, No. 1 (March 2003): 35–49

Roberts, Ken *et al.*, eds., *Surviving Post-communism: Young People in the Former Soviet Union* (Cheltenham: Edward Elgar, 2000)

Robertson, Roland, "Mapping the Global Condition: Globalization as the Central Concept," *Theory, Culture and Society*, 7, Nos. 2/3 (1990): 15–30
Globalization: Social Theory and Global Culture (London: Sage, 1992)

Roeder, Philip G., "Soviet Federalism and Ethnic Mobilization," *World Politics*, 43, No. 2 (January 1991): 196–232

Rorlich, Azade-Ayse, "Islam, Identity and Politics: Kazakhstan, 1990–2000," *Nationalities Papers*, 31, No. 2 (June 2003): 157–76

Rosamond, Ben, "Globalization, European Integration and the Discursive Construction of Economic Imperatives," *Journal of European Public Policy*, 6, No. 4 (April 2002): 147–67

Rose, Sonya, "Cultural Analysis and Moral Discourses: Episodes, Continuities, and Transformations," in Victoria E. Bonnell and Lynn Hunt, eds., *Beyond The Cultural Turn: New Directions in the Study of Society and Culture* (Berkeley: University of California Press, 1999), pp. 217–38

Rosenau, James, *Along the Domestic–Foreign Frontier: Exploring Governance in a Turbulent World* (Cambridge and New York: Cambridge University Press, 1997)

   Distant Proximities: Dynamics beyond Globalization (Princeton and Oxford: Princeton University Press, 2003)

Roy, Olivier, *The New Central Asia: The Creation of Nations* (New York: New York University Press, 2000)

Roy, Srirupa, "Nation and Institution: Commemorating the Fiftieth Anniversary of Indian Independence," *Interventions: The International Journal of Postcolonial Studies*, 3, No. 2 (July 2001): 251–65

Rustamova, Narmina, "Dayirman: Combining Rap, Tradition, and Frustration in Azerbaijan," *Central Asia – Caucasus Analyst*, February 25, 2004, www.cacianalyst.org

Sabonis-Chafee, Theresa, "Communism as Kitsch: Soviet Symbols in Post-Soviet Society," in Adele Marie Barker, ed., *Consuming Russia: Popular Culture, Sex, and Society Since Gorbachev* (Durham: Duke University Press, 1999), pp. 362–82

Said, Edward, *Culture and Imperialism* (New York: Vintage Books, 1994)

Saldanha, Arun, "Fear and Loathing in Goa," *The UNESCO Courier*, 53, No. 7/8 (July/August 2000): 51–3

   "Music, Space, Identity: Geographies of Youth Culture in Bangalore," *Cultural Studies*, 16, No. 3 (May 2002): 337–50

Sarsembayev, Azamat, "Imagined Communities: Kazak Nationalism and Kazakification in the 1990s," *Central Asian Survey*, 18, No. 3 (September 1999): 319–46

Schade-Poulsen, Marc, "The Power of Love: Rai Music and Youth in Algeria," in Vered Amit-Talai and Helena Wulff, eds., *Youth Cultures: A Cross-Cultural Perspective* (London and New York: Routledge, 1995), pp. 81–113

Schafer, Sylvia, *Children in Moral Danger and the Problem of Government in Third Republic France* (Princeton: Princeton University Press, 1997)

Schatz, Edward, "The Politics of Multiple Identities: Lineage and Ethnicity in Kazakhstan," *Europe-Asia Studies*, 52, No. 3 (2000): 489–506

Schelling, Vivian, "Globalisation, Ethnic Identity and Popular Culture in Latin America," in Ray Kiely and Phil Marfleet, eds., *Globalisation and the Third World* (London: Routledge, 1998), pp. 141–62

Schmidt, Gerlind, "New Paradigms of National Education in Multi-Ethnic Russia," in Stephen Webber and Ilkka Liikanen, eds., *Education and Civic Culture in Post-Communist Countries* (New York: Palgrave, 2001), pp. 94–105

Scholte, Jan Aart, "Globalisation and Social Change (Part II)," *Transnational Associations*, 50, No. 2 (March/April 1998): 62–79

Schweller, Randy and David Priess, "A Tale of Two Realisms: Expanding the Institutions Debate," *Mershon International Studies Review*, 41, No. 1 (May 1997): 1–32

Scrase, Timothy J., "Television, the Middle Classes and the Transformation of Cultural Identities in West Bengal, India," *Gazette: International Journal for Communication Studies*, 64, No. 4 (August 2002): 323–42

Searle, John, *The Construction of Social Reality* (New York: Free Press, 1995)

Semenenko, Irina S., "Globalizatsiia i sotsiokulturnaia dinamika: lichnost', obshchestvo, kultura," *Polis*, No. 1 (January 2003): 5–23

Sewell, Jr., William H., "The Concept(s) of Culture," in Victoria E. Bonnell and Lynn Hunt, eds., *Beyond The Cultural Turn: New Directions in the Study of Society and Culture* (Berkeley: University of California Press, 1999), pp. 35–61

Sharma, Suresh, "*Hind Swaraj* as a Statement of Tradition in the Modern World," in Vasudha Dalmia and Heinrich Von Stietencron, eds., *Representing Hinduism: The Construction of Religious Traditions and National Identity* (Thousand Oaks, CA: Sage Publications, 1995), pp. 283–305

Shaw, Roy, "The Cultural 'Animateur' in Contemporary Society," *Cahiers d'Histoire Mondiale*, 14 (1972): 460–72

Shenfield, Stephen, *Russian Fascism: Traditions, Tendencies, Movements* (Armonk, NY: M. E. Sharpe, 2001)

Shevchenko, Olga, "'Between the Holes: Emerging Identities and Hybrid Patterns of Consumption in Post-socialist Russia," *Europe-Asia Studies*, 54, No. 6 (September 2002): 841–66

Shi, Anbin, "Toward a Chinese National-Popular: Cultural Hegemony and Counterhegemony in Maoist and Post-Maoist China," *Social Semiotics*, 10, No. 2 (August 2000): 201–10

Shlegel, Alice, "The Global Spread of Adolescent Culture," in Lisa J. Crockett and Rainer K. Silbereisen, eds., *Negotiating Adolescence in Times of Social Change* (New York: Cambridge University Press, 2000), pp. 71–88

Shnirelman, Viktor, "National Identity and Myths of Ethnogenesis in Transcaucasia," in Graham Smith, Edward Allworth, and Vivien Law, eds., *Nation-Building in the Post-Soviet Borderlands: The Politics of National Identities* (Cambridge: Cambridge University Press, 1998), pp. 48–66

Shulman, Stephen, "Cultures in Competition: Ukrainian Foreign Policy and the 'Cultural Threat' from Abroad," *Europe-Asia Studies*, 50, No. 2 (March 1998): 287–303

Sidorova, Evgenia, "Kazakstan: Soviet Tactics Making Comeback," Institute of War & Peace Reporting, *Reporting Central Asia*, No. 163, November 22, 2002, www.iwpr.net

Sigal, Ivan, and Joshua Machleder, "Independent Media and Alternative Narratives in Central Asia," unpublished paper presented at the Central Eurasian Studies Society annual conference, October 2003

Slezkine, Yuri, "The USSR as a Communal Apartment, or How a Socialist State Promoted Ethnic Particularism," *Slavic Review*, 53, No. 2 (Summer 1994): 414–52

Smith, Anthony D., *Myths and Memories of the Nation* (New York: Oxford University Press, 1999)

Smith, Graham, *The Post-Soviet States: Mapping the Politics of Transition* (New York: Oxford University Press, 1999)

Smith, Kathleen E., *Mythmaking in the New Russia: Politics and Memory During the Yeltsin Era* (Ithaca: Cornell University Press, 2002)

Smith, Michael P., and Luis E. Guarnizo, *Transnationalism from Below* (Piscataway, NJ: Transaction Publishers, 1998)

Smith, Rogers M., *Stories of Peoplehood: The Politics and Morals of Political Membership* (New York: Cambridge University Press, 2003)

Somers, Margaret R., "The Narrative Constitution of Identity: A Relational and Network Approach," *Theory and Society*, 23, No. 5 (October 1994): 605–49

Spillman, Lyn, *Nation and Commemoration: Creating National Identities in the United States and Australia* (Cambridge and New York: Cambridge University Press, 1997)

Springhall, John, *Youth, Popular Culture, and Moral Panics: Penny Gaffs to Gangsta-Rap, 1830–1996* (New York: St. Martin's Press, 1998)

Squier, John, "Civil Society and the Challenge of Russian Gosudarstvennost," *Demokratizatsiya*, 10, No. 2 (Spring 2002): 166–82

Srinivas, Tulasi, "A Tryst with Destiny: The Indian Case of Cultural Globalization," in Peter Berger and Samuel Huntington, eds., *Many Globalizations: Cultural Diversity in the Contemporary World* (New York: Oxford University Press, 2002), pp. 89–116

Steger, Manfred, *Globalism: The New Market Ideology* (Lanham, MD: Rowman and Littlefield, 2002)

Steinmetz, George, "Introduction: Culture and the State," in George Steinmetz, ed., *State/Culture: State-Formation After the Cultural Turn* (Ithaca and London: Cornell University Press, 1999), pp. 1–49

Stetsenko, Anna, "Adolescents in Russia: Surviving the Turmoil and Creating a Brighter Future," in B. Bradford Brown, Reed W. Larson, and T. S. Saraswathi, eds., *The World's Youth: Adolescence in Eight Regions of the Globe* (New York: Cambridge University Press, 2002), pp. 243–75

Stevens, Jacqueline, "Ideology and Social Structure: A Review Article," *Comparative Studies in History and Society*, 39, No. 2 (April 1997): 401–09

Stinchcombe, Arthur, "The Deep Structure of Moral Categories: Eighteenth-Century French Stratification and the Revolution," in Eno Rossi, ed., *Structural Sociology* (New York: Columbia University Press, 1982), pp. 66–95

Suleymanov, Elin, "Azerbaijan, Azerbaijanis and the Search for Identity," *Analysis of Current Events*, 13, No. 1 (February 2001)

Suntharalingam, R., *Indian Nationalism: An Historical Analysis* (New Delhi: Vikas Publishing, 1983)

Suny, Ronald Grigor, *The Revenge of the Past: Nationalism, Revolution, and the Collapse of the Soviet Union* (Stanford: Stanford University Press, 1994)

"Provisional Stabilities: The Politics of Identities in Post-Soviet Eurasia," *International Security*, 24, No. 3 (Winter 1999/2000): 139–79

"Back and Beyond: Reversing the Cultural Turn?" *American Historical Review*, 107, No. 5 (December 2002): 1476–99

Surucu, Cengiz, "Modernity, Nationalism, Resistance: Identity Politics in Post-Soviet Kazakhstan," *Central Asian Survey*, 21, No. 4 (December 2002): 385–402

Swietochowski, Tadeusz, *Russia and Azerbaijan: A Borderland in Transition* (New York: Columbia University Press, 1995)

"Azerbaijan: Perspectives from the Crossroads," *Central Asian Survey*, 18, No. 4 (December 1999): 419–35

Tejapira, Kasian, "The Post-Modernization of Thainess," in Yao Souchou, ed., *House of Glass: Culture, Modernity and the State in Southeast Asia* (Singapore: Institute of Southeast Asian Studies, 2001), pp. 150–70

Thiesse, Anne-Marie, and Catherine Bertho-Lavenir, "Folk Culture and the Construction of European National Identities between the Eighteenth and Twentieth Centuries," in Alain Dieckhoff and Natividad Gutierrez, eds., *Modern Roots: Studies of National Identity* (Aldershot: Ashgate, 2001), pp. 118–29

Thompson, Andrew, "Nations, National Identities and Human Agency: Putting People Back into Nations," *Sociological Review*, 49, No. 1 (February 2001): 18–32

Thompson, Eric, "Rocking East and West: The USA in Malaysian Music (An American Remix)," in Richard King and Timothy Craig, *Global Goes Local: Popular Culture in Asia* (Vancouver: University of British Columbia Press, 2002), pp. 58–79

Tishkov, Valery, *Ethnicity, Nationalism and Conflict in and After the Soviet Union: The Mind Aflame* (London: Sage Publications, 1997)

Tokluoglu, Ceylan, "Definitions of National Identity, Nationalism and Ethnicity in Post-Soviet Azerbaijan in the 1990s," *Ethnic Racial Studies*, 28, No. 4 (July 2005): 722–58

Tolz, Vera, "Forging the Nation: National Identity and Nation Building in Post-Communist Russia," *Europe-Asia Studies*, 50, No. 6 (1998), 993–1022

Tomlinson, John, *Cultural Imperialism: A Critical Introduction* (London: Pinter, 1991)

Globalization and Culture (Chicago: University of Chicago Press, 1999)

Tronvoll, Kjetil, "The Process of Nation-Building in Post-War Eritrea: Created from Below or Directed from Above?" *Journal of Modern African Studies*, 36, No. 3 (September 1998): 461–82

Tsygankov, Andrei P., and Pavel A. Tsygankov, "New Directions in Russian International Studies: Pluralization, Westernization, and Isolationism," *Communist and Post-Communist Studies*, 37, No. 1 (March 2004): 1–17

Turnbull, Jane, "Solomon Islands: Blending Traditional Power and Modern Structures in the State," *Public Administration and Development*, 22, No. 2 (May 2002): 191–201

Turner, Christena, "Locating Footbinding: Variations across Class and Space in Nineteenth and Early Twentieth Century China," *Journal of Historical Sociology*, 10, No. 4 (December 1997): 444–79

Tyrrell, Heather, "Bollywood versus Hollywood: Battle of the Dream Factories," in Tracey Skelton and Tim Allen, eds., *Culture and Global Change* (London: Routledge, 1999), pp. 260–67

Uehling, Greta, "Social Memory as Collective Action: The Crimean Tatar National Movement," in John Guidry, Michael Kennedy and Mayer Zald, eds., *Globalization and Social Movements: Culture, Power, and the Transnational Public Sphere* (Ann Arbor: University of Michigan Press, 2000), pp. 260–87

UNESCO, "Survey of National Cinematography," 2000, available online at www.unesco.org/culture/industries

UNICEF (in coordination with Mery Gardashkhanova, Azerbaijan State Statistical Committee), *Youth at Transition Period in Azerbaijan Republic* (Florence: 2000), www.unicef-icdc.org

Valiyev, Anar, and Yusif Valiyev, "Islamic Extremism in Azerbaijan: Reality and Myth," *Central Asia-Caucasus Analyst*, July 17, 2002, available on-line at www.cacianalyst.org

Van Creveld, Martin, *The Rise and Decline of the State* (Cambridge: Cambridge University Press, 1999)

Van Der Leeuw, Charles, *Azerbaijan: A Quest for Identity* (New York: St. Martins, 2000)

Van Elteren, Mel, "Conceptualizing the Impact of US Popular Culture Globally," *Journal of Popular Culture*, 30, No. 1 (Summer 1996): 47–89

"US Cultural Imperialism: Today Only a Chimera," *SAIS Review*, 25, No. 3 (Summer/Fall 2003): 169–88

Verma, Suman, and T. S. Saraswathi, "Adolescence in India: Street Urchins or Silicon Valley Millionaires?" in B. Bradford Brown, Reed W. Larson, and T. S. Saraswathi, eds., *The World's Youth: Adolescence in Eight Regions of the Globe* (New York: Cambridge University Press, 2002), pp. 105–40

Vertigans, Stephen, and Philip W. Sutton, "Globalisation Theory and Islamic Praxis," *Global Society*, 16, No. 1 (January 2002): 31–46

Vogel, Jerome, "Culture, Politics, and National Identity in Côte d'Ivoire," *Social Research*, 58, No. 2 (Summer 1991): 439–56

Vogel, Steven K., *Freer Markets, More Rules: Regulatory Regimes in Advanced Industrial Countries* (Ithaca: Cornell University Press, 1996)

Von Laue, Theodore H., *The World Revolution of Westernization: The Twentieth Century in Global Perspective* (New York: Oxford University Press, 1987)

Walker, Edward W., *Dissolution: Sovereignty and the Breakup of the Soviet Union* (Lanham, MD: Rowman and Littlefield, 2003)

Wallerstein, Immanuel, *The Modern World-System: Capitalist Agriculture and the Origins of the European World-Economy in the Sixteenth Century* (New York: Academic Press, 1974)

The Modern World-System III : The Second Era of Great Expansion of the Capitalist World-Economy, 1730–1840s (New York: Academic Press, 1989)

Wang, Jing, *High Culture Fever: Politics, Aesthetics, and Ideology in Deng's China* (Berkeley: University of California Press, 1996)

"The State Question in Chinese Popular Cultural Studies," *Inter-Asia Cultural Studies*, 2, No. 1 (April 2001): 35–52

Weber, Eugen, *Peasants into Frenchmen: The Modernization of Rural France, 1870–1914* (Stanford: Stanford University Press, 1976)

Wedeen, Lisa, "Conceptualizing Culture: Possibilities for Political Science," *American Political Science Review*, 96, No. 4 (December 2002): 713–28

Wee, C. J. W.-L., "Representing the Singapore Modern: Dick Lee, Pop Music, and the New Asia," in Yao Souchou, ed., *House of Glass: Culture, Modernity, and the State in Southeast Asia* (Singapore: Institute of Southeast Asian Studies, 2001), pp. 243–69

Weigle, Marcia A., *Russia's Liberal Project: State-Society Relations in the Transition from Communism* (University Park, PA: Pennsylvania State University Press, 2000)

Weiss, Linda, *The Myth of the Powerless State* (Ithaca: Cornell University Press, 1998)

Wendt, Alexander, "On Constitution and Causation in International Relations," *Review of International Studies*, 24, No. 5 (December 1998): 101–17

White, Leslie, *The Concept of Cultural Systems: A Key to Understanding Tribes and Nations* (New York: Columbia University Press, 1975)

Willerton, John P., and Geoffrey Cockerham, "Russia, the CIS and Eurasian Interconnections," in James Sperling, Sean Kay and S. Victor Papacosma, eds., *Limiting Institutions? The Challenge of Eurasian Security Governance* (Manchester and New York: Manchester University Press, 2003), pp. 185–207

Wimmer, Andreas, "Globalizations Avant la Lettre: A Comparative View of Isomorphization and Heteromorphization in an Inter-Connecting World," *Comparative Studies in Society and History*, 43, No. 3 (July 2001): 435–66

Winter, Rainer, "Global Media, Cultural Change and the Transformation of the Local: The Contribution of Cultural Studies to a Sociology of Hybrid Formations," in Ulrich Beck, Nathan Sznaider and Rainer Winter, eds., *Global America? The Cultural Consequences of Globalization* (Liverpool: Liverpool University Press, 2003), pp. 206–21

Wodak, Ruth, Rudolf de Cillia, Martin Reisigl, and Karin Liebhart, *The Discursive Construction of National Identity*, translated by Angelika Hirsch and Richard Mitten (Edinburgh: Edinburgh University Press, 1999)

Wuthnow, Robert, *Meaning and Moral Order: Explorations in Cultural Analysis* (Berkeley and Los Angeles: University of California Press, 1987)

Yan, Yunxiang, "Managed Globalization: State Power and Cultural Transition in China," in Peter Berger and Samuel Huntington, eds., *Many Globalizations: Cultural Diversity in the Contemporary World* (New York: Oxford University Press, 2002), pp. 19–47

Yanik, Lerna K., "The politics of educational exchange: Turkish Education in Eurasia," *Europe-Asia Studies*, 56, No. 2 (March 2004): 293–307

Yee, Albert S., "The Causal Effects of Ideas on Policies," *International Organization*, 50, No. 1 (Winter 1996): 69–108

Yermukanov, Marat, "Kazakhstan after a Decade of Independence," *Central Asia – Caucasus Analyst*, December 18, 2002, available online at www.cacianalyst.org

   "Anti-Drug Efforts of Kazakhstan: Old Methods in New Garbs," *Central Asia – Caucasus Analyst*, February 25, 2004, www.caciananalyst.org

Yoda, Tomiko, "A Roadmap to Millennial Japan," *The South Atlantic Quarterly*, 99, No. 4 (Fall 2000): 629–668

Young, Crawford, *The Politics of Cultural Pluralism* (Madison: University of Wisconsin Press, 1976)

Yu, Keping, "Americanization, Westernization, Sinification: Modernization or Globalization in China?" in Ulrich Beck, Nathan Sznaider, and Rainer Winter, eds., *Global America? The Cultural Consequences of Globalization* (Liverpool: Liverpool University Press, 2003), pp. 134–49

Zachary, G. Pascal, "The World Gets in Touch with its Inner American," *Mother Jones*, 24, No. 1 (January 1999): 50–6

Zorkaia, Natalia, and Nadia Diuk, "Tsennosti i ustanovki rossiiskoi molodezhi," *Polit.ru*, August 21, 2003, www.Polit.ru

Index